Feminine and Feminist Ethics

Feminine and Feminist Ethics

Rosemarie Tong
Davidson College

Wadsworth Publishing Company
Belmont, California
A Division of Wadsworth, Inc.

Philosophy Editor: *Ken King*
Editorial Assistant: *Kristina Pappas*
Production Editor: *Deborah Cogan*
Managing Designer: *Carolyn Deacy*
Print Buyer: *Randy Hurst*
Permissions Editor: *Robert Kauser*
Copy Editor: *Melissa Andrews*
Cover Designer: *Carolyn Deacy*
Compositor: *Scratchgravel Publishing Services*
Printer: *Malloy Lithographing, Inc.*

Cover Art: Judy Rifka, *Square Dress,* 1982
Oil on linen, 51 × 64 ½ in.
Collection of Dr. and Mrs. Jack Eisert
Photo Courtesy of Brooke Alexander

1 2 3 4 5 6 7 8 9 10—97 96 95 94 93

Printed in the United States of America

Library of Congress Cataloging-in-Publication Data

Tong, Rosemarie.
    Feminine and feminist ethics / Rosemarie Tong.
        p.   cm.
    Includes bibliographical references and index.
    ISBN 0-534-17910-X
    1. Feminist ethics.   2. Women—Psychology.   3. Human reproduction—
Moral and ethical aspects.   I. Title.
BJ1395.T66   1993
170'.82—dc20   92-37432

Contents

Preface

This book began three years ago as a study of feminist medical ethics and reproductive technologies. As I tried to tame and tailor the plethora of feminist approaches to reproductive issues, however, I realized there existed a greater need for a book about *general* feminist and feminine approaches to ethics. Indeed, if many of my students wrinkled their noses in confusion at the term "feminist," they became totally bewildered at the suggestion that there might be feminist or feminine approaches to ethics. "Oh no!" they wailed, "Isn't there just one approach to ethics for everyone?!!" I wrote this book for both the undergraduate and the specialist with the hope of dispelling the mystery that too often surrounds all things feminine and feminist. I selected a relaxed, jargon-free style to make a difficult subject less threatening.

The first three chapters give the background necessary to explore the issues further. Chapter 1 introduces and explains the concept of a feminist and/or feminine approach to ethics, as well as offering a case that illustrates the possible difference between masculine and feminine viewpoints. Chapter 2 explains, for the benefit of those without a background in ethics, general definitions of the major traditional ethical theories. Chapter 3 gives a historical background for feminist thinkers and gender debates.

Chapter 4 begins the development of contemporary issues in ethics. This chapter explains twentieth-century approaches to ethics and the contemporary challenges to traditional ontology and epistemology. Chapters 5 through 9 develop in detail feminine, feminist, maternal, and lesbian approaches to ethics. These chapters aim to point up the differences and similarities among these approaches and highlight both their strengths and their weaknesses.

Chapter 10, the conclusion, offers an overview of the book and my own thoughts on what we may gain from feminine or feminist approaches to ethics. My goal, however, is for the reader to develop her/his own ideas on the issues involved. If my attempts to stir the reader's consciousness succeed, many women and men will be encouraged to share their feminine and feminist moral perspectives with each other and the larger community. I look forward to reflecting on their ideas and incorporating a fair share of them in my daily struggle to be a better person tomorrow than I was yesterday.

Acknowledgments

There are many people who have made the task of writing this book easier than it would otherwise have been. In particular, I wish to acknowledge my student research assistant, Susan Peppers, who is planning on entering philosophy graduate school. She is clearly one of those students who will surpass her professor. I also wish to thank two of my other student research assistants: Kristin Garris and Leigh McKeever. They too spent many extra hours in the library on my behalf. Without their help and the able assistance of my secretary, Mrs. Ruth Turner, this book would not have been completed nearly on time. I also want to thank the Wadsworth team, especially Deborah Cogan, Production Editor, and my expert copyeditor, Melissa Andrews. Finally, I want to acknowledge Kenneth King, Philosophy Editor for Wadsworth, and Claudia Card, Professor of Philosophy at the University of Wisconsin in Madison. Their criticisms and comments encouraged me to put forth my best effort. The product may not be perfect, but it is far better than it would have been without their assistance.

I would also like to thank the following reviewers for their comments on the manuscript: Carol W. Anthony, Villanova University; Ann Cudd, Occidental College; Joy Kroeger-Mappes, Frostburg State University; Tom Moody, California State University, San Bernardino; Marilyn M. Pearsall, University of Puget Sound; Bambi Robinson, Southeast Missouri State University.

Feminine and Feminist Ethics

1

Feminine and Feminist Ethics: A First Approximation

CONFUSING MUSINGS

While writing this book, I encountered many articles that asked, in one way or another, if women make better physicians, lawyers, business persons, and politicians than men do. Whenever I read one of these articles, I felt confused, perplexed, and even threatened. I wondered what it meant to say, for example, that women make *better* physicians than men do. Does it simply mean that given current standards of excellence in medicine, women meet these standards more *effectively* and *frequently* than men do? Or does it instead mean that women physicians deliver a *different* kind of health care to their patients than men physicians do? Or does it actually mean that women's medicine is somehow *superior* to men's medicine?

I also wondered about the assumptions that motivated the authors to write their provocative articles. Were they claiming that female hormones cause female physicians to be compassionate, empathetic, and caring, whereas male hormones cause male physicians to be short-fused, arrogant, and cold in manner? Or were they instead claiming that society educates, trains, or otherwise shapes women—much more than it shapes men—to want to minister wholeheartedly to the physical and psychological needs of sick people? Although I was willing to agree that *society* constructs women to be better caregivers than men, I was not willing to agree that *biology* destines women to be the caregivers and men to be the carereceivers. After all, as a feminist who grew up in the late 1960s and early 1970s, I had defended the thesis that sex roles are socialized, and I was reluctant to reconsider one of my basic assumptions about gender identity and behavior.

Nevertheless, even though "different than"/"better than" questions are perplexing and disturbing, I found myself pursuing them. As someone who spends much of her time thinking, teaching, and writing about ethics, I started asking myself questions such as, Do women have a *different* and perhaps even *better* ethics than men do? Are women more proficient in moral reasoning than men are? Is there such a thing as women's ethics? If so, is it true that when confronted with cases like the following one, women will come to one conclusion and men to another?

A CASE TO CONSIDER

Daniel Bocker was worried. The message his secretary had taken merely said, "Go to see Dr. Tai at 3:30 today." He hadn't been asked if 3:30 was convenient for him, and he hadn't been given a reason for coming in.

Mr. Bocker knew it would have to do with his wife, Mary. She had been suffering a lot of pain during her pregnancy, and the preceding week she had been examined by a specialist who Dr. Tai, her gynecologist, had sent her to see. The specialist had performed a thorough examination and taken blood, tissue, and urine samples, but he had told Mary nothing.

"Thank you for coming in," Dr. Tai said. "I want to talk to you before I talk to your wife, because I need your help."

"The tests showed something bad, didn't they?" Mr. Bocker said. "Something is wrong with the baby."

"The baby is fine, but there is something wrong with your wife, something very seriously wrong. She has what we call uterine neoplasia."

"Is that cancer?"

"Yes it is," said Dr. Tai. "But I don't want either of you to panic about it. It's not at a very advanced stage, and at the moment it's localized. If an operation is performed very soon, then she has a good chance to make a full recovery. The standard figures show about 80 percent success."

"But what about the baby?"

"The pregnancy will have to be terminated," Dr. Tai said. "And I should tell you that your wife will not be able to have children after the operation."

Mr. Bocker sat quietly for a moment. He had always wanted children; for him a family without children was not a family at all. He and Mary had talked about having at least three, and the one she was pregnant with now was the first.

"Is it possible to save the baby?" he asked Dr. Tai.

"Mrs. Bocker is only in her fourth month; there is no chance the child could survive outside her body."

"But what if she didn't have the operation? Would the baby be normal?"

"Probably so, but the longer we wait to perform the operation, the worse your wife's chances become. I don't want to seem to tell you what to do, but my advice is for your wife to have an abortion and to undergo the operation as soon as it is reasonably possible."

"But she might recover, even if she had the child and then had the operation, mightn't she?"

"It's possible, but her chances of recovery are much less. I don't know what the exact figures would be, but she would be running a terrible risk."

Mr. Bocker understood what Dr. Tai was saying, but he also understood what he wanted.

"I'm not going to encourage Mary to have an abortion," he said. "I want her to have a child, and I think she wants that, too."

"What if she wants to have a better chance to live?" I think the decision is really hers. After all, it's her life that is at stake."

"But it's not just her decision," Mr. Bocker said. "It's a family decision, hers and mine. I'm not going to agree to an abortion, even if she does want one. I'm going to try to get her to take the extra risk and have the child before she has the operation."

"I think that's the cruelest, most immoral thing I've ever heard," Dr. Tai said.[1]

That women and men might have different moral intuitions about this case is plausible. After all, a woman's body is at stake in an abortion decision in a way that no man's body can be. This fact alone could cause Mrs. Bocker to agree with Dr. Tai that her husband has no right to urge her to continue her pregnancy, that the abortion decision is hers alone to make, and that her right to life is at least as important as that of her fetus. Nevertheless, there are women, including some pregnant women, who might agree with Mr. Bocker rather than Dr. Tai. For example, those women who oppose abortion even when the woman's life or health is imperiled might find their hero in Mr. Bocker. Conversely, there are men who might agree with Dr. Tai rather than Mr. Bocker on the ground that a woman's right to bodily integrity overrides a developing fetus's right to life. Do such ethical agreements between men and women on certain moral issues prove that ethics is gender neutral—that there is neither a women's ethics nor a men's ethics?

Admittedly, if we conceive of women's ethics as some sort of unitary moral point of view to which all and only women must *necessarily* subscribe, then this approach to ethics is doomed. Not only do women disagree among themselves about the right course of action in a case like that of Mr. and Mrs. Bocker, some men and women espouse the same line of moral reasoning. Yet even if there is no women's ethics in the sense of an approach to morality that all and only persons with XX chromosomes can and will embrace, there may still be feminine and/or feminist approaches to ethics open to men as well as to women.

FEMININE AND FEMINIST APPROACHES TO ETHICS

To say that feminine and feminist approaches to ethics, unlike women's ethics, are open to both sexes arouses our curiosity. What is it about feminine and feminist moral perspectives that is capable of speaking to men as well to women? And what, if anything, is the difference between a feminine and a feminist approach to ethics? Philosopher Betty A. Sichel maintains that however similar the terms *feminine* and *feminist* may sound, they refer to different approaches to ethical theory:

> "Feminine" at present refers to the search for women's unique voice and most often, the advocacy of an ethic of care that includes nurturance, care, compassion, and networks of communications. "Feminist" refers to those theorists, whether liberal or radical or other orientation, who argue against patriarchal domination, for equal rights, a just and fair distribution of scarce resources, etc.[2]

Agreeing with Sichel, another philosopher, Susan Sherwin, claims that a feminine approach to ethics "consists of observations of how the traditional approaches to ethics fail to fit the moral experiences and intuitions of women."[3] In contrast, a feminist approach to ethics "applies a specifically political perspective and offers suggestions for how ethics must be revised if it is to get at the patterns of dominance and oppression as they affect women."[4]

Although both Sichel and Sherwin concede that feminine and feminist approaches to ethics are interrelated, and that often it is difficult to classify a specific ethical work as being either "feminine" or "feminist," they refuse to play down the distinctions that separate them, one from the other. They rightly insist that these two approaches to ethics are indeed two different ways of looking at ethical theory and practice, the former occasioned by what I term a "feminine consciousness" and the latter by what many have termed a "feminist consciousness."

FEMININE CONSCIOUSNESS AND FEMININE APPROACHES TO ETHICS

A feminine consciousness regards the *gender* traits that have been traditionally associated with women—in particular, nurturance, compassion, caring—as positive *human* traits. A variety of ethicists and psychologists have developed competing theories about the ultimate source of these traits. One school of thought roots feminine consciousness in women's reproductive role and responsibilities. According to Caroline Whitbeck, for example, biological factors rather than social factors ultimately "influence women, and not men, in their attachment to their children."[5] Among these biological factors "are the *experiences* of pregnancy, labor, childbirth, nursing, and the postpartum recovery."[6] The woman, not the man, carries the child in her body and brings it into the world through the activity of labor. She then nourishes the child with her milk and tends to it in a variety of other ways. These concrete physical experiences shape the woman's consciousness. She starts to view herself as a caregiver and to judge herself in terms of how well she delivers this care to others. Gradually, the woman extends her caring skills out of the home and into the community where she works as a volunteer, for example.

This explanation for feminine caring is a relatively worrisome one, however. If nature has determined that women give care and that men *receive* it, then little can be done to change this state of affairs. Society cannot praise women any more than it can blame men for doing what comes "naturally."

A second school of thought traces feminine consciousness to women's psychosexual development. Nancy Chodorow, for example, observes that unlike sons, who need to disassociate themselves from their mothers to form a masculine identity, daughters can remain emotionally linked to their mothers.[7] As a result, girls develop their capacities for relationships much more quickly and deeply than boys do. Feeling best when they are deeply connected to other people, women worry about their relationships in ways that men do not worry about theirs. Much more than men, women do whatever they have to do to maintain their friendships and family connections. To the degree that men seem to value their ability to stand alone, women seem to value their ability to weave relational networks.

This psychosexual explanation for women's caring is also problematic. Mothers, for example, might wonder if it is a good idea to keep their daughters, any more than their sons, tied to their apron strings.

They might fear that a feminine consciousness unmodified does not permit girls and women much autonomy or psychological freedom to pursue their own desires. Under such a psychosexual view, the links between mother and daughter become very much like the iron chains of biological destiny.

A third school of thought locates feminine consciousness in women's cultural and socioeconomic positions. For a variety of reasons, women have been excluded from participation in public production and relegated to domestic work in the private world of the home. There they cook and clean, but mostly they care for the very young and the very old. To them falls the task of socializing young children and to them falls the task of nursing aged parents. Women *listen* to the babbling of babies, the prattling of teens, and the reminiscences of the old, while men *speak* to each other about business matters, public policies, and professional affairs.

Although less deterministic than its two alternatives, this explanation for feminine consciousness is still flawed. If living in the private realm is what produces a feminine consciousness, then moving into the public realm might alter this consciousness. Yet, change is not always for the better. Women's nurturance, compassion, and caring might be distorted or even destroyed in the public world.

Each of these three theories offers a partial explanation for the generation of feminine gender roles, behavior, and identity. Women's feminine consciousness stems from women's experience. Whether this experience is viewed as primarily biological, psychosexual, or cultural and socioeconomic, one thing about this experience seems certain: It is not *men's* experience—at least it is not the experience of typical men. Even if feminine consciousness is not the exclusive property of women, it remains largely so—a fact whose significance we will probe in later chapters of this book.

FEMINIST CONSCIOUSNESS AND FEMINIST APPROACHES TO ETHICS

Related to, but certainly different from, a feminine consciousness and approach to ethics is a feminist consciousness and approach to ethics. A feminist consciousness is political not only in the sense that it sees that women are subordinated (repressed, oppressed, suppressed) but also in the sense that it seeks to eliminate this subordination. Like feminine consciousness, feminist consciousness is not unitary but multiple. A variety of feminist schools of thought express an equal variety of feminist consciousnesses. Each of these schools of thought—liberal, Marxist, radical, psychoanalytic, socialist, postmodern—addresses the causes of and solutions for women's subordination in its own way, and each emphasizes some ethical considerations over others.

Liberal feminism receives its classic formulation in Mary Wollstone craft's *A Vindication of the Rights of Woman*[8] and in John Stuart Mill's *The Subjection of Women*.[9] Still active in contemporary groups such as the National Organization of Women, liberal feminists find the roots of women's oppression in those cultural constraints that hinder women from competing in the public world: the world of politics, medicine, law, business, and so forth. Because traditional society holds the false belief that women are, by nature, less mentally and physically capable than men, it largely excludes women from the academy, the forum, the marketplace. Excluded from the land of opportunity, women are unable to demonstrate their capabilities: This is a discriminatory state of affairs. Therefore, liberal feminists insist that society should give women the same educational and occupational opportunities that men have; only then will women be able to achieve all that they both can and want to achieve.

In contrast to liberal feminists, Marxist *feminists* believe that it is impossible to secure genuine equal opportunity for anyone, especially women, in a class society. Women's oppression originates, as Frederick Engels said, with the introduction of private property.[10] Private ownership of the means of production by a few persons, originally all male, inaugurated an inegalitarian class system that has its contemporary manifestations in corporate capitalism and imperialism. Reflection on this state of affairs suggests that capital, not men per se, causes women's oppression. If *all* women are to be liberated, and not just the ones who dress for success, then a communist system must replace the capitalist system. Because no one would be economically subordinate to anyone else under communism, women and men would have economic equality.

Also in contrast to liberal feminists, *radical feminists* believe that the patriarchal system that oppresses women—a system characterized by power, dominance, hierarchy, and competition—is so flawed that it cannot be reformed; it must be eliminated. Not only must patriarchy's legal, political, and economic institutions be overturned, so too must its social institutions (especially the family) and its cultural institutions (especially the church and the academy) be extirpated. Furthermore, in contrast to Marxist feminists, radical feminists insist that *men,* not capital, are women's primary oppressors. Because capitalism serves patriarchy rather than vice versa, the destruction of capitalism is at most a necessary condition for women's liberation. As long as patriarchy remains standing, women will not know true freedom.

As radical feminists see it, neither women's economic position nor women's lack of equal rights provides an adequate explanation for women's oppression by men. Rather, women's reproductive roles and responsibilities, as well as the institution of what has been termed "compulsory heterosexuality," are the fundamental causes of female subordination and male domination. Radical feminists debate whether reproduction-controlling technologies such as contraception, sterilization, and abortion and/or reproduction-aiding technologies such as artificial insemination by donor and in vitro fertilization tend to liberate or enslave women; whether the characteristics associated with femininity (caring, compassion, nurturance) are a cause for celebration or simply a trap that lures women into totally sacrificing themselves for others; and, finally, what kinds of intimate relationships are most likely to meet the whole range of women's intellectual, emotional, erotic, and sexual needs.

When it comes to male-female relationships, radical feminists focus on the nature, function, and sheer quantity of the sexual violence men direct against women. Pornography, prostitution, sexual harassment, rape, and women-battery suggest that at some level many men are "women haters."[11] Radical feminists affirm the importance of love between women, agreeing that the ideal of the *feminist* woman who knows herself and is not afraid to love herself and other women must replace the ideal of the *feminine* woman who lives only for her children and/or men.

Like radical feminists, *psychoanalytic feminists* also focus on gender and sexuality, but in a markedly different way than that of radical feminists. Relying on Freudian concepts such as the pre-Oedipal stage and the Oedipus complex, psychoanalytic feminists seek explanations for the differences between male and female sexuality in infant or childhood experiences. According to standard psychoanalytic accounts, in the pre-Oedipal stage all infants are symbiotically attached to their mothers. As far as the infants are concerned, their mothers are omnipotent. The mother-infant relationship is an ambivalent one, however. From the infant's perspective, mother at times gives too much (her presence overwhelms) and at other times gives too little (her absence disappoints).

She is someone to hate as well as to love. During the Oedipal stage, the mother-son symbiosis usually breaks once and for all. The boy gives up his mother in order to escape castration at the hands of his father. As a result of submitting his desires (the id) to the laws of society (the super-ego), the boy fully integrates into culture. Together with his father he will rule over nature and woman, she whose power is just as irrational as nature's. In contrast to the boy, the girl, who has no penis to lose, separates slowly from her mother. As a result, the girl's integration into culture is incomplete. She exists at the periphery or margin of culture, always to be ruled over and never to rule.[12]

Psychoanalytic feminists believe that the best way to rewrite the ending of the Oedipus drama is to promote dual parenting as well as dual careers for heterosexual couples. Were children reared by men as well as by women, they would no longer view the values of authority, autonomy, and universalism as strictly male; and they would no longer view the values of love, dependence, and particularism as strictly female. Rather, they would view all of these values as human values—values mom and dad share in equal measure.

The liberal, Marxist, radical, and psychoanalytic perspectives are not the only ones feminists have developed to explain and overcome women's subordination, but they are some of the main ones. One reaction to the rich diversity of feminist thought has been the attempt of *socialist feminists* to weave these separate streams of thought into a coherent whole. In *Woman's Estate*, Juliet Mitchell argues that four structures *overdetermine* woman's condition: production, reproduction, sexuality, and the socialization of children.[13] Woman's status and function in *all* of these structures must change if she is to be man's equal. Furthermore, as Mitchell adds in *Psychoanalysis and Feminism*, woman's interior world, her psyche, must also be transformed; for unless a women is convinced of her own value, no change in her exterior world can ultimately liberate her.[14]

Alison M. Jaggar develops these and other related thoughts in *Feminist Politics and Human Nature*. She uses the concept of alienation to explain how, under capitalism, everything and everyone that could be a source of women's integration as a person becomes a cause of her disintegration.[15] Women experience nature, work, other people, and even themselves not as allies to be treasured but as aliens to be resisted. Unless society's structures are fundamentally altered, and with them women's self-image, women will remain less happy as well as less free than men.

Recently, attempts such as those of Mitchell and Jaggar to provide women with a *standpoint* from which they can state, for example, what is the best or at least a *better* way to treat women have been challenged by *postmodern feminists* (such as Luce Irigarary, Hélène Cixous, and Julia Kristeva) as instances of so-called "phallogocentric" thought[16]— that is, the kind of "male thinking" that insists on telling as absolute truth *one* and *only* one story about reality.

As postmodern feminists see it, such a story is neither feasible nor desirable. It is not feasible because women's experience is divided by class, race, and culture. There are many stories to be told about individual women—not just one story about "Woman." For this reason, postmodern feminists reject what is sometimes termed woman's "standpoint." As they see it, this standpoint, like any *unitary* standpoint, prevents people from expressing their unique perspectives. Women must feel free to reveal their differences to each other so that they can better resist the patriarchal tendency to center, congeal, and cement thought into a rigid truth that always was, is, and forever will be.

FEMININE AND FEMINIST APPROACHES TO ETHICS: CHALLENGING THE TRADITION

If feminine and feminist consciousnesses are many, then presumably feminine and feminist approaches to ethics are many. Indeed, one of the reasons I prefer to talk about feminine and feminist *approaches* to ethics, rather than feminine and feminist ethics, is simply that the word *approaches* connotes multiplicity.

Yet even though feminine and feminist ethical approaches are many, they tend to share certain features in common. For instance, people who adopt a *feminine* approach to ethics are generally interested in exploring the ethical implications of allegedly feminine concepts such as care and connectedness and contrasting them with the ethical implications of allegedly masculine concepts such as justice and autonomy. Similarly, people who adopt a *feminist* approach to ethics are usually committed to the three normative goals that philosopher Alison Jaggar has identified. As she sees it, to count as a *feminist* approach to ethics, the approach must seek:

1. To articulate moral critiques of actions and practices that perpetuate women's subordination

2. To prescribe morally justifiable ways of resisting such actions and practices

3. To envision morally desirable alternatives that will promote women's emancipation[17]

Finally, no matter what feminine or feminist approach to ethics someone adopts, s/he will assuredly take herself/himself to be doing ethics in ways that depart substantially from traditional approaches to ethics.

In the Western world, traditional ethics consists of those ethical systems that aim to discover, articulate, and interpret the ultimate moral principles that should govern persons' actions. These principles are supposedly universal and impartial, governing everyone irrespective of race, class, gender, and so forth; and the persons they govern are supposedly autonomous (endowed with enough knowledge and power to be able to decide for themselves what is right and wrong). Utilitarian and deontological ethical theories have dominated the moral landscape for at least two centuries. Neither emphasizes feminine values, and neither is particularly concerned about women's subordination or liberation.

What values, then, do utilitarian and deontological theories emphasize? What matters concern them? If these types of ethical theories are neither "feminine" nor "feminist," are they then "masculine" or "masculinist"? Does it ultimately make sense to speak of ethics in gendered terms? Only if we understand traditional ethics can we begin to appreciate its strengths and weaknesses. Likewise, only if we understand "feminine" and "feminist" approaches to ethics can we decide whether these new approaches offer better ways to be moral than the old ones did. If traditional ethics does not motivate us to actually do "the good," can feminine or feminist approaches to ethics inspire us to be as good as we can possibly be? This book seeks to answer this question, however partially and provisionally.

NOTES

1. Ronald Munson, *Intervention and Reflection: Basic Issues in Medical Ethics* (Belmont, Calif.: Wadsworth, 1992), 100–101.
2. Betty A. Sichel, "Different Strains and Strands: Feminist Contributions to Ethical Theory," *Newsletter on Feminism* 90, no. 2 (Winter 1991): 90.
3. Susan Sherwin, *No Longer Patient: Feminist Ethics and Health Care* (Philadelphia: Temple University Press, 1992), 42.
4. Ibid., 42–43.
5. Caroline Whitbeck, "The Maternal Instinct," in Joyce Treblicot, ed., *Mothering: Essays in Feminist Theory* (Totowa, N.J.: Rowman and Allanheld Publishers, 1984), 186.
6. Ibid.

7. Nancy Chodorow, *The Reproduction of Mothering: Psychoanalysis and the Sociology of Gender* (Los Angeles: University of California Press, 1978), 126–140.

8. Mary Wollstonecraft, *A Vindication of the Rights of Women,* ed. Carol H. Poston (Reprint, New York: W. W. Norton, 1975).

9. John Stuart Mill, "The Subjection of Women," in Alice S. Rossi, ed., *Essays on Sex Equality* (Chicago: University of Chicago Press, 1970), 184–185.

10. Frederick Engels, *The Origin of the Family, Private Property and the State* (New York: International Publishers, 1972), 103.

11. Andrea Dworkin, *Women-Hating: A Radical Look at Sexuality* (New York: E. P. Dutton, 1976).

12. Dorothy Dinnerstein, *The Mermaid and the Minotaur: Sexual Arrangements and Human Malaise* (New York: Harper & Row, 1977).

13. Juliet Mitchell, *Woman's Estate* (New York: Vintage Books, 1971).

14. Juliet Mitchell, *Psychoanalysis and Feminism* (New York: Vintage Books, 1975).

15. Alison M. Jaggar, *Feminist Politics and Human Nature* (Totowa, N.J.: Rowman and Allanheld, 1983), 316–317.

16. Phallogocentric: A worldview centered on the penis—that is, on the man. (*Phallus* = representation of penis or testes; *logos* = the word as metaphysical presence; and *centric* = centered on.)

17. Alison M. Jaggar, "Feminist Ethics," in L. Becker and C. Becker, eds., *Encyclopedia of Ethics* (New York: Garland Press, 1992), 361–370.

2

Traditional Types of Ethical Theories: General Definitions

There are about as many definitions of ethics as there are ethicists. Nevertheless, the definitions tend to share certain features. In *Discovering Right and Wrong*, philosopher Louis P. Pojman provides a definition of ethics that merits our close attention:

> "Ethics" (or "moral philosophy," as it is sometimes called) will be used to designate the systematic endeavor to understand moral concepts and justify moral principles and theories. It undertakes to analyze such concepts as "right," "wrong," "permissible," "ought," "good," and "evil" in their moral contexts. Ethics seeks to establish principles of right behavior that may serve as action guides for individuals and groups. It investigates which values and virtues are paramount to the worthwhile life or to society. It builds and scrutinizes arguments in ethical theories, and it seeks to discover valid principles (for example, "Never kill innocent human beings") and the relationship between those principles (for example, does saving a life in some situations constitute a valid reason for breaking a promise?).[1]

Exponents of traditional ethics approve of Pojman's definition. They also praise him for claiming, as he later does, that moral principles play the role that legal statutes, rules of etiquette, and religious commandments play in their respective domains and that to count as a *moral* principle, a principle must be (1) prescriptive, (2) universalizable, (3) overriding, (4) public, and (5) practicable.

A prescription is a formula or recipe that a person needs to follow if certain ends are to be obtained. For example, I take my antibiotics prescription to the pharmacist. If she manages to decipher my physician's scrawled notes correctly, she will be able to provide me with the medicine I need. Moral principles are much like prescriptions. If we closely follow their instructions, we will find ourselves acting in morally acceptable ways. A principle such as "Show respect for all persons," for example, is supposed to influence a fraternity member's behavior toward the coeds at the Homecoming party.

With respect to the element of universalizability, a distinction must be made between abstract moral *principles* and concrete moral *rules*. Whereas moral principles apply in any and all circumstances, moral rules apply only to recurring specific situations. A moral principle like "Always act in such a way as to promote the group's long-term advantage" could easily generate different moral rules. For example, rules permitting infanticide may be moral in societies where goods and resources are scarce, but not in societies where they are abundant.

In addition to being universally applicable, moral principles may override other types of principles. They take precedence over corrupt laws and social institutions, for example. Before the passage of the Civil Rights Act, it was legally permitted, though certainly not morally justified, to keep African-Americans out of for-whites-only restaurants. Similarly, at a state-supported all-male military academy, it is legally permitted but not morally justified to exclude female candidates as cadets, even if the presence of women would destroy what the male cadets regard as the "special" (i.e., chauvinistic) atmosphere of their men-only club. Morality is stronger than opinions, beliefs, and laws.

Of course, if moral principles are to serve as both guides for and standards of our actions, they must be made public. Morality is not a secret to be kept hidden for the chosen few. If women have rights, for example, women cannot sit in their armchairs silently thinking about pursuing life, liberty, and happiness. On the contrary, women must proclaim their rights to all who have ears to hear.

Last, for moral principles to be of value, they must be practicable guides for human behavior. If morality required us to renounce love, sex, property, and family and to retreat into caves to meditate, few people would be prepared to take it seriously. Human limitations must be factored into any viable moral system. Ought always implies can. As a rule, if people do not have the physical and/or psychological capacities to be saints and heroes, then it makes no sense to demand that they behave as saints and heroes. They will fail and morality with them.

According to traditional ethics, the fundamental purpose of prescriptive, universalizable, overriding, public, and practicable moral principles is to help us secure what Pojman identifies as the four interrelated purposes of morality:

1. To keep society from falling apart

2. To ameliorate human suffering

3. To promote human flourishing

4. To resolve conflicts of interest in just ways[2]

Because we need to know what morality demands of us before we can do it, traditional ethicists have carefully examined (1) the *nature* of actions (are they required, forbidden, or merely permitted?); (2) the *consequences* of actions (are they good, bad, or merely indifferent?); and (3) the *motives* behind action (are they self-directed, other-directed, or both?). Because traditional ethicists have come to very different conclusions about the nature, consequences, and motives of moral actions, they have divided themselves into several schools of ethical thought, two of the major ones being utilitarianism and deontology.

UTILITARIANISM: THE ETHICS OF THE GROUP'S GOOD

Utilitarianism is based on the principle of utility: An act is morally right if and only if there is no other act the agent could perform instead that would produce more good. Utilitarians consider both the utility-producing (good) and disutility-producing (bad) features of a set of possible actions, determining to perform the action most likely to produce the most good. For example, given a choice between aborting or not aborting her fetus, a woman must decide whether she will produce more good by terminating or not terminating her pregnancy. Assume that this woman comes from a very religiously conservative family; that her husband wants a child more than anything else in life; and, finally, that her program of graduate studies in philosophy (of all things!) will be interrupted if she has a child at this time. If less harm will be done to her if she quits graduate school than will be done to her family and husband if she terminates her pregnancy, utilitarian tenets obligate her not to terminate her pregnancy. What matters is not simply what is best for her but what is best on the whole.

Because most people do not believe that morality requires extreme levels of self-sacrifice, they may perceive utilitarianism as too demanding.

They may also regard it as impracticable in another sense. On what sort of scale is the woman described above supposed to weigh her good against that of her family and husband? In response to such a query, philosopher Jeremy Bentham (1748–1832) constructed a hedonic calculus. He urged reflective individuals to refer to his calculus's seven components—intensity, duration, certainty, propinquity, fecundity, purity, and extent[3]—to determine the utility yield of particular actions for particular individuals. Bentham's mathematics of morality worked better in the abstract than in the concrete, however. Few, if any, people seemed able to assign numerical values to their good and bad experiences.

Bentham's failure to measure utility—particularly people's subjective experiences of good—provoked his successor, philosopher John Stuart Mill (1806–1873), to distinguish between *quantity* and *quality* of pleasure.[4] What the woman in the above example should weigh is the kind of good she will experience when she receives her Ph.D. against the kind of good her husband will experience when he becomes a father. If judges who have experienced both of these happinesses would prefer "fatherhood" over "doctorhood," then "fatherhood" is a qualitatively better happiness than "doctorhood." We should, says Mill, trust the verdict of these judges since, other things being equal, no experienced, *reasonable* person would ever choose a lower good over a higher good.[5]

But what makes a judge "reasonable"? When a group of experienced judges identifies Dante reading as a better pleasure than bingo playing is this because Dante reading is indeed objectively better than bingo playing, or is it simply because these judges have enough *power* to transform their personal preferences into universal law? Are Mill's experienced, reasonable judges *impartial* judges, or are they instead *partisan* judges, more than likely propertied and privileged men, intent on affirming the values of the group they call their own?

In order to avoid the problem of Mill's judges, twentieth-century preference utilitarians argue that the best way to make intersubjective comparisons of utility is to construct a scale on which people can rank their pleasure preferences from highest to lowest. It is not clear, however, that such a scale can be constructed or that people are able, let alone willing, to identify and reveal their true preferences on it. When people are polled about their preferences, they frequently make mental distinctions between their ideal and actual preferences, reporting the former rather than the latter to pollsters. For example, even though a feminist may prefer Harlequin romances to *Ms.* magazine, because she knows that she *ought* to prefer just the opposite, she may reveal her ideal preference (*Ms.* magazine) to pollsters rather than her actual preference (Harlequin romances).

Preference utilitarians also face the problem of so-called "unacceptable preferences." Because preference utilitarians do not want to defend people's racist or sexist preferences, for example, they attempt to distinguish between unacceptable and acceptable preferences, arguing that whereas the latter preferences are rational, the former ones are irrational. Unfortunately, it is no easier to distinguish rational from irrational preferences than it is to distinguish acceptable from unacceptable preferences. Although the word *rational* has a more objective connotation than the word *acceptable* does, it tends to have the same denotation, namely, "that which most people do and/or think." And even if preference utilitarians were able to provide a more convincing account of rationality than "that which *most* people do and/or think," they, like all other utilitarians, would still need to prove that the individual should be prepared to sacrifice his or her good to that of the group if doing so will produce more total good.

Utilitarians' apparent willingness to sacrifice the rights of one or a few individuals in order to secure the happiness of many individuals weakens their moral credibility. Consider the hypothetical case of Sally, a homeless woman, who is dying in a hospital but whose heart, kidneys, and other bodily organs could be used to save the lives of six other patients currently in the hospital. Assume that Sally's contributions to society are minimal and that she is without family and friends, whereas the other six patients are major social contributors with large families and many friends. Also assume that only Sally can provide the needed organs, since alternative organ sources are not available. Finally, assume that Sally has expressed on several occasions a sense of her own worthlessness. However tempting these circumstances may be, most people will resist the conclusion, "Kill Sally now and save six more worthy lives." Committed utilitarians, however, will not be nearly as resistant. They will view Sally and the six other patients who need her organs as some sort of collective superperson whose aggregate utility demands to be maximized. They will be prepared, therefore, to justify Sally's killing as an unfortunate but necessary means to maximize the group's overall happiness. Individual rights, even the right to life, must give way to the group's good.

In contrast to so-called *act* utilitarians—and so far we have been discussing only those utilitarians who hold that the principle of utility should be applied to particular acts in particular circumstances—so-called *rule* utilitarians do not believe that we may violate the rights of a feeling and thinking individual in order to serve the "good" of some unfeeling and unthinking, indeed nonexistent, superperson. On the contrary, rule utilitarians maintain that even if an isolated violation of an individual's rights produces overall good today, a *rule* permitting—let alone requiring—such violations would not produce more overall good in the long run. Because no one can ever be sure who is going to get the short end of the stick, rational persons would not choose to live in a society that routinely or randomly harms one individual in order to benefit many individuals.

In the course of a careful analysis of utilitarianism, philosopher H. J. McCloskey elaborates on the major difference between act and rule utilitarians. Without indicating whether the utilitarian he has in mind is an act or rule utilitarian, McCloskey asks us to consider the following scenario:

> Suppose a utilitarian were visiting an area in which there was racial strife, and that, during his visit, a Negro rapes a white woman, and that race riots occur as a result of the crime, white mobs, with the connivance of the police, bashing and killing Negroes, etc. Suppose too that our utilitarian is in the area of the crime when it is committed such that his testimony would bring about the conviction of a particular Negro. If he knows that a quick arrest will stop the riots and lynchings, surely, as a utilitarian, he must conclude that he has a duty to bear false witness, causing the punishment of an innocent person.[6]

Yet, even if an *act* utilitarian would lie under such circumstances, a *rule* utilitarian would not. Rather, s/he would argue that from the point of view of utility (total good), people are likely to be much better off in a society with the rule "Don't punish innocent persons" than in a society that lacks such a rule. However tempting it is to punish one innocent person in order to spare many innocent persons from harm, it is morally wrong to do so. Utility will not be maximized in the long run if the rule "Don't punish innocent persons" is broken.

In its respect for rules, rule utilitarianism represents an improvement over act utilitarianism. Still, it is doubtful whether rule utilitarians always honor their utility-maximizing rules. In determining the morality of rules, the principle of utility is, after all, determining the morality of the *actions* those rules govern. If a rule utilitarian could save the whole world from total destruction by punishing one and only one innocent person, would not s/he be permitted/obligated to do so? Are there not exceptions, such as this one, to the *generally* utility-maximizing rule "Don't punish innocent persons"?

DEONTOLOGY: THE ETHICS OF DUTY

The question of when, if ever, to make an exception to a good rule brings us to a discussion of deontology, a set of closely related ethical theories largely based on the work of philosopher Immanuel Kant (1724–1804). Unlike utilitarianism, deontology is a nonconsequentialist ethical theory. Whereas utilitarians insist that an action's moral worth depends on its utility-maximizing consequences, deontologists maintain that it depends on some feature inherent in the action itself.

In the deontologist's world, it does not matter how much or how little utility (good, pleasure, or happiness) one produces as the result of one's actions. Instead, what matters is whether one's actions are motivated by the intent to do one's duty because it is one's duty. Kant himself argues that an action is *morally worthy* only when a person performs it simply because s/he knows it is required, as when a shopkeeper gives the correct change because of the moral law against cheating. The action is *morally unworthy* when a person performs it even though s/he knows it is forbidden, as when a shopkeeper gives less than the correct change despite the moral law against cheating. The action is *morally nonworthy* (neither morally worthy nor morally unworthy) when a person performs it for nonmoral motives, as when a shopkeeper gives the correct change not because of the moral law against cheating but because s/he wants to be perceived as an honest person so that more people do business with her/him.

Because obeying moral rules, or doing one's duty because it is one's duty, is so important for deontologists, they take care to explain precisely what makes a rule a *moral* rule. According to Kant, the rules that we propose to live by are *moral* if they meet all three conditions of the so-called "categorical imperative":

1. Act only on that maxim through which you can at the same time will that it should become a universal law;

2. Act in such a way that you always treat humanity, whether in your own person or in the person of another, never simply as a means but always at the same time as an end; and

3. Never . . . perform an action except on a maxim such as can also be a universal law, and consequently such that the will can regard itself as at the same time making universal law by its maxim.[7]

The first version of the categorical imperative sketches a procedure for deciding whether an act is morally permissible. Suppose, says Kant, that a man needs to borrow money, and he knows that no one will lend it to him unless he promises to repay it. He therefore faces a decision: In order to persuade someone to loan him the money he needs, should he promise to repay the debt even though he knows that he cannot do so? If he were to contemplate making a "lying promise," the rule he would be proposing to act on (what Kant calls a "maxim") would be, "Whenever I need a loan, I will promise to repay it even though I know I cannot do so." Now he must ask himself whether his maxim is one that can be universalized into the law "Whenever anyone needs a loan, s/he will promise to repay it even though s/he knows that s/he cannot do so." Apparently, he cannot universalize his maxim because in doing so he would generate a major inconsistency. Were "lying promises" to become a universal practice, no one would any longer believe "promises," and so no one would continue to make loans to bogus "promise-makers." As Kant himself puts it, "No one would believe what was promised to him but would only laugh at any such assertion as vain pretense."[8]

With respect to the second version of the categorical imperative, Kant reasons that if we judge any object to have value—for example, Leonardo's *Mona Lisa*—the value of that object depends on our valuing it. Were no one of us to place a value on that object, it would literally be worthless. Thus any object that has value only because and insofar as it is valued by some person has merely *conditional* worth; that is, its worth is completely dependent on the condition that some person values it.

In contrast to this state of affairs, the persons who bestow value on objects must regard themselves as belonging to an entirely different category of entities than the entities to which they give conditional worth. Persons cannot easily conceive of themselves simply as objects. To be sure, they can conceive of their bodies as mere objects that have value only to the degree that they serve certain useful functions, but they cannot conceive of their persons (what Kant terms "humanity") as mere objects. To do so, any one person would have to view her/his person as worthless unless it happened to be valued by some other person. But then that person would be the source of value, and there is no reason why one person should be such a source of value and not another (namely, one's self). So each person, as a person, must regard herself/ himself as well as all other persons as having *unconditional* worth: the kind of value that does not depend on any value giver over and above one's self.

It follows from this line of reasoning that if one person treats another person as a mere object, valuable only because of the useful purposes s/he serves, the former person treats the latter person disrespectfully and inconsiderately. Nevertheless, one person can serve the ends of another person and yet not be treated only as an object or *mere* means by that other person. For example, patients go to physicians to regain their health. In one sense then, patients use physicians as means to their own ends, but they are not thereby using physicians as mere means to their own ends. To do that patients would have to treat their physicians as less worthy of respect and consideration than they take themselves to be. In other words, they would have to exploit their physicians in some manner or another, for example, by refusing to pay them for their services or by manipulating them in any number of ways without any concern for their own happiness and self-development.

The third version of the categorical imperative instructs people that unless agents act autonomously, their "right" actions as well as their "wrong" actions are morally worthless. When people act heteronomously, they see themselves as being coerced or forced to obey a rule that they have *no reasons* to obey and therefore *no moral obligation* to obey. In contrast, when persons act autonomously, they see themselves as having reasons to obey a rule. Because it is their own will—not anyone else's—that prescribes this rule, they see themselves as under a *moral* obligation to follow it. Moreover, because their reasons for obeying this rule are the same reasons any autonomous person would have, they prescribe it for themselves.

Like the principle of utility, the categorical imperative is not unproblematic. If the universalizability condition is applied to lies *in general*, a clear inconsistency can be derived. An equally clear inconsistency cannot be derived in the case of each and every *specific* lie, however. We may not be willing to universalize the maxim "Lie in order to get rich quick," but we may be willing to universalize the maxim "Lie in order to save your child from ruthless kidnappers."

Second, although slave owners certainly treat their slaves as mere means to their own ends, infertile couples who contract women to gestate their embryos do not necessarily treat these women merely as "things," as rented wombs. On the contrary, they may show these women much respect, attending to their wants and needs. Whereas a slave has no say whatsoever about the conditions of his/her servitude, a gestated mother may have considerable say about the conditions of her employment.

Third, and finally, we tend to think that when we act autonomously, we are following the imperatives of our own subjectivities. Had Kant not told us otherwise, it would never have dawned on us that to act autonomously is to follow the "imperative" of a universal and objective order that arguably transcends and judges our particular subjectivities.

Beyond the specific problems that weaken each version of Kant's categorical imperative, there exist general problems that tend to weaken most formulations of deontology. Because of their stress on the absolute character of moral rules, deontologists struggle to adjudicate so-called "conflicts of duty." If both the rule "It is wrong to lie" and the rule "It is wrong to permit the murder of innocent people" are absolute, then I may fall prey to an irresolvable moral dilemma on some occasion or another. For example, assume that I am hiding a battered woman from her husband. If this man comes to me, brandishing a loaded gun, and asks me if I know where his wife is hiding, I can lie to him, or I can tell him where his wife is. In either event, I will have done something "wrong." To be sure, deontologists could argue that one or the other of these rules is not really absolute; or that God would never permit two really absolute moral rules to conflict; or that a moral rule is absolute only in the "abstract" and not in the context of certain concrete circumstances. But none of these strategies enables me to prioritize *genuinely absolute* but also *conflicting* moral rules.

Finally, some versions of deontology, especially Kantian ones, claim that our feelings neither add nor subtract from the moral worth of our actions. It is this point, more than any other, that weakens the credibility of deontology. *If* it is possible for me to fulfill my parental duties to my sons either grudgingly or cheerfully, it strikes me that doing so cheerfully is morally preferable to doing so grudgingly. Doing the right thing counts for a lot but not as much as doing the right thing with the right feelings. Reading to our children, buying them quality clothes, and sending them to the best schools all out of a sense of "duty" cannot make up for a lack of emotion and love. No one wants to feel cared for out of a sense of "obligation." Indeed, the realization that our parents or guardians labored to raise us only because they felt morally compelled to do so can psychologically scar us. A sense of duty devoid of emotion may be worse than no sense of duty at all. Contrary to Kant, I think that our feelings can and do contribute, either positively or negatively, to the moral worth of an action, so much so, that I also think that duty alone is not always enough to make an action morally worthy.

TRADITIONAL ETHICS CHALLENGED

The claims of traditional ethics are indeed powerful. When I began graduate school, I was convinced that if I could only combine the best points of utilitarianism and deontology, I would be able to create the ideal ethical theory. My theory would be equally attentive to the consequences of and motives for action; it would be no more concerned about group happiness than about individual rights; and it would bring everyone somehow closer together. (The last thought was my own; my ethics professors would have regarded it as "sentimental" or worse.)

After a semester or so, I gave up. I wondered how all the bizarre hypothetical cases presented in my classes related to me or anyone else I knew. My ethics classes began to bore me, even alienate me.

We spent enormous amounts of time trying to decide if what made an action right was its intended, actual, or projected consequences: If Harry Truman intended to maximize utility by dropping an A-bomb on Hiroshima—as it seemed at the time it would—was his action still "right" years later when his intent had, in fact, produced more harm than good to humankind? We also spent hours cleverly wording obviously immoral maxims that could nonetheless be universalized as laws of nature: Whenever anyone is 5 feet 4 inches tall, is blond-haired and green-eyed, has a birthmark on her upper left arm, has two crooked teeth, and so on, then she will promise to make good on her promises knowing full well that she cannot. We debated whether persons were really obligated to do an action simply because it would add one more "hedon" (unit of pleasure or well-being) to the pile of overall good: If society will get 70 hedons if a woman gives up her brilliant career so that she can be the best mommy ever, but only 69 hedons if she keeps on working full time, cutting a maternal corner here and there, does she *have* to limit her professional potential to provide that one extra hedon to society? And we debated whether persons were always obligated to follow the categorical imperative no matter the consequences: If "Thou shalt not kill" is a universal law, but a man much stronger than you is raping your four-year-old daughter, do you have to stand by and watch? Under such circumstances, don't you have the right to shoot—and possibly kill—him to stop the violation? It was all so rational, so distant from real life, so tidy on paper.

Yet even though I was convinced that utilitarianism and deontology were flawed ethical theories, I could not quite articulate what they lacked until I started to study a variety of feminine and feminist approaches to ethics. Some of these works aimed to *reinterpret* traditional ethics, to move its boundaries closer to feminine and/or feminist territories. Others sought to *supplement* the traditional ethics of justice and rights with an ethics of care and responsibilities. Still others worked to *replace* traditional ethics with new approaches to ethics based on a nondualistic worldview (that is, a worldview that does not split reason from emotion, self from other, nature from culture, and so on).

As we will repeatedly see, these three specific projects—reinterpretation, supplementation, and replacement—intersect, as do the more general projects of developing feminine and feminist approaches to ethics. Nevertheless, these general projects are distinct from each other. By appreciating and analyzing the ways in which feminine and feminist approaches to ethics make up for what traditional ethics lacks, we can meet the challenge that currently confronts us: reconceiving ethics on the basis of an ontology, epistemology, and politics that have been corrected to incorporate women's ways of being, knowing, and doing.

NOTES

1. Louis P. Pojman, *Discovering Right and Wrong* (Belmont, Calif.: Wadsworth, 1990), 2.
2. Ibid., 13.
3. Jeremy Bentham, "An Introduction to the Principles of Morals and Legislation," in *Utilitarianism and Other Writings* (New York: The New American Library, 1962), 65.
4. John Stuart Mill, "Utilitarianism," in *Utilitarianism, Liberty, and Representative Government* (London: J. M. Dent & Sons, 1936), 7–8.
5. Ibid., 9.
6. H. J. McCloskey, "A Non-Utilitarian Approach to Punishment," *Inquiry* 8 (1965).
7. Immanuel Kant, *Groundwork of the Metaphysics of Morals*, trans. H. J. Paton (New York: Harper & Row, 1956), 74–75.
8. Ibid., 40.

3

Women's Morality:
Precursory Feminine and
Feminist Approaches to Ethics

Although feminine and feminist approaches to ethics may strike us as late twentieth-century developments, in fact they have a long history. Among others, Jean-Jacques Rousseau, Mary Wollstonecraft, John Stuart Mill, Harriet Taylor, Catherine Beecher, Elizabeth Cady Stanton, and Charlotte Perkins Gilman all discussed what is probably best termed "woman's morality."[1] Each of these thinkers pondered questions such as, Are women's positive feminine traits "natural" and their negative ones "socially constructed"? Is there a gender-neutral standard available to separate "good" from "bad" psychological traits? If moral virtues as well as psychological traits are connected with one's emotional repertoire, indeed with one's physiology, shouldn't we expect men and women to excel at different moral virtues as well as to manifest different psychological traits? Should all individuals be urged to cultivate precisely the same set of psychological traits and moral virtues, or should there be room for specialization, provided that this specialization does not split down gender lines?

In this chapter, we will see that eighteenth- and nineteenth-century representatives of "women's morality" formulated diverse answers to some of the questions on which not only women's but also men's goodness depends. Their insights continue to inspire twentieth-century "feminine" and "feminist" thinkers who, like their predecessors, seem more interested in motivating people to actually do the good than in formulating totally consistent theories that may or may not speak to the concerns of ordinary people. In the course of retrieving "women's

morality" from its historical archives, we will better position ourselves
for the critical readings feminine and feminist approaches to ethics demand.

WOMAN'S MORALITY AND
ARISTOTELIAN VIRTUE ETHICS

Because the topic of virtue is quite complex, it is important to define
what virtue is and to make some preliminary observations about it. In
Chapter 2, we focused on utilitarianism and deontology as paradigms of
traditional ethics. There are, however, other paradigms of traditional
ethics. So-called "virtue ethics" is probably the most frequently mentioned paradigm. It differs from its utilitarian and deontological counterparts in that it focuses on the goodness or badness of people's *characters* as opposed to the rightness or wrongness of people's *actions*.

Perhaps the most well-known exponent of virtue ethics is the Greek
philosopher Aristotle (384–322 B.C.), who claimed that the ultimate goal
of human action is personal happiness (*eudaemonia*), understood as a
state of total well-being.[2] Given that we all desire this state of affairs,
said Aristotle, we all want to know how to attain it. But unless we are
able to understand what our purpose in living is—that is, our essential
human function—we cannot know what will make us happy let alone
how to attain it. Aristotle considered several candidates for the honor of
essential human function. First, we exist to take nourishment and grow.
Second, we exist to feel emotions and to perceive the external world
through complex perceptual structures. Third, we exist to somehow use
our capacity for reasoning.

By the first hypothesis, human life is indistinguishable from plant
life; by the second, it is indistinguishable from nonsapient animal life.
But because humans can do much more than plants and nonsapient animals can do, Aristotle argued that the *essential* human function must
have to do with that function *only* humans can perform. Because our
capacity for rationality and language supposedly separates us from all
other entities (mineral, plant, and even animal), Aristotle concluded
that the purpose of human life must somehow involve this capacity.
Thus, for Aristotle, the aim of human existence, *eudaemonia,* "turns out
to be activity of soul in accordance with virtue, and if there are more
than one virtue, in accordance with the best and most complete"[3]—that
is, *reason.*

If the happy life is the active life, the life in which we freely exercise our capacities, tendencies, and functions, then it is also the life of a practitioner. Depending on his/her physical and psychological capacities, a person may derive considerable satisfaction from any number of human activities—for example, parenting, golfing, teaching, and film-making—each of which constitutes a coherent and complex form of socially established cooperative human relationships.

What is difficult about human activities is not *enjoying* them, however, but *prioritizing* and *coordinating* them. Aristotle's answers to questions like "Which of my activities should I regard as primary?" and "How should I relate my concerns to yours?" are ones that lead him away from appeals to anything like Mill's principle of utility or Kant's categorical imperative. Not even the most sophisticated weighing of hedons (units of pleasure) and dolors (units of pain) can tell a man whether it is good for him to get more pleasure from building a corporate empire than from parenting his daughter. Similarly, not even the most scrupulous application of the categorical imperative can tell a woman whether her duties as a wife should take precedence over her duties as a daughter or mother. What will mediate such situations, however, is practical wisdom, or intelligence in directing human activities to the goal of human well-being, flourishing, or thriving.

Practical wisdom—the ability to know the right thing to do—has two indispensable functions. First, it enables us to know not only the *means* to certain desired ends but also which *ends* are worthy of desire. The person who is merely clever is able to find the means appropriate to the attainment of all sorts of ends, be they good or bad. Although the person of practical wisdom is also gifted with this technical skill, s/he exercises it only on behalf of good ends—that is, those ends that, when taken together, properly ranked, and gradually achieved, constitute "what is best" or "the human good." Second, practical wisdom enables us to exercise those virtues we need to exercise in order to attain both the *specific good* internal to any worthy practice and the *general good* toward which all worthy practices tend—namely, the good of flourishing as an individual in a community. Unless a person is practically wise, s/he will exhibit not virtue but either its excess or its defect. So, for example, the woman who lacks practical wisdom will act not courageously but either rashly or cowardly. Likewise, the man who lacks practical wisdom will act not in a magnificent manner but in either a stingy or a vulgar one.

Although Aristotle's virtue ethics has much to recommend it, what complicates its adoption as an ethical theory is that there are two kinds of Aristotelian virtue: intellectual and moral. Aristotle defined virtue generally as an activity of the soul (state of mind) that merits praise because it leads us to make "right" choices about what will contribute to our happiness.[4] An intellectual virtue like practical wisdom (knowledge of how to secure the ends of human life) or intuitive reason (knowledge of the principles from which science proceeds) is a product of "teaching."[5] We praise people who exhibit intellectual virtues because they are able to *discern* what it is that will make them happy. In contrast, a moral virtue like courage, temperance, or justice is "a result of habit."[6] We praise people who exhibit moral virtues because they are able to *perform*, almost spontaneously, those actions that do in fact make them happy.

Unlike Aristotle, contemporary ethicists choose a narrower definition of virtue that reserves the term for *moral* virtue only. Moreover, their list of moral virtues tends to be more restricted than Aristotle's, whose scheme includes courage, temperance, liberality, magnificence, pride, ambition, good temper, friendliness, truthfulness, ready wit, shame, and justice.[7] If a moral virtue is a cultivated behavioral disposition that makes a person not merely *acceptable* in his or her own society but *good* in any recognizably human society, then only some of the "moral" virtues on Aristotle's list are actually *moral* virtues—or what we might call "character traits." The rest are merely nonmoral virtues—or what we might call "psychological traits." We do not care whether our saints and heroes display ready wit or give magnificent dinner parties, for example. We do, however, care whether they have sterling characters—that is, whether they are disposed to obeying moral principles. What we want to know, then, is what makes a virtue a moral character trait that manifests goodness as opposed to a nonmoral psychological trait that determines our degree of social acceptability.

MORAL VIRTUE AND NONMORAL VIRTUE: THE CONFLATION OF CHARACTER TRAITS WITH PSYCHOLOGICAL TRAITS

Although twentieth-century ethicists do not have a final answer to this fundamental question about moral versus nonmoral virtue, their preliminary conclusions may still prove helpful in interpreting eighteenth- and nineteenth-century views on "woman's morality." One factor that may distinguish moral from nonmoral virtues is that the former seem to be related to recognized moral principles in ways that the latter are not. Because honesty, benevolence, nonmalevolence, and fairness are associated with such recognized moral principles as the duty not to deceive, the duty to be beneficent, the duty not to harm, and the duty to be just, they are generally recognized as moral virtues. In contrast, because optimism, rationality, self-control, patience, endurance, industry, cleanliness, and wit—to name a few—are not associated with any recognized moral principles, they are classified as nonmoral virtues.

Another factor that may separate moral from nonmoral virtues is that moral virtues are more closely linked "with what has been deemed essential for the moral life and incompatible with the immoral life"[8] than nonmoral virtues are. It is much harder, for example, to conceive of a nonmalevolent murderer than a self-controlled robber. We can perhaps imagine a witty robber, but not an honest one.

Yet another factor that may distinguish moral from nonmoral virtues is that compared to nonmoral virtues, moral virtues are more directly tied to *ungendered character traits* (traits that any person, male or female, has to cultivate in order to be regarded as a good person). In contrast, compared to moral virtues, nonmoral virtues are more directly tied to *gendered psychological traits* (traits that women have to cultivate in order to be regarded as "feminine" and men have to cultivate in order to be regarded as "masculine"). Although society may describe a "masculine" woman as unattractive and unappealing, society must concede that she is a *good* person, her masculinity notwithstanding, if she exhibits such character traits as courage, justice, and temperance.[9] Similar points could be made about society's reactions to and judgments about "feminine" men whose characters are nonetheless exemplary.

In this chapter it will become clear, first, that most eighteenth- and nineteenth-century thinkers did not in fact distinguish between moral and nonmoral virtues or between character and psychological traits. Instead, they mixed these virtues and traits together, dividing them into what they sometimes termed "male virtues" and "female virtues." For the most part, the virtues they classified as *male* included a variety of masculine psychological traits (strength of will, ambition, courage, independence, assertiveness, hardiness, rationality, and emotional control) as well as a few distinctively human moral virtues: honesty and justice, to name two. Similarly, for the most part, the virtues they classified as *female* included a variety of feminine psychological traits (gentleness, modesty, humility, supportiveness, empathy, compassion, tenderness, nurturance, intuitiveness, sensitivity, and unselfishness) as well as a few distinctively human moral virtues: benevolence, or caring, to name the one most often mentioned.[10]

Second, we will discover that most eighteenth- and nineteenth-century thinkers tended to favor male virtues over female virtues. As a result, an allegedly male virtue like justice was regarded as superior to an allegedly female virtue like benevolence or caring, and masculine psychological traits like independence and rationality were generally regarded more highly than feminine psychological traits like empathy and emotionality. On occasion, however, a female virtue took pride of place, as moralists doffed their hats in the direction of "femininity."

Finally, we will discover that most eighteenth- and nineteenth-century thinkers tended to identify social acceptability with moral goodness. Yet, as we can easily recognize, there is more to virtue than popularity. An extremely independent and assertive man may be socially acceptable but unable to cultivate the crucial virtue of caring. Similarly, a very humble and supportive woman may be socially acceptable but unable to cultivate the virtue of justice. Simply because a woman is perfectly "feminine" and a man is perfectly "masculine" does not mean that they are entirely good.

EIGHTEENTH- AND NINETEENTH-CENTURY PRELUDES TO TWENTIETH-CENTURY FEMININE AND FEMINIST APPROACHES TO ETHICS

Like their twentieth-century counterparts, eighteenth- and nineteenth-century exponents of "women's morality" generally approached their subject matter in one of three ways: (1) They instructed women to maintain their distinct and unique virtue; (2) they told women to walk along *men's* moral pathways; or (3) they encouraged some combination of the former two approaches. As we will see in the following sections, each of these recommendations to women has its weaknesses as well as its strengths. Clearly, the empirical, conceptual, and normative problems that trouble twentieth-century proponents of feminine and feminist approaches also troubled their forerunners. Apparently, the sign of a genuine moral problem is that solutions to it tend to be partial and provisional.

Rousseau's Reflections on Women's Morality

We find a prime example of the first approach in the work of the eighteenth-century philosopher Jean-Jacques Rousseau. In his classic of educational philosophy, *Emile,* Rousseau claimed that morality is not the same in men and women. Thus, any attempt to inculcate men and women with the same virtues is a misguided educational endeavor. Rousseau portrayed the development of rationality as the most important educational goal for boys but not for girls.[11] Committed to a view that makes "Rational Man" the perfect complement for "Emotional Woman" and vice versa, Rousseau believed that the more men and women differ, the more likely they are to need each other and to bond together into a long-lasting union. But because men's and women's natural differences are not diametrically opposed to each other, these natural differences must be heightened and deepened (indeed exaggerated) through education.

Rousseau's ideal male student, Emile, is schooled in moral virtues such as temperance, justice, and fortitude, whereas Sophie is schooled not in moral virtues but in nonmoral virtues, specifically, the feminine psychological traits of patience, docility, good humor, and flexibility. Emile studies the humanities, the social sciences, and the natural sciences, all the while perfecting his civic leadership skills; Sophie dabbles in music, art, fiction, and poetry, all the while refining her domestic skills. Rousseau claimed that the development of Emile's mental capacities would make him a rational, moral, self-governing, self-sufficient citizen and husband/father, while the development of Sophie's sensitivities would make her both an understanding, responsive wife and a caring, loving mother. Highly differentiated gender roles are the ultimate purpose of a Rousseauvian education—an education that reinforces the boundaries between the public and the private world, as well as the lines between male and female.

Rousseau believed that even though women *could* develop masculine psychological traits, they *should* not.[12] He warned mothers that should their daughters develop masculine psychological traits, their daughters would suffer dire consequences. A woman, he claimed, cannot "be nurse today and warrior tomorrow"[13] without making herself and everyone else with whom she deals miserable: "A brilliant wife is a plague to her husband, her children, her friends, her valets, everyone."[14] To be virtuous, Sophie must develop precisely those feminine psychological traits that Emile lacks: "A perfect woman and a perfect man ought not to resemble each other in mind any more than in looks."[15] Whereas a man ought to be physically strong and mentally active, a woman ought to be physically weak and mentally passive. Together they will constitute a harmonious whole.

One worrisome point about Rousseau's vision of heterosexual complementarity is that almost all of the virtues Rousseau classified as "female" are merely feminine psychological traits. Indeed, most of them are the kind that impede moral development (for example, coquetry, guile, and subservience). In contrast, his list of "male" virtues is a blend of masculine psychological traits and moral virtues. Apparently, Rousseau believed that women are unable to cultivate *human* moral virtues, the kind of virtues that transcend the personality types favored by particular societies. Rousseau attributed what he perceived as women's moral deficiencies to their lack of autonomy, that is, to what contemporary philosophers have described as some persons' inability "to think and act independently of the customs, opinions and fashions of one's social world."[16] Women lack autonomy, said Rousseau, because autonomy requires certain material conditions, particularly economic independence. Thus, because women are usually economically dependent on men, they are destined to a life of heteronomy, that is, to a life in which they march to the beat of male drummers. For this reason, Rousseau limited women's morality to the cultivation of those feminine psychological traits that serve the desires of their material benefactors—men:

> Women and men are made for one another, but their mutual dependence is not equal. Men depend on women because of their desires; women depend on men because of both their desires and their needs. We would survive more easily without them than they would without us. For them to have what is necessary to their station, they depend on us to give it to them, to want to give it to them, to esteem them worthy of it. They depend on our sentiments, on the value we set on their merit, on the importance we attach to their charms and their virtues.[17]

What Rousseau said about women lends itself to some very disturbing interpretations. Men do not really need women to feel good about themselves but women really do need men to feel good about themselves. If men stopped telling women how wonderful women are—if they stopped attaching value to women's "charms" and "virtues"— women would question their *worth* in ways that men would not question their worth were women to stop loving, honoring, and obeying them. As it happens, however, women are in luck! Like most men, Emile happens to *desire* women, and so Sophie, his chosen woman, is not forced to search for the real ground of her being—that is, her true self.

If my interpretation of Rousseau is accurate, what he offers us is not a recipe for heterosexual complementarity but one for a lopsided state of affairs in which women do all the giving and men do all the taking. Whether they are apart or together, Sophie and Emile are incomplete persons, "monstrosities"—what Dorothy Dinnerstein has termed a "mermaid" and a "minotaur."[18] When they are apart from each other, they simply lack a wide range of psychological traits that could improve their separate selves, and when they are together, they are more likely to bring out the worst in each other than the best.

Mary Wollstonecraft's Reflections on Women's Morality

In her 1792 monograph, *A Vindication of the Rights of Women,* Mary Wollstonecraft had the intellectual independence to reply "What nonsense!" to Rousseau's theories.[19] Although Wollstonecraft did not use terms such as "socially constructed gender roles," she denied that women are *by nature* more pleasure seeking and pleasure giving than men. If men were confined to the same "cages" women find themselves locked in, as are low-ranking military men, for example, they would develop the same kind of weak characters women arguably develop.[20] Denied the chance to develop their rational powers, to become moral persons who have concerns, causes, and commitments over and beyond personal pleasure, men as well as women would become overly "emotional," a condition Wollstonecraft associated with hypersensitivity, extreme narcissism, and excessive self-indulgence.

Because she regarded the ability to reason rather than the capacity to feel as the characteristic that distinguishes humans from brutes, Wollstonecraft predictably approved of Emile's educational program but not of Sophie's. She perceptively contrasted "decorum," which is "manners," such as any automaton might master, with "morals," which require an educated understanding."[21] Whereas society teaches men morals, it teaches women manners. More specifically, society encourages women to cultivate negative feminine psychological traits like "cunning," "vanity," and "immaturity," all of which impede the proper development of positive feminine psychological traits. Even worse, society twists and turns women's genuine virtues into vices. Wollstonecraft commented, for example, that when *strong* women practice gentleness, it is a grand, even godly, virtue; but when *weak* women practice it, it is a demeaning, even subhuman, vice. The positive psychological trait of gentleness is transformed into the negative psychological trait of obsequiousness "when it is the submissive demeanor of dependence, the support of weakness that loves, because it wants protection; and is forbearing because it must silently endure injuries; smiling under the lash at which it dare not snarl."[22]

Distressed by her female contemporaries' negative feminine psychological traits (and rightly so, because they are the ones that keep women subservient), Wollstonecraft concluded that the quickest way for women to be regarded as moral is for them to become "men"—that is, for women to display the psychological traits usually associated with men. Yet, it is doubtful that Wollstonecraft believed that "masculinity" is the *best* way for women to develop personally and morally under any and all circumstances. She may simply have believed that it is the most *prudent* way for them to develop personally and morally within a patriarchal society that prefers male values to female values.

Just because Wollstonecraft lamented women's moral deficiencies does not mean that she totally blamed women for not being as good as they possibly could be. On the contrary, she claimed that because women are politically and economically oppressed, they do not have the material means necessary to develop their moral potential:

> But to render her really virtuous and useful, she must not, if she discharges her civil duties, want individually the protection of civil laws; she must not be dependent on her husband's bounty for her subsistence during her life, or support after his death; for how can a being be generous who has nothing of its own; or virtuous who is not free?[23]

If a woman is free, she does not have to develop a "masculine" personality in order to become moral. Like a free man, a free woman may cultivate whatever psychological traits most contribute to her moral development. Women may focus on the supposedly masculine psychological traits of strength and bravery, even as men may focus on the supposedly feminine psychological traits of empathy and nurturance. Under conditions of freedom, socially constructed gender boundaries cease to restrict *human* moral development.

John Stuart Mill's and Harriet Taylor's *Reflections on Women's Morality*

Debates about what makes a character good and a personality socially acceptable did not end with Mary Wollstonecraft. Writing a century after Wollstonecraft, John Stuart Mill agreed with his predecessor that virtue is gender neutral and that society is wrong to set up an ethical double standard according to which women's morality is to be assessed differently than men's morality. Indeed, as Mill saw it, society is wrong to set up *any* gender-based double standards:

> I do not know a more signal instance of the blindness with which the world, including the herd of studious men, ignore and pass over all the influences of social circumstances, than their silly depreciation of the intellectual, and silly panegyrics on the moral nature of women.[24]

Reflecting further on women's alleged moral superiority, Mill concluded that, first, women's "moral nature" is not the result of innate female propensities but of systematic social conditioning. To praise women on account of their great "virtue" is merely to compliment patriarchal society for having inculcated in women those feminine psychological traits that serve it well:

> All women are brought up from the very earliest years in the belief that their ideal of character is the very opposite to that of men; not self-will and government by self-control, but submission and yielding to the control of others. All the moralities tell them that it is the duty of women, and all the current sentimentalities that it is their nature, to live for others, to make complete abnegation of themselves, and to have no life but in their affections.[25]

Second, some of the "virtues" that society inculcates in women but not in men turn out to be disguised versions of the very vices they are intended to overcome. Mill cited "unselfishness" as a case in point, arguing that women are no less selfish than men are. It is just that whereas in men selfishness assumes an individualistic, ego-oriented form, in women it assumes a communal, family-oriented form. "Family selfishness" may seem less *selfish* than "individual selfishness," but only because it wears an "amiable gaze"[26] and easily passes for duty.

Confined to the private, or domestic, realm, the typical woman is preoccupied with the immediate concerns of her family and friends. She overestimates her loved ones' wants and needs and underestimates those of society in general. As a result, she spares no effort to further her husband's career, to put her sons through school, and to marry her daughters well, but she neglects her larger civic duties. Because this kind of "unselfishness" does not require a woman to regard a stranger's, or even a neighbor's, good as valuable as her family's and friends' good, it is not utilitarian.

In Mill's estimation, what will enable women to display true unselfishness—that is, the kind of utilitarian unselfishness that takes *everyone's* interests into account—is women's access to education and suffrage. Provided that society gives women the same educational opportunities and political rights it gives men, women will have the means to understand the connections between the private and public realms. They will be prepared to think like genuinely moral agents.

Harriet Taylor's suspicions about women's allegedly superior moral virtues equaled those of Mill. An independent thinker, Taylor did not let her marriage to Mill interfere with the development of her own thinking. As she saw it, Mill's proposed cure for women's moral infirmities was no panacea. Women need more than educational opportunities and political rights if they are to become moral. They need, as Wollstonecraft had earlier suggested, economic security. As long as a woman has no income of her own, she will feel beholden to the men (husband, father, brother, son) who support her, and they will feel justified in articulating the terms of her existence.[27] "Buying power," as well as "thinking power" and "voting power," is a necessary condition for a woman's freedom without which she cannot hope to be moral.

Whatever their disagreements about women's need to work outside of the home, however, Mill and Taylor were both adamant that sexual inequality is an impediment to the cultivation of moral virtue. In fact, Mill proclaimed that "the present constitution of the relation between men and women" is the source of "all the selfish propensities, the self-worship, the unjust self-preference, which exist among mankind."[28] However exaggerated this claim may be, it is not one to be lightly dismissed. Male-female inequalities—in particular, patterns of male domination and female submission—have caused men and women to develop such *negative* masculine and feminine psychological traits as male arrogance and female servility. These negative psychological traits make it difficult for men and women to cultivate moral virtues. For example, consider the moral virtue honesty, which philosopher Alasdair MacIntyre defines as the ability "to listen carefully to what we are told about our own inadequacies and to reply with the same carefulness for the facts."[29] An arrogant man cannot be honest, for he will not *be able* to listen to anyone itemize his actual inadequacies. Likewise, a servile woman cannot be honest, for she will not *be willing* to challenge those who label her virtues "vices." People whose daily lives are encumbered by structures of domination and submission may find it extraordinarily difficult to become moral. In fact, to the degree that people are unfree, they *cannot* be honest or benevolent or fair or conscientious. All they can be is the distortions of these ways of being: a truly vicious state of affairs.

Catherine Beecher's Reflections on Women's Morality

In contrast to Mill and Taylor, other nineteenth-century thinkers denied that virtue is one. Instead, they forwarded either a "separate-but-equal" theory of virtue according to which male and female psychological traits are simply *different,* or a "separate-and-unequal" theory of virtue according to which female virtue is ultimately *better* than male virtue. Significantly, this diverse group of thinkers disagreed among themselves whether the virtues typically associated with women (nurturance, empathy, compassion, self-sacrifice, kindness) are (1) full-fledged moral virtues to be developed by men as well as by women; (2) *positive* feminine psychological traits to be developed by women alone; or (3) *negative* feminine psychological traits to be developed neither by women nor by men.

Catherine Beecher belonged to this group of thinkers. Even though she believed that women's place is in the home, she did not believe that women's minds and bodies are somehow inferior to those of men. On the contrary, she worked, says Barbara Cross, "to replace the languishing, corseted lady of wealth, the worn, extravagant housewife, and the 'fainting, weeping, vapid, pretty plaything' of society with an energetic and enlightened figure, clad 'in the panoply of Heaven and sending the thrill of benevolence through a thousand youthful hearts.'"[30] Women do not need to become politically and economically active in order to justify their existence. Rather, all they need to do is to perform their domestic duties with determination, drive, and discipline.

Beecher agreed with Wollstonecraft that women's domestic duties are demanding ones and that women must be properly educated in order to discharge these duties effectively. But even though she conceded that women, like men, must be educated in "mental discipline," she did not think that men and women should receive the *same* education. With the remarkable proviso that women's work be recognized as more *fundamental* than men's, Beecher thought, like Rousseau, that men and women should learn different things to fit their different social roles. Unless women succeed in their domestic and reproductive tasks, men will lose their reason for working:

To man is appointed the out-door labor—to till the earth, dig the mines, toil in the foundries, traverse the ocean, transport merchandise, labor in manufactories, construct houses, conduct civil, municipal and state affairs, and all the heavy work, which, most of the day, excludes him from the comforts of a home. But the great stimulus to all these toils, implanted in the heart of every true man, is the desire for a home of his own, and the hopes of paternity.[31]

To guide civilization in positive directions, women must create the kind of homes and families for which men will want to live and, if necessary, to die. Regrettably, because society neither takes women's all important task seriously nor educates them for it, "family labor is poorly done, poorly paid, and regarded as menial and disgraceful."[32]

In an effort to bolster the status of "family labor," Beecher created "domestic science." In *The New Housekeeper's Manual,* she and her sister Harriet enumerated all the things women must learn to do in order to run proper Christian households. The list is staggering. Women must know *everything* including "how dampers and air boxes should be placed and regulated, how to prevent or remedy gas escapes," and how to manage "ball corks and high and low pressure on water pipes."[33] Most important, women must know how to mother.

A single woman herself, Beecher sought to mother society's "soul" as well as the young, the old, the infirm, and the poor. She asserted that it was *women's* role to make society "Christlike"—that is, submissive, self-sacrificial, and benevolent. Sheltered safely in the private realm, where they are largely insulated from the siren calls of wealth, power, and prestige that pervade the public sphere of politics and economics, women are supposedly better situated to cultivate what Beecher and her sister termed the "grand peculiarity of the character of Christ . . . *self-denying benevolence.*"[34] By acting as moral exemplars for their children, husbands, fathers, and brothers, women can teach Christlike virtue to all their relatives. The better that women are, the better that everyone else will be. Apparently, only women are active moral agents; children and men are simply the passive recipients of women's goodness.

What is perplexing and perhaps even self-contradictory about Beecher's line of reasoning is her apparent belief that "self-denying benevolence" is both a feminine psychological trait—that is, a nonmoral virtue in which *women* specialize—and a required *human* moral virtue. "Christian" society requires men as well as women to practice the virtue of self-denying benevolence *in theory*. Yet, because men supposedly have a harder time than women emulating Christ, "Christian" society expects very little in the way of self-denying benevolence from men *in practice*. As a result, "Christian" society asks women to guide men slowly down the path of virtue, picking up the moral slack whenever their charges falter.

To her credit, Beecher portrayed women as morally powerful rather than morally deficient persons. Yet is it *women's* role to make *men* good? Are not all human beings, male or female, responsible for their own goodness, for their own moral character? Are only women obliged to be submissive, self-sacrificial, and benevolent—to hang, so to speak, with Christ on the cross? If so, we must wonder what kind of moral virtue self-denying benevolence is if only half the members of society (that is, women) are really expected to cultivate it.

Elizabeth Cady Stanton's Reflections on Women's Morality

Elizabeth Cady Stanton's position on men's and women's morality is extremely complex. On the one hand, she suggested that women's alleged virtue and men's alleged vice are the products of socialization:

> In my opinion, [man] is infinitely woman's inferior in every moral quality, not by nature, but made so by [a false] education. . . . Woman has now the noble virtues of the martyr. She is early schooled to self-denial and suffering. But man is not so wholly buried in selfishness that he does not sometimes get a glimpse of the narrowness of his soul, as compared with woman. Then he says, by way of excuse for his degradation, "God made woman more self-denying than man. It is her nature. . . ."[35]

On the other hand, she suggested that beyond socialization, there is a "feminine element" that determines how "good" a woman is going to be and a "male element" that determines how "bad" a man is going to be.

> The male element is a destructive force, stern, selfish, aggrandizing, loving war, violence, conquest, acquisition, breeding in the material and moral world alike discord, disorder, disease and death. See what a record of blood and cruelty the pages of history reveal! Through what slavery, slaughter, and sacrifice, through what inquisitions and imprisonment, pains and persecutions, black codes and gloomy creeds, the soul of humanity has struggled for the centuries, while mercy has veiled her face and all hearts have been dead alike to love and hope! The male element has held high carnival thus far, it has fairly run riot from the beginning, overpowering the feminine element everywhere, crushing out all the diviner qualities in human nature. . . .[36]

But whether her final view is that men's and women's diverging moralities are the result of socialization or biological nature, Stanton consistently argued that men's nonmoral virtues—specifically, their *negative* masculine psychological traits—have set the standard for behavior in the public world. Women's nonmoral virtues—including their *positive* feminine psychological traits—have been either suppressed or ignored to the detriment of the public world. If the public world is to survive, let alone thrive, women must enter it. Exerting influence over one's husband and children in the style of Beecher is not enough. Working in the economic world and participating in the political scene is also crucial.[37]

Stanton exposed the error of struggling for the human rights of "mankind" without also struggling for the human rights of "womankind."[38] In her *Declaration of Human Sentiments*, a document modeled on the Declaration of Independence, Stanton proclaimed that women as well as men "are created equal."[39] In her later works, she further specified the ways in which men have failed to treat women as their equals—that is, as full human persons with their own unique destinies. While addressing the Senate Committee on Women's Suffrage in 1892, for example, Stanton asked the assembled senators to reflect on the fact that women are not merely "functions" or "roles"—that is, mothers, wives, sisters, and daughters. Rather they are also individuals, citizens, and, yes, *women*. According to Stanton, it is unfair for men to subordinate women's rights to women's duties, since they do not subordinate men's rights to men's duties.[40]

Although Stanton frequently celebrated women's values in her efforts to secure the franchise for them, she had reservations about idealizing women as totally self-sacrificial human beings. It occurred to her that until women have the same political and economic power as men have, it may be truly *self*-denying (indeed, *self*-annihilating) for women to specialize in benevolence. Paradoxically, benevolence may presently be a negative feminine psychological trait, even if it is ultimately a *required* human moral virtue. In the course of interpreting a biblical passage in which Jesus praises a widow for giving her last few coins to the poor, Stanton suggested that an oppressed group cannot always afford to be entirely good—not without destroying itself. Agreeing that the widow's small gift was indeed a precious one, Stanton nonetheless cautioned women that women's self-sacrifice may effectively perpetuate women's second-class status:

This woman, belonging to the impoverished class, was trained to self-abne-gation; but when women learn the higher duty of self-development, they will not so readily expend all their forces in serving others. "Self-development is a higher duty than self-sacrifice," should be woman's motto henceforward.[41]

Although the duty of self-sacrifice is morally required in the abstract, "ought" implies can. Because few women in a patriarchal society have the political and economic means to practice benevolence without men taking advantage of them, they cannot always afford to be "nice."

Charlotte Perkins Gilman's Reflections on Women's Morality

In her feminist utopian novel, *Herland*, Charlotte Perkins Gilman por-trays an all-female society in which the women are able to serve others without sacrificing themselves to these others. As a result of an earth-quake that permanently cut off Herland's women from their men, Herland's women became self-sufficient. No longer did they need men to survive either on a short-term basis or, thanks to the miracle of par-thenogenesis, on a long-term basis.

Herland is a mother-dominated society in which reproduction rather than production is the leitmotiv. But just because Herland is child-cen-tered does not mean that all life is somehow "private," or "domestic life." The women of Herland have a public life that encompasses both economic and political aspects; they till the soil, harvest the crops, build the houses, make the laws, and administer justice. Indeed, Gilman would have had it no other way, for she believed that to the degree that women have been kept out of the public realm, to that same degree has their moral growth been retarded. What Gilman seeks to offer women in *Herland,* then, is a sufficiently broad arena for their full moral devel-opment. Competitive individualistic approaches to life, with their hos-tility toward connectedness, disappear in Herland, and its women are able to relate to each other without dominating each other.

No wonder that the three American explorers—Terry, Van and Jeff—who stumble on Herland are shocked and confused. Before they arrive, they joke about the mythical land, assuming that there *must* be men in it, since women could not possibly cooperate well enough, or be competent enough, to run a country. When they see how successfully Herland is run, at least one of them, Terry, a macho "womanizer" and exploiter of women, prefers to question the femininity and moral char-acter of his hostesses rather than to concede their competence:

They've no modesty . . . no patience, no submissiveness, none of that natural yielding which is woman's greatest charm.[42]

Terry does not regard Herland's mothers as virtuous in any sense of the term, since for him female virtue is nothing more or less than a set of negative feminine psychological traits including deference, girlish charm, and fragility. For a woman to be assertive, to lack submissiveness, is for her not only to be unfeminine but also to be *bad*.

In contrast to Terry, who has real contempt for women, Jeff, a physician with a poet's heart, idolizes women. Jeff does not want to rule women; rather he wants to serve, even worship, them. He quickly comes to the conclusion that femininity can take different forms in different societies but that this does not matter as long as women continue to symbolize for men everything that is good, true, and beautiful. Whereas Terry wants a female slave (more specifically, a female sexual slave), Jeff wants a goddess.

Significantly, the women of Herland do not want to be goddesses any more than they want to be slaves. In fact, because they have no idea of "masculinity" or "femininity" to compare and contrast, the women of Herland are rather bewildered by Jeff's and Terry's discourses on femininity and female virtue. As they see it, the relevant categories are *humanity* and *virtue,* and only Van, who represents the "objectivity" of science (he is a sociologist), is in any position to understand what they think about themselves and why. Van seems to the women of Herland more human, less prone to confuse what his society calls "maleness" with the kind of "humanness" that transcends social construction:

"We like you best . . . because you seem most like us." "More like a lot of women!" I thought to myself disgustedly, and then remembered how little like "women," in our derogatory sense they were. . . .

"We can quite see that we do not seem like—women—to you. Of course, in a bisexual [that is, one with two sexes] race the distinctive feature of each sex must be intensified. But surely there are characteristics enough which belong to People, aren't there? That's what I mean about you being more like us—more like People."[43]

As he gets to know the women of Herland better, however, Van begins to realize that they are more than *genderless persons*. They are *women*. Specifically, they are what feminist philosopher Mary Daly terms "natural" women—women who have not been socially constructed to reflect the false image of what a "real woman" should supposedly be—that is, the "Totalled Woman"[44] who is patient (with men), who submits (to men), and who yields (to men). Like Semele, the "mother" of Dionysus who served only as a temporary maternal vessel— Zeus's lightning consumed her when she was six months pregnant—the Totalled Woman is so mesmerized by men that she longs to be wrecked by them in a head-on collision from which she will not recover. Indeed, she permits men to deprive her not only of her self but of any extension of that self. She lets the male Zeus/God rob her of what would seem to be the quintessential female energy: the creative power to birth chil dren. After all, the story of Semele ends with Hermes sewing up the six-month-old Dionysus in the thigh of Zeus who, three months later, delivers him into the world.[45]

Gilman uses the characters in *Herland* to demonstrate her awareness that society has inculcated women with the kind of negative feminine psychological traits that tend to "total" women. Yet, she also uses the characters in *Herland* to testify to women's capacity to resist "totalization" by developing, in addition to positive feminine psychological traits, what amounts to real moral virtue—the kind of character traits men as well as women should be eager to develop. For example, speaking on behalf of his fellow adventurers, Van summarizes their past and present views on Herland's women as follows:

> We had expected them to be given over to what we called "feminine vanity"—"frills and furbelows," and we found they had evolved a costume more perfect than the Chinese dress, richly beautiful when so desired, always useful, of unfailing dignity and good taste.
>
> We had expected a dull submissive monotony, and found a daring social inventiveness far beyond our own, and a mechanical and scientific development fully equal to ours.
>
> We had expected pettiness, and found a social consciousness besides which our nations looked like quarreling children—feebleminded ones at that.
>
> We had expected jealousy, and found a broad sisterly affection, a fair-minded intelligence, to which we could produce no parallel.
>
> We had expected hysteria, and found a standard of health and vigor, a calmness of temper, to which the habit of profanity, for instance, was impossible to explain—we tried it.[46]

Clearly, "untotalled" women are exemplary human beings.

Of course, *Herland* is a fictional, utopian work in which imagined social, economic, and ideological conditions permit women to develop in morally good as well as psychologically healthy ways. In her nonfictional, "real world" work, *Women and Economics,* Gilman wrote that to the degree that women are economically dependent on men, both they and men will tend to exhibit negative psychological traits. Women will be known for their blind faith, complete submission, and self-destructive self-sacrifice, and men will be known for their "pride, cruelty, and selfishness."[47] Only when women are men's economic equals will women and men be able to develop the kind of positive psychological traits that are compatible with moral virtue.

What Gilman neglects in *Women and Economics,* however, is the sexual and reproductive independence from men that is also necessary for women's moral development. Economic freedom is not enough. Perhaps the absence in Herland of what Stanton described as the tension between "self-abnegation" and "self-development" stems from the lack of men. There is no one to take advantage of women's natural or required tendency to care. It is safe for women to mother in Herland because every citizen of Herland shares in its essential maternal activities. Not only do mothers "mother," they are also "mothered."

CONCLUSIONS

As we have seen, some past thinkers believed that virtue is the same, or largely the same, for both men and women. Nevertheless, even among these thinkers, there was a tendency to favor the virtues that society associated with men over those that society associated with women. Wollstonecraft, for example, suggested that if a woman wishes to cultivate true moral virtues, she must first cultivate a set of "masculine" personality traits such as independence and assertiveness. No doubt, Wollstonecraft's realization that many eighteenth-century feminine psychological traits impeded women's moral development, even if they enabled certain middle-class women to charm the men on whom they depended, motivated her suggestion that "masculinity" is a precondition for morality. Writing with the purpose of exposing just how hollow society's praise of women's "virtue" is,[48] Wollstonecraft chose to focus on what was wrong about women's "morality" rather than what was right about it. As a result, Wollstonecraft did not praise women nearly enough, sometimes giving the impression that she preferred men's ways of being, thinking, and acting to women's. Her position becomes more understandable if we recall that, as a *writer,* she was struggling to succeed in a man's world.

In addition to thinkers like Wollstonecraft who urged women to cultivate men's virtues, other past thinkers encouraged men to practice *manly* virtues and women to practice *womanly* virtues. Unfortunately, such divisions of virtue tended to be more separate than equal. For example, Rousseau offered Emile a much more impressive set of virtues than he offered Sophie—the implication being that Sophie lacks the kind of spine necessary to be moral. Even though Beecher maintained that women's virtues are at least as good as men's virtues, she did not want women to test their moral mettle in the public world. Yet if women are good, why did Beecher fear that they would not be able to withstand the evils of the public world when they were already withstanding the evils of the private world? Was Beecher so prone to nineteenth-century idealizations of the "home" as a safe and pure haven in a dangerous and corrupt world that she actually believed life is nasty, brutish, and short only in the public world? Did she think that one's capacity for morality is likely to be tested only outside of one's home? Did her happy homemaker never struggle with the evils of incest or woman battering?

Unlike Beecher, Stanton did not doubt women's ability to remain moral in the public world. She reasoned that if women could maintain their goodness in the private domain, they could also maintain it in the public domain. Still, even if Stanton was convinced about women's ability to act morally even under adverse circumstances, she did not want women to cultivate this ability entirely at their own expense. In the end, Stanton chose the virtue of self-development over the virtue of self-abnegation for women, not because she did not value self-abnegation but because she did not want women's *goodness* to be used against women.

In contrast to all of these thinkers, Gilman sought to create a utopia for women. Only there could women successfully cultivate the best "masculine" as well as "feminine" psychological traits. The women in Herland are independent, assertive, and hardy as well as empathetic, nurturant, and compassionate. Still, Herland is more traditionally "feminine" than "masculine." Herland's leaders stress the moral virtues that emanate from benevolence far more than those that flow from justice (for example, honesty and fairness). Although the women in Herland are honest and fair persons capable of delivering justice, for them virtue is ultimately about mothering—that is, about being attentive to individuals' particular needs and desires. And although Gilman recommends that men as well as women become "mothers," she ultimately concludes in *Herland* that only a few men are capable of cultivating the moral virtues associated with benevolence.

Although eighteenth- and nineteenth-century thinkers failed to answer all the questions that they had about women's morality, they demonstrated people's tendency to think of morality as gendered. Traditionally, certain personality traits and moral virtues have been associated with men and others with women. We have inherited this legacy. As I see it, it is incumbent on us to determine whether a gendered or an ungendered conception of morality is most likely to successfully guide our moral development. But before we can make this determination, I think it is important for us to first understand the kinds of *worldviews* that lead to either gendered or ungendered conceptions of morality.

In the next chapter we will analyze some of the ontological and epistemological assumptions that guide feminine and feminist approaches to ethics, comparing and contrasting them with traditional assumptions and approaches. We will see that there is no way to separate our reflections about goodness from our reflections about personhood and truth. The task of feminine and feminist approaches to ethics is, then, to provide us with a strong sense of self and a clear vision of reality that will enable us to do what we are required to do.

NOTES

A version of some sections of this chapter was published as "Feminist Justice: A Study in Difference." *Journal of Social Philosophy* XXII, no. 3 (Winter 1991): 81–91. Used by permission of the editor.

1. Jane Roland Martin, *Reclaiming a Conversation: The Ideal of the Educated Woman* (New Haven, Conn.: Yale University Press, 1985), 104.

2. *The Nicomachean Ethics*, Bk I, Ch. 7, in W. D. Ross, ed., *The Works of Aristotle Translated Into English* (London: Oxford University Press, 1963).

3. Ibid.

4. Ibid., Bk I, Ch. 13, 1103[a].

5. Ibid., Bk II, Ch. 1, 1103[a].

6. Ibid.

7. Ibid., Bk II, Ch. 7.

8. See Louis P. Pojman, *Ethics: Discovering Right and Wrong* (Belmont, Calif.: Wadsworth, 1990), 120.

9. It is, of course, conceivable that society would, as it has in the past, claim that the only "goodness" woman is capable of is the perfection of her feminine traits.

10. This list of psychological traits is found in Mary Vetterling-Braggin, ed., *"Femininity," "Masculinity," and "Androgyny"* (Totowa, N.J.: Littlefield, Adams, and Co., 1982), 5–6.

11. Jean-Jacques Rousseau, *Emile*, trans. Allan Bloom (New York: Basic Books, 1979).

12. Rousseau, as quoted in Martin, *Reclaiming a Conversation*, 41.

13. Rousseau, as quoted in ibid.

14. Rousseau, as quoted in ibid., 52.

15. Rousseau, as quoted in ibid., 53.

16. John Exdell, "Ethics, Ideology, and Feminine Virtue," in Marsha Hanen and Kai Nielson, eds., *Science, Morality and Feminist Theory* (Calgary: The University of Calgary Press, 1987), 175.

17. Jean-Jacques Rousseau, *Emile*, 364.

18. Dorothy Dinnerstein, *The Mermaid and the Minotaur: Sexual Arrangements and Human Malaise* (New York: Harper & Row, 1977).

19. Mary Wollstonecraft, *A Vindication of the Rights of Women*, ed. Miriam Brody (London: Penguin Books, 1988), 108.

20. Ibid., 105.

21. Ibid., 106.

22. Ibid., 117.

23. Ibid., 259.

24. John Stuart Mill, *On the Subjection of Women* (New York: Frederick A. Stokes Company, 1911), 169.

25. Ibid., 32

26. John Stuart Mill, "Periodical Literature: Edinburgh Review," *Westminster Review* I, no. 2 (April 1824):526.

27. Harriet Taylor Mill, "Enfranchisement of Women," in Alice S. Rossi, ed., *Essays on Sex Equality* (Chicago: University of Chicago Press, 1970), 105.

28. Mill, *On the Subjection of Women*, 176.

29. Alasdair MacIntyre, *After Virtue* (Notre Dame, Ind.: University of Notre Dame Press, 1981), 178.

30. Barbara Cross, ed., *The Educated Woman in America* (New York: Teachers College, Columbia University, 1965), 7.

31. Catherine E. Beecher and Harriet Beecher Stowe, *The American Woman's Home: Principles of Domestic Science* (New York: Arno Press & the New York Times, 1971), 19.

32. Ibid., 13.

33. Catherine E. Beecher and Harriet Beecher Stowe, *The New Housekeeper's Manual* (New York: J. B. Ford and Company, 1873), 14ff.

34. Beecher and Beecher, *The American Woman's Home*, 234.

35. Elizabeth Cady Stanton, "Address Delivered at Seneca Falls," in Ellen Carol Dubois, ed., *Elizabeth Cady Stanton/Susan B. Anthony: Correspondence, Writing, Speeches* (New York: Shocken Books, 1981), 30.

36. Stanton, as quoted in Mari Jo Buhle and Paul Buhle, eds., *The Concise History of Women's Suffrage* (Urbana: University of Illinois Press, 1978), 252–253.

37. Ibid., 253.

38. Ibid.

39. Ibid., 94.

40. Ibid., 325–326.

41. Stanton, *The Woman's Bible*, 131.

42. Charlotte Perkins Gilman, *Herland: A Lost Feminist Utopian Novel* (New York: Pantheon Books, 1979), 98.

43. Ibid., 89.

44. Mary Daly, *Gyn/Ecology: The Metaethics of Radical Feminism* (Boston: Beacon Press, 1978), 64.

45. Ibid., 65.

46. Gilman, *Herland: A Lost Feminist Utopian Novel*, 81.

47. Gilman, *Women and Economics* (New York: Harper & Row, 1966), 319.

48. I owe this point to Claudia Card, professor of philosophy at the University of Wisconsin.

4

The Ontological and Epistemological Conditions for Feminine and Feminist Approaches to Ethics

Eighteenth- and nineteenth-century thinkers like Mary Wollstonecraft, John Stuart Mill, Harriet Taylor, Catherine Beecher, Elizabeth Cady Stanton, and Charlotte Perkins Gilman did much to develop what we would call feminine and feminist approaches to ethics. In fact, they began to pointedly question the ontological and epistemological assumptions on which traditional approaches to ethics are based. As we will see in this chapter, whether they be feminine or feminist, twentieth-century approaches to ethics, even more than any of their precursors, aim to challenge such traditional ontological assumptions as that the more separate the self is from others, the more autonomous, unique, and generally superior that self is. Moreover, these recent approaches try to dispute such traditional epistemological assumptions as the necessarily universal, abstract, impartial and rational nature of reliable knowledge. Given the intimate connections between ethics, ontology, and epistemology, we need, then, to understand precisely what theories of self and knowledge guide feminine and feminist approaches to ethics. If these new approaches to ethics do not rely on the traditional assumptions, to what new assumptions do they appeal?

TRADITIONAL ONTOLOGY CHALLENGED

A number of thinkers, not all of them "feminine" or "feminist," complain that the self that grounds traditional ethics is an "excessively individualistic" self[1]—a self that even takes a measure of delight in separating *himself* from others. I use the reflexive pronoun *himself* deliberately here since, historically, philosophers have spoken of "autonomous *man*" rather than of "autonomous *woman*." Although their intent may have been to use the term man generically, applying it to men and women equally, the consequence of their semantic choice has been anything but gender neutral.

Most people picture autonomous man as a biological male: an independent self, geared toward maximizing his self-interest effectively, efficiently, and expediently. Such a self is always on guard against the ominous "other" who, at any moment, may interfere with his life projects. Even when the "other" seduces him to establish cooperative relations in a community, autonomous man proceeds very cautiously. Apparently, he never manages to totally suppress his fundamental suspicion that every individual he encounters is a potential threat—a competitor for resources that are, in some way or another, scarce. Ever ready for combat, autonomous man guards his rights vigilantly. He tries as hard as possible not to be distracted by considerations of what he owes to others for fear that those others will take advantage of him. Isolated, hostile, fearful, and competitive, autonomous man seems an unlikely candidate for moral development.

Caroline Whitbeck on a Different Reality

Among the thinkers most troubled by the "autonomous man" conception of the self is Caroline Whitbeck. She argues that traditional philosophers, most of whom have been men, have unnecessarily segmented reality by coupling concepts and terms as pairs of polar opposites.[2] Examples of these dichotomous duos are activity/passivity, sun/moon, culture/nature, day/night, high/low, and, of course, male/female.[3] Since this kind of oppositional dualism stems from two male-based worldviews, one preeminently patriarchal and the other insistently individualistic, Whitbeck believes that it favors "masculine" over "feminine" interpretations of reality. Originally, the fathers (or monarchs) ruled all. Then the sons (or propertied male citizens) rebelled against the fathers. Their rebellion constituted their basic self-understanding: "us" against "them." As an extension of this primordial consciousness, reality split into the "twos" that plague us to this day. Ontology became a matter of separating the self from the other, and ethics became a matter of defending one's own interests against those of others.

In order to heal the rifts that such personal alienation and social conflict generate, Whitbeck insists that we must develop a new ontology

and, as its accompaniment, a new ethics. What we need is a nonopposi-
tional, nondualistic, nonhierarchical ontology. That is, we need an approach to reality that does not define the self *against* the other, viewing
that other as an entity that must be either controlled or eliminated.

According to Whitbeck, people come to understand their selves
through others, not *against* them. We are historical creatures, shaped
by our relationships with our parents, siblings, friends, and colleagues.
Although we differ from one another, we relate to each other reasonably well because we also have much in common. For example, because
I recognize the similarities between our bodies, I can imagine that the
diseases and wounds that cause me pain cause you pain. I come to know
you, and you me, through *analogy* rather than through *opposition*. Indeed, were reality as oppositional as traditional ontology claims, I could
not know you at all. There would be no points of contact between you
and me. We would be lonely, solipsistic atoms.

Whereas autonomous man is the paradigm for traditional ontology,
the mother-child duo is the paradigm for Whitbeck's relational ontology. Whitbeck claims that this relationship is so symbiotic that nothing
belongs to the mother that does not belong to the child, especially during pregnancy and the child's infancy. To reinforce her point, Whitbeck
refers to the World Health Organization's conception of "maternal-child
health."[4] Although a woman may think that her health is her personal
business—after all, it is *her* body that is at stake—a mother's health cannot be entirely separated from that of her fetus or infant. If a mother is
malnourished or drug- or alcohol-addicted, then her fetus's or infant's
health may be negatively affected. Similarly, if a fetus or infant has certain toxic conditions or certain contagious infections, its mother's health
may be imperiled.

The choice between a self-versus-other ontology guided by the autonomous man paradigm on the one hand and a self-in-and-through-
others ontology guided by the mother-child paradigm on the other is
not without significant ethical consequences. If I define myself in *opposition* to you, by way of whatever we do not have in common, then I will
probably view you as a threat—at least as someone who could not possibly understand me or share my interests. My fear of you and your fear
of me will lead us to construct a political, social, and moral order in
which "Do no harm" will serve as the foundational rule. In such a world,
our relationships with each other will be guarded and markedly legalistic. We will make contracts with each other, and we will arm ourselves
with the protective coating of our rights. If I have a right to something—be it property or even life—then you have a duty not to take it

away from me. If you dare to violate one of my rights or entitlements, then I am free to retaliate against you. Our contractual rights and duties create the only relationships we have. We are bound together by our intentions: our promises, our words of honor, our oaths. Our relationships are no stronger than the contractual rights and duties on which they are based.

In contrast to this rights-based morality, Whitbeck offers a relationship-based morality. If we define the self in terms of her/his relationships to others, then responsibility becomes the primary moral notion. We may think here of Confucian ethics (a connection Whitbeck does not make). This ethical system is founded on five reciprocal relationships: husband-wife, parent-child, brother-brother, friend-friend, and ruler-subject. A man is not a self *first* and *then,* for example, a husband, parent, brother, friend, or ruler. Rather, a man becomes a self to the degree that he is good at relating to the other people who together define him. The more he fulfills his responsibilities toward his wife, child(ren), brother(s), friend(s), or subject(s), the more a man is able to constitute himself as a self.[5] Rights have only an auxiliary role to play in an ethical system such as this one; they are, as Whitbeck states, merely "claims upon society and upon other people that are necessary if a person is able to meet the responsibilities of her or his relationships."[6] I have a *right* to life, liberty, and the pursuit of happiness because without these rights I will not be able to rear my children. Because my children are dependent on me for their well-being, they, as well as I, will suffer if I become a jobless, homeless, "shopping-bag" lady.

Virginia Held on Noncontractual Society

Like Whitbeck, Virginia Held believes that the mother-child paradigm is the most appropriate substitute for the "autonomous man" paradigm. In order to emphasize how, in advanced capitalist societies, traditional ontology's ideal person pursues the so-called "bottom line" in the name of enlightened self-interest, Held refers to "autonomous man" as "economic man." She notes that economic man's paranoid tendencies cause him either not to relate to others or to relate to others only contractually. Because others are not to be trusted, one's dealings with them must be specified in terms of a set of contractual rights and duties held in place by a set of sanctions. Those who default on a contract, or who in any way violate one of its terms, must be appropriately penalized. In contrast to economic man, Held is not pleased that, increasingly, contracts regulate our private as well as public lives. Men and women sign prenuptial agreements, marriage contracts, and divorce settlements; parents promise to leave their children an inheritance on condition that their children behave in certain ways; children sign study contracts at school and work contracts at home; fertile women contract their reproductive services to infertile couples; and so on. Held suggests, however, that our growing reliance on contracts may be a sign of social disease rather than health. Unless we forsake economic man's adversarial ontology and replace it with a more relational ontology, our society may not be able to survive, let alone thrive. Sheets of paper cannot hold people together in the way that blood, sweat, tears, and laughter can.

Held urges us to compare a society guided by the mother-child paradigm with one guided by the contract paradigm and to ask ourselves in which one of these societies we would prefer to live. As she sees it, the mother-child paradigm differs from the contract paradigm in at least six ways. First, the relationship between a "mothering person"[7] and a child is not *voluntary,* especially from the point of view of the child who has been called into an existence s/he did not request but also from the point of view of the mothering person who may or may not know/want what the relationship of "mothering" actually demands. The kind of "deals" parents strike with their children are quite different from the kind of deals stockbrokers strike with their clients. If I say to my sons, "I'll send you to the college of your choice now, so that later on you'll put me in the retirement community of my choice," I know full well that only their love for me will motivate them to set me up in style when my gray hairs finally overtake my black hairs. No court of law will force them to make my last years golden ones. Of course, I doubt that I would want to "bargain" with my sons about our present or future plans to care for one another, for as I see it, the essential goal of mothering is not to get something out of it like a condo in Miami Beach but is simply "to give of one's care without obtaining a return of a self-interested kind."[8] When my sons ask me what I want for my birthday, I usually mutter something like, "Nothing, just be good kids." Presumably, I say this because as Held reiterates:

> The emotional satisfaction of a mothering person is a satisfaction in the well-being and happiness of another human being, and a satisfaction in the health of the relation between the two persons, not the gain that results from an egoistic bargain.[9]

Second, the relationship between a mothering person and child is permanent and nonreplaceable. Next to the ephemeral rules of our supply and demand marketplace, parental ties—no matter how tenuous—are permanent and unique. For example, trends in art—indeed, what counts as "good" art—may depend on the highest bidder. Today's "pile of junk" may be tomorrow's masterpiece or vice versa. What one would not have traded for the world yesterday finds its way into the corner of the attic or basement today. Everything that economic man buys and sells may be reduced to "a merely replaceable commodity."[10] Compared to these kinds of transactions, the relation between a mothering person and a child is enormously stable. Mothering persons are not inclined to assess the value of their children on the basis of what other people would give for them. Nor are they eager to trade this year's "model" for a new and improved one.

Third, the relationship between a mothering person and a child is a relationship between unequals. Supposedly, contracts are made between equals, and the equality at stake is that of equal rights. When people move out of the state of nature into civil society, they relinquish some of their freedom to do as they please in exchange for certain guarantees, such as the right to vote. In an election, each citizen's vote counts as much as any other citizen's. In contrast, whatever kind of relationships exist in the family, they are not, as Held correctly insists, relationships between equals. Although each member of a family deserves equal respect and consideration, a decision whether to spend more money on Junior's education than on grandma's health care involves much more than equal rights. At stake is the family's spirit of cooperation, sense of solidarity, and capacity for love. It does not really matter if Junior has more of a *right* to the family's income than grandma does—not if everyone is going to hate Junior for using all of the family's money to attend Harvard University while grandma languishes in a low-quality long-term care facility.

Fourth, the relationship between a mothering person and a child is one based on positive rights (rights to be benefited) as well as on negative rights (rights not to be harmed). In traditional political theory, economic man apparently treasures the right not to be interfered with, to be left to his own devices, more than any other right. Yet, the right to be helped is probably as important as the right not to be hindered. In fact, Held maintains that if society has the resources with which to benefit people, there are few, if any, excuses, let alone justifications, for failing to do so. It is not enough for society to let starving infants scream at the top of their lungs without interference; it should provide them with the bottles of milk without which they will die.

Fifth, the relationship between a mothering person and a child constitutes a symbiotic whole: a community of two. The problem for economic man is how to build community. If selves are utterly atomistic and fixated on their own individual gain, what can possibly motivate them to get together and to stay together? In contrast, the problem for mothering persons and children is achieving separation. They have community; what they need is individuality. "For the child," says Held, "the problem is to become gradually more independent. For the mothering person, the problem is to free oneself from an all-consuming involvement."[11]

Sixth, and finally, Held describes the relationship between the mothering person and the child as a "caring"/"relying" relationship.[12] Worried that he may not always be able to secure the so-called "upper hand," economic man seeks to negotiate the kind of contracts that will equalize the balance of power between himself and others. Were mothering persons to view their relationships to their children primarily as struggles for power, however, their children would suffer enormous harm. They would grow up the victims of physical, psychological, and sexual abuse, ready to do unto their children the violence that had been done unto them. That we view this situation as pathological to the extreme speaks to our belief that a good relationship between a mothering person and a child is not a domination-subordination relationship. There is more to power than the power to control other(s)—the sort of essentially brute and destructive power that leads to the development of increasingly unlivable societies.

In order to make our societies livable, Held suggests that we reconceive power—that we recognize its humanizing and creative possibilities:

> The power of a mothering person to empower others, to foster transformative growth is a different sort of power than that of a stronger sword or dominant will. And the power of a child to call forth tenderness and care is perhaps more different still.[13]

Held believes that our political, economic, and social lives would look very different if we exorcised economic man from our collective imagination and replaced him with the image of the mothering person/child duo. No "Pollyanna," Held does not argue that all we need to do is to replace bombs with bonbons and the world will be beautiful. She simply invites us to reexamine society's assumption that things like bombs stand for true "power," whereas human affection does not. Held challenges the vocabulary with which we formulate our ideas of power. True *empowerment* comes from growth and love, not from death and domination.

Lorraine Code and Annette Baier on "Second" Persons

Like Whitbeck and Held, Lorraine Code is eager to challenge autonomous or economic man. But she rejects the mother-child paradigm as the appropriate basis for a new relational ontology and ethics, since she believes this paradigm "works to suppress and/or condemn ambivalences often characteristic of mother-child relationships."[14] As Adrienne Rich writes in *Of Woman Born,* many mothers are just as likely to react to their infants and children with "anger" as with "tenderness." No matter how much a mother loves her child, its constant needs can tax her patience and, with no relief from her husband or any other adult, ultimately make her feel frustrated or worse. In fact, Rich recounts her less than consistently benign attitude toward her own children as follows:

> I remember being uprooted from already meager sleep to answer a childish nightmare, pull up a blanket, warm a consoling bottle, lead a half-asleep child to the toilet. I remember going back to bed starkly awake, brittle with anger, knowing that my broken sleep would make the next day hell, that there would be more nightmares, more need for consolation, because out of my weariness I would rage at those children for no reason.[15]

Rich's point is not that women do not love their children but that no person can be expected to remain always cheerful and kind unless his or her own physical and psychological needs are met.

Perhaps Code has something like Rich's experience in mind when she suggests that the most appropriate model for what constitutes an ideal human relationship is not the mother-child relationship but some other, yet unspecified relationship. Whatever this mysterious relationship may be, however, Code concedes that given autonomous (or economic) man's flaws, Whitbeck's and Held's mother-child paradigm certainly offers a better foundation for ethics than, for example, seventeenth-century philosopher René Descartes's solitary self, trying to prove his very existence to himself.

In Code's estimation, Descartes's announcement "Cogito ergo sum" ("I think therefore I am") is counterintuitive. The "I" *cannot think, or even exist*, unless it is first, and perhaps always, a "you." Had my parents not taught me how to speak, for example, I would never have learned how to think. I would be like the "Wild Child of Averyon," left as a babe in France to survive on his own in the forest. No mother ever asked the Wild Child, "What do *you* want to do today?" No father ever asked him, "What do *you* want to do when you grow up?" Indeed, no one ever asked the Wild Child a "you" question. The Wild Child could not become a *self* because he had never been an *other* for anyone. He could not meaningfully use the first-person singular pronoun, "I," with reference to himself; nor could others convincingly use the third-person singular pronoun "he" with reference to "him." In sum, the Wild Child was not "recognizably human" because he had never been anyone's "you"—that is, anyone's "*second person.*"[16]

Code notes that Annette Baier, who coined the term *second person*, uses it *descriptively*—simply to denote the ways in which normal infants are related to their parents in particular. In contrast to Baier, Code wishes to use the phrase *prescriptively*—as a recommendation about how all persons should relate to each other. We can view our interdependence as a curse and struggle to get out from under each others' thumbs, or we can view our interdependence as a blessing and continue to grow as second persons "through identification and differentiation, through learning and speaking with each other."[17] The choice is ours, but if we wish to be human there is only one right choice: the choice of interdependence.

Code believes that we can improve human interaction if we adopt an ontological perspective like that of Whitbeck or Baier—a perspective that sees self and others always in *relation*. As a rule, we should approach people confidently and trustfully rather than warily and distrustfully, and we should try to view our encounters with them as an opportunity to change ourselves for the better. To be sure, our generally positive attitude toward people will not always be rewarded. The minuses as well as the pluses of the human condition are rooted in human interdependence. Some of our relationships will prove to be person-enhancing, but others will prove to be person-diminishing. Yet if we want never to be harmed by others, we must be prepared never to be benefited by them. In fact, to live in isolation means receiving nothing at all. Life without relation would mean life robbed of its humanity. Without ties to others, we would be reduced to a Wild Child existence, incapable of thought or emotion, more animal than human.

Jean Grimshaw and Diane Meyers on Autonomy

As deficient as traditional ontology may be, Jean Grimshaw and Diane Meyers believe that some of its concepts not only can but should be retrieved from the patriarchal web that ensnares them. For example, autonomy is not necessarily a negative word. Individuals can become self-determining and self-actualizing without becoming solipsistic. Autonomous individuals can create cooperative communities. They do not have to engage in competitive combat with each other.

Relying on Aristotle's conception of autonomy, Grimshaw notes that whether a decision/action is autonomous depends on *where* that decision/action originates. Actions that originate from "within" oneself are autonomous (voluntary), but those that originate from "outside" oneself are not. Examples of actions that originate outside of oneself are those that are performed because of external influences, pressures, compulsions, or constraints.

As interpreted by Grimshaw, Aristotle's conception of autonomy meshes well with the ordinary person's conception of autonomy. Most of us associate autonomy with free choice and the ability to plan our lives; conversely, most of us associate a lack of autonomy with being determined, controlled, or coerced by external forces:

> . . . if a person is prevented from doing what they would otherwise intend or desire to do, or if they are coerced into doing what they would *not* otherwise want or desire to do, they are not acting autonomously. Under this interpretation, actions which originate from "inside" the self are those which are seen as in accordance with conscious desires or intentions, and those which originate from "outside" the self are those which ones would not do if one were not coerced.[18]

Autonomy, then, is just as valuable for women as it is for men. All human beings—and not just biological males—need to be free in order to develop morally.

Insofar as women's actions originate from "outside" of themselves—the product of physical violence, economic dependence, sexual harassment, and discriminatory laws—Grimshaw concedes that women are not autonomous. She doubts, however, that women's lack of autonomy runs any deeper than this. Specifically, Grimshaw disagrees with Mary Daly, Marilyn Frye, and Kate Millet, whom she regards as maintaining that most women's desires and intentions are merely the residue of centuries of patriarchal conditioning. She rejects their belief that women have been conditioned, brainwashed, and indoctrinated to want certain things (for example, to serve men's needs—especially their sexual needs) that they would not have wanted had they not been under patriarchy's thumb. She also rejects their belief that women will remain unfree until women's true, authentic, or feminist selves are rescued from their false, inauthentic, or patriarchal selves.[19]

Clearly, Grimshaw refuses to take seriously the possibility that most women are *indeed* the victims of what is generally termed "false consciousness," a distinctively nonautonomous state of awareness. Instead, she catalogs what she perceives as the main political and philosophical problems associated with a commitment to the view that "the monolithic brutality and psychological pressures of male power have reduced women almost to the state of being 'nonpersons.'"[20]

The main political problem with some women seeking to deliver other women from a "false" consciousness they do not regard as false, says Grimshaw, is that if the latter women refuse to be rescued, the former women may label them "unenlightened," "willfully blind," or "mindless." In an effort to justify their decisions and actions, the labeled women may react defensively, or even hostilely, against their "labelers." Absent any real means to heal the kind of wounds that are the inevitable result of women accusing each other of "sins" for which they may or may not be responsible, the cause of sisterly solidarity would be set back.

The main philosophical problem with a commitment to the "false consciousness" doctrine, says Grimshaw, is that it requires an equal commitment to the belief that the self "is, at least potentially, a unitary, rational thing, aware of its interests";[21] that "splits" in the self are the result of social conditioning; and that the way to overcome these "splits" is to access one's real self through an entirely "rational process."[22] Grimshaw's challenge is most provocative. Yet, just because Daly, Frye, and Millet distinguish between true and false consciousnesses does not automatically commit them to the further view that true consciousness is the product of a unitary self, whereas false consciousness is the product of a split self.[23] A woman who perceives herself not as a unitary self but as a multiplicity of selves clamoring for continual reinterpretation can nonetheless be in a state of true consciousness, cognitively aware of the ways in which patriarchy has and still is conditioning her. The fact that we are always pulling ourselves together does not mean that we are blind to what is going on around us. On the contrary, it may be a sign that we are in control of our identities, adaptively shaping and reshaping them to ward off those who would destroy them.

Grimshaw is on firmer ground when she comments that women, including feminist women, are a study in contradictions, inconsistencies, and incoherencies.[24] For example, I may indulge any number of Harlequin romance fantasies in my dream life without ever intending to actualize any of them in my real life—largely because I know that if I had to face the kind of macho man that populates these romances over breakfast every day of my life, I would go stark raving mad. Similarly, I may know that "beauty" and "thinness" are traps for women. Yet when my feelings of "ugliness" and "fatness" overwhelm me, I may nonetheless start doing things to my body that I *know* are abusive; worse yet, I may actually *feel* better after I *do* them.

Despite the fact that some of my thoughts and actions indicate a lack of full autonomy, I still trust that Daly, Millet, and Frye would accuse me of *akrasia* (weakness of will—that is, knowing what is right but failing to do it), before they would label me a totally benighted, helpless, and hopeless victim of false consciousness. Like true consciousness, autonomy is not a state of being that women either achieve or fail to achieve once and for all. On the contrary, autonomy is, as Grimshaw correctly observes, a dialectical process "in which a constant (but never static or final) search for control and coherence needs balancing against a realism and tolerance born out of effort to understand ourselves (and others) better."[25]

Like Grimshaw, Meyers believes that autonomy is a dialectic process, that is, that it makes sense to view oneself as both autonomous and not autonomous. According to Meyers, the challenge for women is to admit what is true—namely, that women have been oppressed, suppressed, and repressed—along with what is also true—namely, that women are not altogether heteronomous. Just because society socializes women in ways that limit their options, and just because women tend to develop deep emotional relationships and to orient themselves more toward home-centered than work-centered concerns, does not make them utterly incapable of autonomous thought and action.[26]

First, Meyers argues that men, no less than women, are strongly socialized. To be sure, men have more career and life-style options than women have, but if men are going to attain personal autonomy, they have to attain it within a society that instructs them to be "macho" rather than "wimpy." A man who wants to be a nurse, for example, will probably meet with as much resistance as a woman who wants to be a construction worker.

Second, Meyers argues that although women, far more than men, may let their loved ones' needs and wants eclipse their own needs and wants, all persons—male or female—need affection, intimacy, or love. If we interpret personal autonomy as aloofness, as total psychic separation from others, it becomes a very unappealing way of being. In fact, it becomes a sign that one has failed rather than succeeded as a human being.

Third, Meyers argues that there is no good reason to associate personal autonomy with public, as opposed to private, achievements. The businessman in the gray flannel suit and the Ford-motor assembly-line worker are certainly in the public sphere, but neither of them is an exemplar of personal autonomy. On the contrary, both of these employees are, to a greater or lesser extent, economically dependent on their bosses, and often they must keep their opinions to themselves for fear of being fired.

Having argued that socialization works against men's as well as women's ability to be autonomous, and that autonomous persons can be emotional and "private" as well as rational and "public," Meyers notes that there are many types of autonomy. Among these types of autonomy are programmatic, episodic, and partial access autonomy. Each of these ways of taking charge of one's life brings a person that much closer to achieving full autonomy.

People manifest *programmatic* autonomy when they ask themselves questions about the direction of their lives. These questions can be very broad—Meyers suggests "Do I care more about material gain or spiritual life?"—or they can be quite narrow—"Should I spend Sundays at church or in my office?" Although a woman who, after a few minutes reflection, decides to spend Sundays at church may not have asked herself any truly soul-searching questions, she is nonetheless exhibiting programmatic autonomy—albeit to a lesser degree than those churchgoers who have plumbed their souls to their very depths. Comments Meyers:

> Although people who query themselves regarding the most general aspects of their life plans are plainly more autonomous than people who by and large conform to social expectations and only attend to themselves regarding the minutiae of their lives, the latter may display narrowly programmatic autonomy.[27]

Even if a woman goes to church only to gain the approval of her neighbors, she is programmatically autonomous insofar as she decides to lead a life in accordance with social mores. She has made a decision about the direction of her life, even if that decision is merely to accede to social pressure.

Episodic autonomy differs from programmatic autonomy in that it is not directly related to the broader strokes of one's life, that is, to decisions that extend over a considerable length of time and that seriously affect the course of one's entire destiny. In face of a possibly boring Saturday afternoon, a woman exhibits episodic autonomy when she asks herself, "What do I *really want* to do today?" Simple as it sounds, such a question can serve as an occasion for introspection. People who try to figure out what they really want to do on boring Saturdays, "give greater expression to their own beliefs and desires"[28] than people who spend boring Saturdays simply being bored, or who engage in whatever activities their families or friends like even if they themselves dislike such activities.

When individuals gain limited insight into what Meyers terms their "authentic self," they achieve *partial access* autonomy. As an example of partial access autonomy, Meyers points to a fundamentalist woman who is upset by her daughter's teacher's cavalier dismissal of creationism. Although this woman has never questioned her faith and is heteronomous on this account, she is "autonomous" enough to defend her unexamined beliefs against ridicule.[29] To be sure, Meyers's use of the term *autonomous* here is worrisome. Ordinarily, one would think that even though the woman Meyers describes is being assertive, she does not gain insight into her authentic self merely by verbally assaulting her daughter's teacher (unless, of course, one's authentic self is simply the self one happens to be at any given point in time). Indeed, it strikes me that unless this woman uses the teacher's challenge as an opportunity to question her unexamined faith for the first time, rather than as an excuse to build up her walls of defense all the more fiercely, she is definitely *not* accessing her "authentic self."

Whatever problems may trouble Meyers's account of autonomy, however, she is correct to insist that throughout history women have consistently exhibited *some* measure of programmatic, episodic, and partial access autonomy. If we cease to view autonomy as an "all" or "nothing" matter, we can celebrate women's achievements under conditions of oppression. Although few women have been entirely able to control the course of their own destinies, labeling most women *total* victims places an unfair burden on their shoulders. It is, in fact, to admit defeat. For how could *total* victims ever rise up and demand equality?

TRADITIONAL EPISTEMOLOGY CHALLENGED

Like traditional ontology, traditional epistemology affects the character of traditional ethics. Because ontology and epistemology are intimately related, we cannot easily separate questions about how knowledge differs from belief and how reason is or is not related to emotion from questions about the nature of reality and the identity of persons (selves and others). For example, inquiries about the emotions raise both ontological questions such as "Are we more or less integrated persons when we feel intensely?" and epistemological questions such as "Do our feelings help us to reason better and to see reality as it truly is, or do our feelings hinder us and show us reality simply as we would prefer it to be?" Similarly, analyses of autonomy generate both ontological discussions about self-sufficiency and epistemological discussions about rationality.

Given the conceptual connections between ontology and epistemology, those who criticize traditional ontology also tend to criticize traditional epistemology. Specifically, critics attack traditional epistemology's (supposed) emphasis on rationality in general and on abstraction, universality, and impartiality in particular. They claim that such emphases contribute to the formation of a distorted worldview that inhibits proper moral development.

The Abstract Versus the Concrete

To criticize the role of "abstraction" in traditional ethics, says Grimshaw, is generally to criticize its tendency to "discount" or "think away" the unique or particular features of those persons or situations about which a moral judgment needs to be made.[30] Through the process of abstraction, the traditional ethicist "distances" himself from the "human consequences" of his judgments and actions.[31] In other words, he blocks from his consciousness the degree to which his decision to follow a moral rule may cause real men, women, and children to bleed, to sweat, to cry, and even to die.

Clearly, at least deontology and perhaps also utilitarianism tend toward abstraction. These ethical approaches ask us to submit all of our moral experiences to a single, overreaching behavioral index such as the categorical imperative or the principle of utility. Kantians bid us to have equal respect and consideration for persons simply because they are persons: to disregard their gender, race, age, socioeconomic class, physical beauty, and mental acumen. Similarly, utilitarians ask us to regard each sentient creature as one and no more than one. The fact that sentient creature x is one's father and sentient creature y is a stranger is, in and of itself, morally irrelevant.

Although the Kantian emphasis on persons *qua* persons does counteract our tendency to favor our loved ones' interests over those of strangers no matter what, it may lead to a failure of moral imagination. It may be easier for me *never* to lie—not even for a good reason—than to focus on the exact ways in which certain individuals will be harmed or benefited as a result of my lying, or not lying, in a particular instance. If I can block from my imagination the suffering of the woman who will lose her husband if I tell him the truth about her one and only infidelity, then I may be better able to follow the demanding dictates of the categorical imperative, according to which it is always wrong to lie, no matter what the consequences of telling the truth.

Like the categorical imperative, the principle of utility may lead to some failures of moral imagination. Under certain circumstances (for example, scare resources), the principle of utility may require us to deprive a child of a life-saving but extremely expensive bone marrow transplant in order to fund adequate prenatal care for hundreds of pregnant women. By refusing to focus on the child's plight—by ignoring the terror in his eyes—I may find it easier to sacrifice him for the sake of the common good.

Grimshaw agrees that readily sacrificing flesh and blood people "to large-scale goals, whether they be obedience to God or the dictates of a nationalistic militarism, or a fight against social injustice or exploitation"[32] is a morally dubious tendency. Nevertheless, she maintains that it is not the case that *all* norms are necessarily hostile to the ethical enterprise. Even if *rules* encourage abstraction in our moral lives, *principles* do not usually have this effect.

For Grimshaw, a rule is a prescription for action "whose purpose is to eliminate the need for reflection, except in marginal or problematic cases."[33] Rules like "Don't kill" exist as moral conveniences. We follow rules automatically and fairly unquestioningly. Although Grimshaw does not make the point, rote rule following probably makes us morally lazy—inattentive to those features of a specific case that serve to challenge the rules that ordinarily apply to cases of its kind.

In contrast to rules, principles invite us to be morally reflective or conscientious. Comments Grimshaw:

> Principles are, I think, best expressed in the form of "Consider. . . ." Consider whether your action will harm others; consider what the consequences for other people will be if you do this; consider whether the needs of others should outweigh consideration of your own.[34]

If principles are indeed considerations of this type, then feminine and feminist approaches to ethics are no less "principled" than traditional approaches to ethics. It is just that feminine and feminist ethicists voice principles—for example, "Consider whether your behavior will stand in the way of maintaining care and relationships"[35]—that traditional ethicists have not often invoked or even recognized.

In the same way that principles/considerations play a legitimate role in feminine and feminist approaches to ethics, so too does a certain kind of distancing. Grimshaw concedes that distancing can play a deleterious role in morality. People often use language to transform human beings into things. It is easier for a soldier to kill a "Gook" than to kill a sixteen-year-old Vietnamese boy. Nevertheless, distancing is not always bad. Indeed, it is sometimes very good:

> A surgeon, or an ambulanceman or a nurse have to be able to distance themselves emotionally from the human sufferings and tragedies they may work with in order to be able to do their job at all. Sometimes an incessant emotional dwelling on actual or possible honors may be counterproductive or oppressive.[36]

Were a feminine or feminist approach to ethics to forbid all forms of distancing, it would impose a severe demand on our psyches. Indeed, it would require us to keep our feelings churning even when they threaten to render us unfit for decision or action of any sort.

Universality Versus Particularity

Although universality plays a role in utilitarianism as well as in deontology, its role is particularly clear in Kantian ethics. According to Kant, for an action to be moral it must be capable of being universalized: "Act only on that maxim through which you can at the same time will that it should become a universal law."[37] This statement sketches a procedure for deciding whether an act is morally permissible. When a person contemplates doing a particular action, s/he should ask what rule s/he would be following if s/he were to do that action. (This will be the maxim of the act.) Then s/he should ask whether s/he can consistently will that everyone follow that rule (maxim) all of the time. (Her/his consistent willingness will make the rule [maxim] a universal law in the relevant sense.) If s/he discovers that s/he cannot do this, then s/he must not act on the proposed rule (maxim).

Kant provides several examples to explain the above procedure. Suppose, he says, a man is so tired of his unhappy life that he decides to commit suicide. Before doing so, however, he must ask himself whether such an action goes against his duty to his being. Can he consistently will to make a universal law out of the maxim "Whenever life gets difficult, and there seems more of a possibility of pain than pleasure, one should commit suicide"? According to Kant, the man cannot universalize his maxim, since "a system of nature by whose law the very same feeling whose function (*Bestimmung*) is to stimulate the furtherance of life should actually destroy life would contradict itself and consequently could not subsist as a system of nature."[38] To act "inconsistently" is to act "irrationally," and to act "irrationally" is to undermine the foundation of morality.

A significant point that may not be immediately apparent here is that in order to perform a *morally worthy* action, it is not enough for me to do the right thing (for example, to tell the truth). Rather, I must do the right thing for the right reason (namely, the reason that the moral law commands me to tell the truth). If I tell the truth only because I want people to think well of me, or only because I do not want to hurt gullible people, then my action is *morally worthless*. Altruistic actions based on human-hearted concern for others as well as selfish actions based on bold self-interest are both rooted in what Kant terms "inclination." Because inclination is an ephemeral phenomenon—our feelings fluctuate from day to day—Kant refuses to base morality on such shifting sands. Rather, he bases morality on supposedly steady reason.

Those who espouse feminine and feminist approaches to ethics dispute Kant's claim that only an action done for duty's sake—out of respect for the moral law—is morally worthy, whereas the same action done strictly for an individual's sake—out of sheer love for him/her—is not. Philosopher Lawrence A. Blum doubts, for example, that the sacrifices I have made for my children must be motivated by some universalizable law like "People ought to take care of their children's physical and psychological needs" in order to be morally worthy. He calls his approach to ethics a "direct altruism" view. According to this view, an action is morally good if it is "motivated by a regard for the good of others."[39] The sacrifices I make for my children are morally worthy, then, if they are motivated by my wanting to contribute to their well-being *because I love them.*

Not only does Blum deny that agents must regard their morally good actions as universalizable, he also denies that they must regard them as "morally obligatory or morally incumbent"[40] on themselves. What makes my dinner invitation to a lonely old couple with whom I have nothing in common, for example, a morally good action is not some universal principle that people ought whenever possible to extend dinner invitations to lonely old couples, but my "direct response" or regard for their "good." Here the critic may object that even though I do not describe my action as being motivated by its universalizability, in fact what makes it morally good *is* its universalizability. If I look puzzled, the critic will ask me how I would morally assess a friend who refuses to extend dinner invitations to lonely old couples when she could easily do so. Am I not logically required to say that if *I* am morally obligated to invite lonely old couples to dinner, so is anyone in circumstances similar to mine?

One way for me to reply to this criticism, says Blum, is for me to deny that my friend's circumstances are, in fact, nearly identical to mine. I can protest, for example, that compared to me, she is an awkward conversationalist and a mediocre cook. Or I can assert that just because I am required to do a good deed does not mean that everyone else is equally required to do the same good deed:

> To regard an act as right generally carries the implication that anyone similarly situated ought to perform it, that it is right not only for me but for any agent in my situation (taking into account relevant differences between the agents, etc.). But to act merely out of a direct regard for another's good does not carry this implication and does not require taking up the stance of "any moral agent." One is simply moved by another's suffering to help him; one need not, in addition, hold the belief that this consideration which has moved one is binding on others as well.[41]

Blum later concedes, however, that there may be a sense in which inviting lonely old couples to dinner is universalizable. Because Kant's principle of universalizability (act only on that maxim through which you can at the same time will that it should become a universal law) is rightly interpreted to mean that anyone in circumstance x is *permitted* to do action y, then my action is universalizable. Anyone *may* invite lonely old couples to dinner. It is not wrong to do so. It is only if Kant's principle of universalizability is wrongly interpreted to mean that everyone in circumstance x is *required* to do y that I should, in Blum's opinion, deny that my act is universalizable. Just because anyone *may* invite lonely old couples to dinner does not mean that anyone, let alone everyone, *must* do so.

Blum's point stresses the importance of concern and particularity over obligation and universalizability. We need not mull over what others would or should do in our situation, but we do need to respond with care for the good of the persons before us. This is not to say that universalizable actions are not morally worthy: It simply means that universalizability is not a *necessary* condition for moral worth. As important as duty may be, it tells only a chapter of the moral story, the bulk of which is about "being responsive to the weal and woe of others."[42]

Impartiality Versus Partiality

Related to the issue of universality versus particularity is that of impartiality versus partiality. According to traditional philosophers, moral reasoning must be impartial—that is, free of prejudice or bias. All persons must be treated as persons. When it comes to meeting the legitimate needs of a person qua person, his/her *relationship* to me is irrelevant. It does not matter whether s/he is my best friend or my worst enemy.

Moral impartiality requires us to detach ourselves from everything that makes us different from everyone else. But, as Marilyn Friedman points out, such detachment is not always feasible, since we cannot easily escape the specifics of our history.[43] Nor is it necessarily desirable. In requiring us to manifest attitudes "such as detachment from personal concerns and loyalties, disinterest, dispassion, and a regard for the generalized moral equality of all persons,"[44] impartiality may force us to jeopardize our closest relationships—relationships that demand attachment. We would hurt the people closest to us if they thought that the "goodness" we direct toward them is no different than the "goodness" we direct toward strangers.

Yet, even though Friedman believes that we neither can nor should seek to transcend our histories—that is, our race, class, gender, age, physical condition, and so forth—she believes that the social conception of the self is subject to two dangerous distortions. First, the *social* self needs to be distinguished from the *conventional* self. Partiality can take all sorts of forms, only some of which generate morally attractive consequences. Friedman notes that "the same social traditions that confer prerogatives of favoring loved ones have permitted, to those with greater power, privileges of hurting those same loved ones."[45] Parents who beat their children often argue that they know what is best for them; likewise, husbands who rape their wives sometimes claim that they know their wives' "real" desires. In view of such abuses of "partiality," those who are developing feminine and/or feminist approaches to ethics may wish to claim that partiality is morally justified only when it *benefits* rather than *harms* those toward whom it is directed.

Second, "being partial" is not a synonym for "being parochial." In their desire not to be parochial—that is, concerned only with the interests of one's immediate family and friends as opposed to those of one's region, nation, and the world—moral impartialists have insisted that "proximity and close relationship carry no moral weight and that moral responsibilities—for example, to those who are starving—extend equally to all members of the global village."[46] As an extreme example of this impartialist perspective, Friedman points to the eighteenth-century philosopher William Godwin. Should it come to choosing between the life of "my beloved but socially worthless parent" on the one hand and the life of François de Salignac de La Mothe-Fénelon, the archbishop of Cambray, on the other hand, I must, said Godwin, choose the archbishop. "Impartial truth"[47] demands that simply because *my* father is *mine*, I must in no way favor his insignificant (!) life over the significant (!) life of the archbishop.

Although Friedman believes that few moral impartialists are as extreme as Godwin, she nonetheless claims that most of them are committed to pushing charitable duty beyond the parameters of familial and friendly relationships—and rightly so. Our desire to attend to the needs of our loved ones should not become an excuse for the kind of moral laziness that impedes our ability to expand our conception of self to include more persons than those who immediately surround us. Still, our moral energy is limited. Although we must strive to overcome those aspects of ourselves that cause us to be parochial, we can expand ourselves only so far before we collapse. Charity has its endings as well as its beginnings. Unless morality permits us to be somewhat partial, we will go stark raving mad.[48] I simply cannot react to the pain of distant peoples in the same way that I react to my children's pain. As it is, I can scarcely cope with my two children's pain, let alone with the pain of *millions* of distant peoples.

Reason Versus Emotion

Traditionally, reason has been associated with the universal, the abstract, the mental, the impartial, the public, and the male, whereas emotion has been associated with the particular, the concrete, the physical, the partial, the private, and the female. Although traditional philosophers did not always split reason totally from emotion, glorifying the former and denigrating the latter, modern thinkers have come to interpret emotion as the opposite of reason. If reason is objective, then the emotions are subjective; if reason brings us closer to the facts, then the emotions simply reflect our values; and if reason is something to develop, the emotions are something to overcome.

Alison M. Jaggar on the Emotions

According to Alison Jaggar, the bifurcation between reason and emotion, and the concomitant privileging of reason over emotion, is misguided. No less than reason, the emotions can bring us closer to the truth, for the emotions are not simply a way of feeling but of knowing. Jaggar points out that, historically, the so-called "Dumb View" of the emotions, according to which they are entirely noncognitive responses to environmental stimuli, has prevailed in traditional philosophical circles. The Dumb View teaches that there is a virtual equivalence between the emotions on the one hand and "the physical feelings or involuntary bodily movements that typically accompany them"[49] on the other.

Recently, so-called cognitivists have challenged the Dumb View on the grounds that the emotions are most appropriately identified not with the physiological sensations that accompany them but with the mental judgments that differentiate among them. What I feel is not simply my stomach churning but my *anxiety* about the lecture I must deliver at 8:00 P.M. Although Jaggar believes that cognitivist interpretations of the emotions represent a significant advance over the Dumb View, she is still dissatisfied with them. In her estimation, cognitivists tend to reinstantiate the split between reason and emotion when they distinguish between the cognitive and noncognitive aspects of our emotions.[50]

As an alternative to both Dumb View and cognitivist interpretations of the emotions, Jaggar forwards a view of the emotions according to which they are both social constructs and active engagements with our world. Because our culture teaches us what feelings to have and how to express them appropriately, our emotions are *learned* responses to life's "ups" and "downs." Solitary individuals, impervious to culture's lessons, are emotionless as well as speechless. In the same way that we learn how to speak, we learn how to feel. It is false, therefore, to argue that our emotions are "uncontrollable and irrational."[51] Although our feelings are not nearly as deliberate as our thoughts, neither are they entirely spontaneous. My feelings of anger, for example, are those "habitual responses"[52] I have developed to deal with certain kinds of situations. So habituated have I become to "flying off the handle" when confronted with an unreasonable demand that I fail to think twice before I start screaming at the top of my lungs that "No, I won't do X, Y, or Z. You're being unfair to me!" Nevertheless, if I tried, I could think twice, calm myself down, and proceed to handle matters differently.

Jaggar joins her argument that the emotions are social and public phenomena with her claim that we are largely in charge of our emotions to suggest that our emotions are ways of knowing. She comments that "just as observation directs, shapes, and partially defines emotion, so too emotion directs, shapes, and even partially defines observation."[53] Knowledge is not neutral. Our passions draw us to study certain matters and to ignore others. Some facts speak more loudly to us than others precisely because we are more interested in them. Nevertheless, traditional philosophers have defined true knowledge as knowledge of objective facts undistorted by subjective values. According to this view, emotion is the enemy of reason, and it must be repressed. This view of knowledge is dangerous for two reasons. First, it tends to discredit women, since culture has associated women with emotionality and men with rationality. If the emotions impede reason, then women must be silenced because their "emoting" constitutes an impediment to human progress. Second, it is false. There is no way to entirely separate facts from values. Someone's values are going to guide what we perceive or do not perceive, and what history teaches us is that whoever has the most power in society will tend to control our perceptions. Jaggar comments:

> Within a capitalist, white supremacist, and male-dominant society, the predominant values will tend to be those that serve the interests of rich white men. Consequently, we are all likely to develop an emotional constitution

that is quite inappropriate for feminism. Whatever our color, we are likely to feel what Irving Thalberg has called "visceral racism"; whatever our sexual orientation, we are likely to be homophobic; whatever our class, we are likely to be at least somewhat ambitious and competitive; whatever our sex, we are likely to feel contempt for women.[54]

Despite the fact that our emotional repertoire is largely under the control of the powers that be, Jaggar nonetheless insists that people often experience "outlaw" or "conventionally unacceptable"[55] emotions. For example, even though society still instructs women to react to sexist jokes with at least a forced smile, a woman might instead rage against them. Women often feel crazy when they experience such outlaw emotions for the first time, refusing to trust these feelings unless they are corroborated by other women who have had similar experiences. Jaggar admits that it would be incorrect to think that an outlaw emotion is somehow more appropriate than a conventional emotion simply because it is experienced by a woman or by a member of another oppressed group. She suggests instead that what makes an emotion appropriate is that by displaying it, one contributes to the formation of a society "in which all humans (and perhaps some nonhuman life too) thrive."[56] An example of an appropriate emotion would be to feel anger when a rape victim is, for all practical purposes, put on trial together with the man who raped her.

Although Jaggar's concept of an appropriate emotion is an underdeveloped one, it is also a promising one. To type emotions as either appropriate or inappropriate is to suggest that emotions are not only a way to know but a way to act. If one fails to feel and even to display anger in the face of injustice, then one's fault is ethical as well as epistemic. Ethics is not only a matter of knowing what is right and doing what is right; it is also about having certain sorts of feelings when one does what one knows is right. To be sure, it is better for others that I do the right thing—that I not hurt them—even if I do not have any human-hearted feeling towards them, but it is better for *me* if my right actions are accompanied by appropriate feelings. Only then do I have a chance to become a fully integrated person who does not experience herself as a mind-body split, a battleground in which emotion and reason are always in conflict.

Lawrence A. Blum on the Emotions

Another thinker who believes that emotions play a crucial role in our moral development is Blum. As he sees it, traditional ethics has separated reason from the emotions, suggesting that whereas reason is a necessary condition for morality, the emotions are not. Referring to Kant in particular, he laments the fact that traditional ethics tends to view the emotions as the enemy of reason—that which slows down rather than speeds up one's moral development:

> Feelings and emotions are entirely distinct from reason and rationality. They do not yield knowledge, and can in fact divert us from morally directed thinking and judgment. In order to obtain a clear view of the rights and wrongs in a situation we must *abstract* and *distance* ourselves from our feelings and emotions.[57]

Supposedly, the emotions not only fail to help us in moral decisions but also prevent us from finding the "right" moral path to follow. Particularly dangerous are altruistic emotions because they are generated by and directed toward specific people in specific situations.

For example, we hear that Johnny, an appealing indigent child, will die without a bone marrow transplant, and so we work feverishly to raise the funds for his operation. What is not quite right about our working feverishly on behalf of Johnny is the fact that had Johnny not been an appealing indigent child, but a crotchety indigent adult, very few efforts would have been made on his behalf. To act merely from altruistic feelings is, in Kant's estimation, to act from inclination, a phenomenon far removed from the real foundation of morality, that is, reason or rationality. Unlike inclination, reason will instruct us that Johnny's life is no more worthy than that of the crotchety adult's.

Admittedly, there is something very appealing about the thought that reason has the power to blind us to those particularities about specific people that would otherwise cause us to favor or disfavor, accept or reject, support or abandon them. We know that favoritism can cause an employer to hire cousin Joe rather than a far more qualified stranger, or to promote Mary, a beautiful and "bubbly" secretary, over her competition, Sarah, who is exceedingly plain and never cracks a smile. Aware of our own human frailties, we easily succumb to the view that morality is about fighting human "weakness," or "softness":

> The Kantian view has obvious affinities with a definite Protestant tradition of morality—the emphasis on subjection to duty, on control of feelings and inclinations from one's selfish lower nature, on conscientious action on principle, rather than emotional spontaneity. That tradition has deeply affected the moral thinking and experience of Anglo-Americans.[58]

No wonder that traditional ethics has favored justice over caring, a virtue that seems to be ruled by the "head" and not by the "heart."

As Blum sees it, however, the Kantian tradition has unnecessarily condemned the emotions. It has apparently forgotten what Aristotle knew about the emotions, namely, that when the emotions are properly educated, they serve as reliable indexes for human virtue and vice. Proper feelings of honor and shame enable us to be courageous (rather than cowardly or foolhardy) and self-respectful (rather than servile or arrogant), for example. What is more, there is a major difference between a raw emotion and an altruistic emotion. Whereas a raw emotion is little more than a visceral gut feeling, an altruistic emotion is a tendency to do good to others that has been reflectively cultivated for many years, beginning with our parents' admonition that we ought to think of other people's feelings.

Convinced that feelings have a major role to play in morality, Blum argues that far from undermining morality, feelings, especially altruistic emotions, usually enhance it. Indeed, Blum claims that such altruistic emotions as sympathy, compassion, human concern, and friendship are necessary components of morality. Not surprisingly, Kantians approach Blum's view with suspicion. As they see it, only one aspect of a person's inner life directly affects the moral worth of his/her actions, and that is his/her motivational structure. Provided that persons have the proper motivation for their actions—that is, that they act out of respect for the law (doing a duty for duty's sake) as opposed to merely acting in accord with the law (doing a duty to gain power, prestige, or profit)—their actions are morally worthy. Irrespective of the good or bad consequences of their actions, they have acted as they should have.

Blum wonders whether it is correct to separate the "rightness of the act" from the "moral good of the motive."[59] Whereas many traditional ethicists argue that if a social worker saves a woman from her abusive husband only in the hopes of getting some favorable newspaper publicity, the act itself is "right" independent of the "badness" of its motive, Blum does not. Instead, he joins emotion with action to assess the appropriate moral *response* to the situation. Although the selfish social worker's actions relieve the battered wife by removing her from the situation, they do not convey concern to the battered wife. Because the selfish social worker's "right" action fails to express the "good" motive of concern, the action is not *really* right in Blum's estimation. As far as he is concerned, "Emotion itself is often part of what makes the act morally right or appropriate in a given situation."[60]

Blum does not reject the motive-act split as totally deficient, however. For a certain range of actions it may make sense to split the goodness of the motive from the rightness of the action. Things go wrong; the material world resists our motives; bad luck breaks our best laid plans into pieces. Misinformation, coupled with the best morally good motive, can still lead to a wrong act. In such situations, giving the agent credit for morally good motivation—as separated from the consequent action—makes sense. Nevertheless, Blum still insists that for an equally wide range of actions the motive-act split makes no sense whatsoever. In the case of such actions, the *goodness* of the motive cannot be separated from the *rightness* of the act; that is, the act cannot be right unless the motive is good.

For example, consider a date-rape victim being consoled by one of her friends. Much of the good that she will derive from this act of consolation is the feeling that her friend really cares about her. If she senses that her friend is only doing her "duty" in consoling her, it is hard to imagine her friend's gesture being of any real consolation to her. But, says Blum,

> this means that the motive of the action cannot be separated from the action itself, when one is considering the act as the morally appropriate act of beneficence which it is. In this situation there can be no sharp separation between assessment of motive and assessment of act.[61]

Even if the friend's action is motivated by a desire to do the right thing, her action is at best the right, or beneficent, action of *pretending to console* a friend; it is not, strictly speaking, the right, or beneficent, action of *actually consoling* a friend.

After a loved one's death, a hug from a close friend will mean much more than the lip service of dutiful strangers. Kindly deeds mean little or nothing without the emotion of sympathy behind them. Sympathy must be the motive for a kind deed for it to convey an authentic good to the mourner, for, as Blum sees it, "part of the good" that an action brings to a recipient *is* the emotion that the action expresses.[62]

To take away an altruistic action's emotional base is to take away much of its moral meaning. To be sure, such a subtraction does not necessarily take away *all* of an action's moral meaning. Consider, for example, a welfare mother who receives help from a rich person who cares nothing about her personally but is only fulfilling his obligations to society. Clearly, the welfare mother benefits from this dutiful citizen's actions; it is just that she would benefit even more were she to receive the same help from a caring friend who may have once suffered what she is now suffering. Though the welfare mother will benefit financially irrespective of the emotional basis of her respective donors' contributions, the good conveyed to her by her friend's gift would be more profound than is the good conveyed to her by the rich person's handout.

Blum's analysis goes even deeper than this, however. Altruistic emotions can convey goods even when they do not lead to action. Blum uses the following example. Joan is an astronaut. While circling the moon, something goes wrong, and her life-support system begins to fail. She radios the people at headquarters, and they do what they can from the ground. All attempts fail, however. They are left with the awful task of telling Joan that she has only a very short time to live. Nothing remains but to talk with her through the rest of her ordeal, until death overcomes her. Joan has two friends, Dave and Manny, who hear of her predicament. They react to the news in ways that are typical of their temperament/character. Manny, an obsessive-compulsive type, "considers that he has an obligation to Joan to make certain that everything possible be done to try and save her."[63] He runs around, reenacting all the previously futile attempts to save her. Yet when he is fully satisfied that nothing can be done, he feels that he has done *all* that he can do. He has "lived up to his obligation to his friend."[64] Observing that he can do nothing else, Manny goes on with his day.

Dave reacts differently—and, Blum would say, above and beyond Manny's more obligational approach to Joan's dilemma. He, too, tries all possible actions to save Joan's life. Yet when he realizes that he can do nothing to save her, he continues his *caring* commitment to Joan:

> . . . throughout the inquiry he is fervently hoping that the life support mechanism can be fixed. He is picturing Joan's situation, pained by her likely suffering, hoping she is not suffering too horribly, hoping that she can find consoling thoughts, wanting her to know how much she has meant to him, and lamenting his own loss. When he reaches the conclusion that nothing can be done, he does so with anguish in his heart. He continues to be taken up with thoughts and feelings for Joan. Yet he does not engage in fruitless and hopeless activity. He recognizes the situation for what it is.[65]

Although Dave and Manny perform the same actions, Dave possesses something Manny does not—namely, an emotional response to the situation. Dave shows care and concern for Joan, not just a sense of duty. Suppose Joan can predict her friends' reactions. Surely, knowing that Dave is suffering with her and thinking of her will be more of a comfort to Joan than knowing that Manny, having fulfilled his "obligations," is already off somewhere watching situation-comedy reruns on television while she asphyxiates in space. Blum points out the crucial difference in their reactions (Dave—emotion-action; Manny—action alone).

Clearly, having the proper sentiments, feelings, or emotions is, for Blum, essential to an action's total goodness; they are not mere frosting on the moral cake. Blum argues that moral growth lies in our learning the emotional responses of sympathy, care, and concern. Emotions are not only morally relevant but also are morally necessary. Saving a drowning child out of obligation rather than human kindness does not win high marks in Blum's book.

CONCLUSIONS

Clearly, any ethics based on an ontology that stresses the interdependencies between the self and the other will be very different from one that is based on an ontology that separates the self from the other. What is more, any ethics based on an epistemology that values the concrete, the particular, the partial, and the emotional will be very different from one that insists that these values are false values that ultimately work against the moral enterprise. In the next five chapters, we will have the opportunity to assess whether feminine and/or feminist approaches to ethics are, as a result of their reliance on nontraditional ontological and epistemological assumptions, better equipped than traditional approaches to ethics to make us want to be better persons. A feminine or feminist approach to ethics that helps persons to actually bridge the gap between thinking the good and doing the good will be an improvement over those traditional approaches to ethics that have failed to persuade us that what makes life worth living may be the desire to be a better person tomorrow than one was today.

NOTES

1. Susan Sherwin, "A Feminist Approach to Ethics," *Dalhousie Review* 64, no. 4 (Winter 1984–1985):704.
2. Caroline Whitbeck, "A Different Reality: Feminist Ontology," in Ann Garry and Marilyn Pearsall, eds., *Women, Knowledge, and Reality: Explorations in Feminist Philosophy* (Boston: Unwin Hyman, 1989), 51.

3. Hélène Cixous, "Sorties," in Betsy Wing, trans., *The Newly Born Woman* (Minneapolis: University of Minnesota Press, 1986), 63.
4. Whitbeck, "A Different Reality: Feminist Ontology," 65.
5. Fung Yu-Lan, *A Short History of Chinese Philosophy* (New York: The Free Press, 1948), 197.
6. Whitbeck, "A Different Reality: Feminist Ontology," 66–67.
7. This is Held's term. Because she believes that men as well as women can rear children, Held prefers the term *mothering person* to the term *mother.*
8. Virginia Held, "Non-contractual Society: A Feminist View," in Marsha Hanen and Kai Nielsen, eds., *Science, Morality and Feminist Theory* (Calgary: University of Calgary Press, 1987), 127.
9. Ibid.
10. Ibid., 128.
11. Ibid., 130.
12. Ibid., 131.
13. Ibid., 132.
14. Lorraine Code, "Second Persons," in Marsha Hanen and Kai Nielsen, eds., *Science, Morality and Feminist Theory* (Calgary: University of Calgary Press, 1987), 367.
15. Adrienne Rich, *Of Woman Born* (New York: W. W. Norton, 1979), 13.
16. Annette Baier, "Cartesian Persons," in Annette Baier, *Postures of the Mind: Essays on Mind and Morals* (Minneapolis: University of Minnesota Press, 1985), 84.
17. Code, "Second Persons," 366.
18. Jean Grimshaw, "Autonomy and Identity in Feminist Thinking," in Morwenna Griffiths and Margaret Whitford, eds., *Feminist Perspectives in Philosophy* (Indianapolis: Indiana University Press, 1988), 91.
19. Ibid., 92.
20. Ibid., 93.
21. Ibid., 95.
22. Ibid.
23. I owe the insight for this point to Claudia Card, professor of philosophy at the University of Wisconsin.
24. Grimshaw, "Autonomy and Identity in Feminist Thinking," 98–101.
25. Ibid., 106.
26. Diane Meyers, "Personal Autonomy and the Paradox of Feminine Socialization," *The Journal of Philosophy* 84, no. 11 (November 1987):622.
27. Ibid., 625.
28. Ibid.
29. Ibid., 626.
30. Jean Grimshaw, *Philosophy and Feminist Thinking* (Minneapolis: University of Minnesota Press, 1986), 204.
31. Ibid., 205.
32. Ibid., 219.
33. Ibid., 207.
34. Ibid.

35. Ibid., 209.
36. Ibid., 213.
37. Immanuel Kant, *The Groundwork of the Metaphysics of Morals*, trans. H. J. Paton (New York: Harper & Row, 1964), 88–89.
38. Ibid., 89.
39. Lawrence A. Blum, *Friendship, Altruism and Morality* (London: Routledge & Kegan Paul, 1980), 84.
40. Ibid., 86.
41. Ibid., 90.
42. Ibid., 100.
43. Marilyn Friedman, "The Social Self and the Partiality Debates," in Claudia Card, ed., *Feminist Ethics* (Lawrence, Kans.: University of Kansas Press, 1991), 164.
44. Ibid., 163.
45. Ibid., 170.
46. Ibid., 174.
47. Ibid.
48. Ibid., 176.
49. Alison M. Jaggar, "Love and Knowledge: Emotion in Feminist Epistemology," in Ann Garry and Marilyn Pearsall, eds., *Women, Knowledge and Reality* (Boston: Unwin Hyman, 1989), 132.
50. Ibid., 133.
51. Ibid., 136.
52. Ibid.
53. Ibid., 138.
54. Ibid., 143.
55. Ibid., 145.
56. Ibid., 146.
57. Blum, *Friendship, Altruism and Morality*, 2, my emphasis.
58. Ibid., 3.
59. Ibid., 141.
60. Ibid., 142.
61. Ibid., 143.
62. Ibid., 144.
63. Ibid., 146.
64. Ibid.
65. Ibid., 147.

5

Carol Gilligan's
Ethics of Care

Although twentieth-century feminine and feminist approaches to ethics are distinguishable one from the other, they share many ontological and epistemological assumptions. Whether a "feminine" and/or "feminist" thinker is celebrating or critiquing the virtue of care, s/he will tend to believe that the self is an interdependent being rather than an atomistic entity. S/he will also tend to believe that knowledge is "emotional" as well as "rational" and that thoughtful persons reflect on concrete particularities as well as abstract universals. This is certainly true of Carol Gilligan, whose ethics of care is definitely rooted in "women's ways" of being and knowing.[1]

The questions that Gilligan poses about the relationship between gender and morality are similar to the ones that Wollstonecraft, Mill, Taylor, Beecher, Stanton, and Gilman posed. Is virtue the same or different in men and women? What is moral virtue, what is nonmoral virtue, and how are the two related? Does society encourage women to cultivate empowering or disempowering feminine psychological traits? What makes a feminine psychological trait either empowering (positive) or disempowering (negative)?

Gilligan's answers to these questions are provocative ones. In her first major book, *In a Different Voice,* Gilligan claimed that on the average, and for a variety of cultural reasons, women tend to espouse an ethics of care that stresses relationships and responsibilities, whereas men tend to espouse an ethics of justice that stresses rules and rights.[2] Even though Gilligan has qualified her gender-based claims over the years, she has not given them up entirely. In one of her more recent studies involving eighty educationally privileged North American adults and adolescents, two-thirds of the men and women raised considerations of both justice and care. Nevertheless, these men and women tended to focus on one more than the other of these two ethical perspectives. Whereas the women were just as likely to focus on justice as on care, only one man focused on care.[3] Thus, for Gilligan, care retains its connection to the "feminine."

Our task is to interpret and assess Gilligan's claims and claims like them. "With focus defined as 75 percent or more of the considerations raised pertaining either to justice or to care,"[4] it is, after all, puzzling why only one of Gilligan's male subjects focused on care, while several of her female subjects focused on justice. Could it be that men have good reason not to be carers? Is caring always a risky business? Or is it risky only in certain kinds of societies? Specifically, is it dangerous for women and other vulnerable people to espouse an ethics of care in a patriarchal society?

EXPLANATIONS OF GILLIGAN'S ETHICS OF CARE

Gilligan represents her work as a response to the Freudian notion that men have a well-developed moral sense whereas women do not. As Gilligan sees it, Freud condemned women twice. On the basis of what amounted to little more than his own personal reflections, Freud simply declared that women "show less sense of justice than men . . . are less ready to submit to the great exigencies of life, . . . [and] are more often influenced in their judgments by feelings of affection or hostility."[5] Later Freud underscored his observations by attributing women's supposed moral inferiority to a developmental difference, namely, "the strength and persistence of women's pre-Oedipal attachments to their mothers,"[6] attachments that men successfully break. Freud claimed that girls are much slower than boys to develop a sense of themselves as autonomous moral agents personally responsible for the consequences of their actions or inactions. Because the female id (unconscious desires) is supposedly more resistant to society's rules and regulations than is the male id, women are not as "civilized" as men.

Freud's account of women's "moral inferiority" is by no means peculiar to him. Traditionally, many psychologists and philosophers have reasoned from an androcentric point of view, seeing women's moral *inferiority* where they should have seen women's moral *difference* in Gilligan's estimation:

> My research suggests that men and women may speak different languages that they assume are the same, using similar words to encode disparate experiences of self and social relationships. Because these languages share an

overlapping moral vocabulary, they contain a propensity for systematic mistranslation, creating misunderstandings which impede communication and limit the potential for cooperation and care in relationships.[7]

Because these "mistranslation(s)" and "misunderstandings" contribute to a gross misrepresentation of women's morality, Gilligan aims to correct them.

Her main target for criticism is her former mentor, educational psychologist Lawrence Kohlberg, who claims that moral development is a six-stage process. Stage One is "the punishment and obedience orientation." To avoid the "stick" of punishment and/or to receive the "carrot" of a reward, the child does as s/he is told. Stage Two is "the instrumental relativist orientation." Based on a limited principle of reciprocity— "You scratch my back and I'll scratch yours"—the child does what satisfies his or her own needs and occasionally the needs of others. Stage Three is "the interpersonal concordance or 'good boy-nice girl' orientation." The adolescent conforms to prevailing mores because s/he seeks the approval of other people. Stage Four is "the law and order orientation." The adolescent begins to do his or her duty, show respect for authority, and maintain the given social order for its own sake in order to be recognized as an honorable, as opposed to a shameful, person. Stage Five is "the social contract legalistic orientation." The adult adopts an essentially utilitarian moral point of view according to which individuals are permitted to do as they please, provided that they refrain from harming other people in the process. Stage Six is "the universal ethical principle orientation." The adult adopts an essentially Kantian point of view that provides a moral perspective universal enough to serve as a critique of any conventional morality. The adult is no longer ruled by self-interest, the opinion of others, or the force of legal convention, but by self-legislated and self-imposed universal principles such as those of justice, reciprocity, and respect for the dignity of human beings as intrinsically valuable persons.[8]

Kohlberg's six-stage scale appeals to many people schooled in traditional ethics. Yet the popularity of a theory of moral development is not an index of its truth. We must ask ourselves whether Kohlberg's six stages of moral development are indeed (1) universal, (2) invariant (a always precedes b, b always precedes c, and so on), and (3) hierarchical (b is "more adequate" than a, c is "more adequate" than b, and so on).[9] Should we interpret the fact that women rarely climb past Stage Three on Kohlberg's scale, whereas men routinely ascend to Stage Five, to

mean that women are less morally developed than men are? Or should
we, like Gilligan, question Kohlberg's methodology, claiming that his
scale provides an account of *male* moral development rather than of *human* moral development?[10]

In order to determine the truth of Gilligan's claim, we need to understand how Kohlberg's methodology works. For the most part,
Kohlbergian researchers present their subjects with hypothetical moral
dilemmas that they are asked to resolve. The case of Heinz, a husband
who wants to buy his grievously ill wife a drug that might cure her, is
typical among these dilemmas. A druggist has overpriced the needed
drug, and Heinz cannot afford to buy it. The question is, then, "Should
Heinz steal the drug?"[11]

When Kohlbergian researchers asked this question of two eleven-
year-old children named Jake and Amy, they gave very different answers. Viewing a moral dilemma as "a math problem with humans,"[12]
Jake set up the dilemma like an equation and produced an appropriate
Kohlbergian answer. Heinz should steal the drug because Heinz's wife
is worth more than the druggist's business: That is, the right to life is
greater than the right to property. In contrast, Amy failed to produce
an appropriate Kohlbergian answer. Viewing a moral dilemma as "a
narrative of relationships that extend over time,"[13] she made no attempt
to compare the value of life to the value of property. Instead, she immediately focused on the concrete effects that Heinz's theft would have
on the relationship between him and his wife:

> If he stole the drug, he might save his wife then, but if he did, he might have
> to go to jail, and then his wife might get sicker again, and he couldn't get
> more of the drug, and it might not be good. So, they should really just talk it
> out and find some other way to make the money.[14]

Despite the reasonability of Amy's response, the Kohlbergian researcher insisted that she focus on the question at hand: "Should Heinz
steal the drug, after all?" Fearing that she was not producing the "right"
answer to the "right" question, Amy began to hesitate, a fact that the
researcher used to mark her down on Kohlberg's scale. Apparently,
doubt and intellectual soul-searching are not a part of "mature" moral
agents.

Gilligan contrasts the two children's differing responses not to negate
Jake's way of handling Heinz's dilemma but to affirm Amy's way of handling it. As the result of several empirical studies, including interviews

with twenty-nine relatively diverse women who were deciding whether to have an abortion, Gilligan concluded that women's *ontologies* and *epistemologies* as well as *ethics* typically diverge from men's. Because women tend to view the self as an interdependent being and morality as a matter of responsibilities for others, women do not do as well on Kohlberg's scale as do men, who tend to view the self as an independent, autonomous being and morality as a matter of ranking individual's rights.

Gilligan's controversial claims about men's and women's differing ontologies, epistemologies, and ethics are not, by her own admission, altogether unique. She relies, for example, on the theories of psychologist Nancy Chodorow, who roots men's and women's different conceptions of the self in what she maintains are the different "object-relational" experiences they have as infants with their mothers and fathers. As Chodorow sees it, the pre-Oedipal stage is sexually charged for boys in a way that it is not for girls. Feeling a sexual current between himself and his mother, the son senses that his mother's body is not like his own. As he enters the Oedipal stage, the son realizes how much of a problem his mother's otherness is. Though overwhelmingly in love with her, he cannot remain attached to her without risking his father's wrath. Not willing to take this risk, the son separates from his mother. What makes this process of separation less painful for the son is his dawning realization that power and prestige come from identification with men—in this case, the father. It is disturbing that social contempt for women helps the boy define himself in opposition to the female sex that his mother represents.[15]

In contrast to the mother-son pre-Oedipal relationship, "prolonged symbiosis" and "narcissistic over-identification characterize the mother-daughter pre-Oedipal relationship."[16] Because both the mother and the daughter are female, the daughter's sense of gender and self is continuous with that of her mother. Nevertheless, during the Oedipal stage, the mother-daughter symbiosis begins to weaken. What prompts a girl to distance herself from her mother is what her father symbolizes: namely, an independent being who presumably has what it takes to (sexually) satisfy women. Thus, as Chodorow interprets it, girls "envy" the penis because it signifies male power in the bedroom as well as in the boardroom.

Chodorow believes that the disparate psychosexual development of boys and girls has profound social implications. The boy's separation from his mother is the source of his inability to relate deeply to others.

This inability prepares him for work in the public sphere, which values single-minded efficiency, a down-to-business attitude, and competitiveness. Similarly, the girl's oneness with her mother is the source of her capacity for relatedness. This capacity is necessary for her role as nurturant wife and mother in the private sphere. If men have a major problem, it is with intimacy; if women have a major problem, it is with self-individuation.

Focusing on the asymmetrical role of intimacy and self-individuation in men's and women's lives, Gilligan notes that the importance of separation and autonomy for men often leads them to center discussions of morality around issues of justice, fairness, rules, and rights, whereas the importance of family and friends for women often leads them to center discussions of morality around people's wants, needs, interests, and aspirations. Gilligan also suggests that for women, much more than for men, moral development means learning how to integrate other-directed demands with self-centered concerns. During the process of their moral development, women supposedly move in and out of three stages: (1) an overemphasis on self; (2) an overemphasis on others; and (3) a proper emphasis on self in relation to others. Although a woman's moral development from an overly self-centered position (Level One), to an overly other-directed position (Level Two), and finally to a self-in-relation-to-others position (Level Three) is never final, as a woman morally matures, an increasing number of her decisions will follow Level Three patterns.

At Level One, the self is the sole object of a woman's concern. This self is a beleaguered self: a powerless and disappointed self, so afraid of being hurt that it prefers isolation to connectedness. As one woman in Gilligan's abortion study asserted, this is a self that wants *above all* to survive:

> I think survival is one of the first things in life that people fight for. I think it is the most important thing, more important than stealing. Stealing might be wrong, but if you have to steal to survive yourself or even kill, that is what you should do. . . . Preservation of oneself, I think, is the most important thing. It comes before anything in life.[17]

No wonder, then, that some of Gilligan's subjects initially regarded a baby as someone who would help them survive by loving them. However, as these women struggled through their abortion decisions, many of them concluded that a baby, no less than themselves, is a vulnerable person in need of love. Gradually, they began to reinterpret their *self-interest* as *selfishness*. So, for example, a seventeen-year-old, who at first wanted to carry her baby to term to assuage her loneliness, finally decided that it would be wrong for her to do so because she did not have the means to take care of a baby:

> What I want to do is to have the baby, but what I feel I should do, which is what I need to do, is have an abortion right now, because sometimes what you want isn't right. Sometimes what is necessary comes before what you want, because it might not always lead to the right thing.[18]

Like this seventeen-year-old, any woman who makes the transition from "wish" to "necessity"—that is, from "the 'selfishness' of willful decision" to "the 'responsibility' of moral choice"[19]—will reach Level Two of moral development. What motivates a woman to move from Level One to Level Two is a desire to establish connections with others and to participate in social life. In many ways, the Level Two woman is the conventional, nurturant woman who equates goodness with self-sacrifice and who tries to subjugate her wants to those of other people. In extreme cases, such a woman comes to believe that it is *always* "selfish" for her to do what she wants. In Gilligan's abortion study, for example, one woman who wanted to continue her pregnancy was being pressured by her lover to terminate it. Because this woman wanted both the baby and her lover's approval, she found herself in a moral "no-win" situation.

On the one hand, aborting the fetus would be "selfish." She would thereby secure one of *her* wants, namely, her lover's approval. On the other hand, not aborting the fetus would also be "selfish." She would thereby secure another of *her* wants, namely, a baby. The woman reasoned that no matter what she decided to do, she would hurt someone: either her lover or her fetus. In the end, the woman decided to have the abortion, consoling herself that it was not really *her* decision, but her *lover's*. Because the woman resented her lover's "decision," however, her resentment gradually turned to anger, souring the very relationship for which she had sacrificed her child.[20]

The moral of Gilligan's anecdote is that a woman can suppress her wants only so long before she reaches a destructive boiling point. To avoid becoming a resentful, angry, even hateful person, a woman needs to push beyond Level Two to Level Three of moral development, where she will learn how to care for herself as well as for others. As a woman moves to Level Three, the decision to abort, for example, becomes a complex choice she must make about how best to care for the fetus, herself, and anyone likely to be deeply affected by her decision. One of the women in Gilligan's study explains her decision to have an abortion as just such a choice:

> I would not be doing myself or the child or the world any kind of favor having this child. I don't need to pay off my imaginary debts to the world through this child, and I don't think that it is right to bring a child into the world and use it for that purpose.[21]

Gilligan characterizes the move from Level Two to Level Three as a transition from goodness to truth. A woman moves from pleasing others—being the conventionally good, always self-sacrificing woman—to recognizing her own needs as part of any relationship. In sum, a woman attains moral maturity when she stops opposing her needs in favor of others', simultaneously recognizing the falseness of this polarity and the truth of her and others' interconnectedness.

If we compare Gilligan's account of *women's* moral development with Kohlberg's account of *human* moral development, we can begin to appreciate why she thinks his account is really one that describes *men's* moral development. A "formal logic of fairness" informs Kohlberg's mode of reasoning and style of discourse; his scale structures moral phenomena in terms of a set of rights and rules. In contrast, a "psychological logic of relationships" informs Gilligan's mode of reasoning and style of discourse; her scale structures moral phenomena in terms of a set of responsibilities and connections.[22] To be sure, Gilligan's scale is no more a scale of *human* moral development than is Kohlberg's. Far from denying this fact, however, Gilligan instead suggests that students of moral development should not expect men and women to achieve moral personhood in precisely the same way. Rather, researchers should be attentive to the different ways in which men and women describe the beginnings and endings of their distinctive moral journeys, viewing them as alternative ways to achieve the goals of a morality that ultimately requires both rights and responsibilities.[23]

In her most recent work, *Mapping the Moral Domain*, Gilligan further develops the position she introduced in *In a Different Voice*.[24] Several recent studies of adolescents' moral development indicate that by the age of eleven, most children are able to use either a justice approach or a care approach to solve a moral problem. They can, in other words, speak the language of both rights and responsibilities. The fact that a child favors one of these languages over the other in everyday speech is not, however, a clear sign that s/he is using his/her *preferred* moral language. On the contrary, it may merely be a sign that s/he wishes to use whatever moral language his/her peers favor. For example, in one dual-sexed high school, where the justice perspective predominated among boys and girls alike, "students of both sexes tended to characterize care-focused solutions or inclusive problem-solving strategies as utopian or outdated; one student linked them with impractical Sunday school teachings, another with the outworn philosophy of 'hippies.'"[25] Presumably, students in the school who voiced care strategies would encounter negative reactions from their peers and even be rejected as definitely not "cool."

Rather than being disheartened by this adolescent behavior, Gilligan consoles herself that the "cool" response to a moral problem is a *learned* response that can, after all, be either *unlearned* or *never learned* in the first place. It encourages Gilligan that early childhood psychologists no longer view young children as isolationists, capable only of "parallel play,"[26] instead viewing them as skilled social interactors capable of creating relationships with their peers. It also encourages her that an increasing number of adolescent psychologists have replaced asking the question "Why has this sixteen-year-old *not* developed relational capacities x, y, and z yet?" with the question "Why has this sixteen-year-old *lost* so many of the relational capacities s/he had when s/he was eleven, or seven, or even three?"[27]

Recently, several studies have concluded that most children (but especially girls) express a "deep sense of outrage and despair over disconnection"[28] as they enter adolescence. They perceive that the adult world is inhospitable to the kind of intense and intimate relationships that make childhood special. Because girls, even more than boys, treasure their close friendships, they are particularly distressed at the parental admonition, "Growing up is about standing on one's own two feet." They fear that adulthood is not so much about autonomy as it is about aloneness, that is, about "being excluded, left out, and abandoned."[29]

As Gilligan sees it, teachers routinely communicate to students the message that "caring is for kids," that adults do not have time to build a strong network of relationships. Our whole educational system stresses only certain kinds of thinking. Teachers encourage students to analyze arguments; to be scientific, objective, and rational; to abstract and universalize their thoughts. As a result, students begin to view the humanities as so much frivolous fluff—subjective stuff for sentimental softies. Rather than providing students with the strategies and skills for *communal* life, teachers provide them with the strategies and skills for *competitive* life.

Although Gilligan criticizes overly analytical, objective, and neutral teachers in general, she saves her harshest words for those educational psychologists who interpret children's relationships as unhealthy attachments or growth-limiting dependencies. There is nothing "sick" about children's relationships in Gilligan's estimation. Far from being impediments to moral development, such "attachments" or "dependencies" are actually a sign of growth. Rather than encouraging children to be detached and independent, adults should encourage them to be responsive to other people's needs and wants.[30]

CRITICISMS OF GILLIGAN'S ETHICS OF CARE

Despite the appeal of Gilligan's ethics of care, critics have raised several plausible objections against it. First, Gilligan misunderstands or misinterprets Kohlberg. Second, the distinction between justice and care is not a new one, but an old one. Third, justice and care are not so much two *different* approaches to morality as they are two *complementary* approaches to morality. Fourth, justice and care are two different approaches to morality, but care is not as good an approach to morality as justice is. Fifth, justice and care are not gender correlated. Sixth, whether or not justice and care are gender correlated, the cultural identification of women with care has negative consequences for women. Seventh, "justice" and "care" are inappropriate descriptions of the ethical perspectives in question. Indeed, if "justice" and "care" are nothing more than the perspectives of the oppressor and oppressed, valorizing care may worsen the position of the oppressed.[31] Finally, to laud care as *the* "woman's voice" ignores the sometimes hurtful selectivity and even exclusivity of care: Racism, classism, and lesbophobia within women's ranks turn care itself into a questionable approach to morality.[32] We must examine *who* cares about *whom* and *why* before we give the feminist stamp of approval to a "caring" act.

Criticism One

There is some reason to think that in attacking Kohlberg, Gilligan is attacking a "straw man."[33] For example, researchers Catherine G. Greeno and Eleanor E. Maccoby claim that, overall, Kohlberg's paradigm does not show women fixating at Stage Three of moral development as men climb on toward the pinnacle of moral perfection. On the contrary, sixty-one Kohlbergian studies show female children and adolescents scoring approximately the same in moral reasoning as male children and adolescents. They also show female and male adults achieving nearly identical moral development scores, with the exception of those studies that include in their sample relatively uneducated and unemployed housewives.[34] Because the ability to move from Stage Three to Stages Four and Five on Kohlberg's scale largely depends on actively participating in the public world, it stands to reason that housewives would remain fixed at Stage Three. Not women's gender but their lack of experience in the public world causes their moral underdevelopment.

There are at least two ways to answer Greeno and Maccoby's criticism, both of which challenge the assumption that one's educational and occupational experiences rather than one's gender most strongly affect one's ultimate moral development. The first way is to concede that career women do better than housewives on Kohlberg's tests but to explain the "success" of career women as a function of their *acquired masculine gender* and not of their educational and occupational levels per se. For the most part, the public world is a "male" world. Women who succeed in it tend to think and act like conventional men who, more often than not, sacrifice intimacy for autonomy. Women who fail in the public world tend to think and act like conventional women who, more often than not, sacrifice autonomy for intimacy. Because Kohlberg's scale of moral development is structured to fit the contours of the public world, a woman will climb high on the scale to the degree that her moral voice is recognizably "masculine" (that is, "justice" rather than "care" inflected). Thus, a career woman who speaks like a man will strike a Kohlbergian researcher as more morally developed than a housewife who speaks like a woman. It is at once as simple and as complex as this.

The second way to resist the claim that not gender but educational and occupational experiences play the crucial role in one's moral development is simply to deny that whereas housewives speak in a "feminine" voice, career women speak in a "masculine" voice. Gilligan herself disputes Greeno and Maccoby's empirical findings by contrasting them with those of Diana Baumrind. According to Baumrind, the *most* educated women are the ones *least* likely to speak the masculine language of justice.[35] One possible explanation for Baumrind's results is that the truly educated woman—that is, the woman with a mind of her own—will refuse to become a "man" in exchange for social approval. The accolades of society are no substitute for the kind of pride and pleasure that a self-confident woman derives from the knowledge that she is her own person.

Criticism Two

Despite the fact that Gilligan writes as if she has discovered a different moral voice, her ethics of care may not be that novel. For example, philosopher George Sher claims that Gilligan's contrast between women's approach to morality—an approach that is supposedly concrete, non-principled, personal, care-driven, and responsibility oriented—and men's approach to morality—an approach that is supposedly abstract, principled, impersonal, duty-driven, and rights oriented—is a distinction that traditional ethicists such as Kant and Schopenhauer have already made. Comments Sher: "The opposition of concrete and abstract, personal and impersonal, duty and care are not recent empirical discoveries but generic determinants of the moral problematic."[36]

Sher's point is worthy of consideration. William K. Frankena, a traditional ethicist, reduces all moral principles to two fundamental ones: (1) justice or equality and (2) benevolence.

> There are two basic principles of prima facie obligation: that of benevolence and that of justice or equality. From the former follow various less basic principles of prima facie obligation: the principle of utility, the principle of not injuring anyone, the principle of not interfering with another's liberty, and so on. From the latter follow others, for instance, equality of consideration and equality before the law. Possibly some others like keeping promises follow from both.[37]

Yet even though Frankena's distinction between justice and benevolence is similar to Gilligan's distinction between justice and care, philosopher Marilyn Friedman argues that it is not the same as Gilligan's distinction. Gilligan's care reasoners, unlike Frankena's benevolence reasoners, consider persons in their *particularity* rather than in their *universality*.[38] Care reasoners do not attend to everyone in general, but to the individual men and women, boys and girls, to whom they are specifically related. *Whom* one benefits or harms is of essential and intrinsic concern to them.

Criticism Three

To the degree that caring and justice are actually complementary rather than conflicting approaches to the moral life, Gilligan may be exaggerating the differences between caring and justice. For example, Sher insists that no matter how "abstract" an ethicist is, he still has to attend to matters of context to determine whether an action does in fact constitute adultery, murder, rape, or arson. Similarly, no matter how "concrete" an ethicist is, she cannot possibly focus on each element of a moral situation *equally* without being overwhelmed by detail.[39]

Sher's commonsensical objection to Gilligan is quite compelling. To meet with our full approval, the just person must be caring, and the caring person must be just. Far from being dichotomous moral concepts, justice and care are at least mutually compatible if not actually symbiotically related.

Friedman has effectively explored the interconnections between justice and care. As she sees it, justice is relevant to care in at least three ways. First, if we view a personal relationship as a "miniature social system which provides valued mutual intimacy, support, and concern for those who are involved,"[40] we will find that frequently one person in the relationship becomes the giver, and the other becomes the receiver. This mode of injustice characterizes many heterosexual relationships, for example. Women typically serve men's physical and psychological needs and wants rather than the other way around; it is women who feed men's egos, and it is women who tend men's wounds.[41] Unless this inequitable state of affairs is remedied over time, women's caring acts are gradually transformed into masochistic acts.

Second, if we think about it, a personal relationship creates "special vulnerabilities to harm."[42] When someone I care about and who supposedly cares about me harms me, justice demands that this wrong be "righted." The fact that someone cares for me does not give him or her license to exploit and oppress me. On the contrary, any injustice perpetrated in the context of a caring relationship is worse than it would otherwise be. An argument can be made, for example, that rape by an acquaintance inflicts deeper psychological wounds than rape by a stranger because the "date rapist" takes advantage of his victim's trust.

Third, if we focus on some of our closest relationships, especially our familial relationships, we will discover that they are fraught with the potential for myriad injustices. Should mom and dad give their son, Jim, privileges they are not willing to give their daughter, Sue? Should Mr.

and Mrs. Jones pay for Grandpa Jones's much-needed vacation or for daughter Beth's summer camp? Should Mr. Smith give up an excellent job so that he can move with Mrs. Smith, who has a mediocre job, to a city where she will have an excellent job but he will have only a mediocre one?

Although Friedman does not specify care's effects on justice in as much detail as she specifies justice's effects on care, several examples quickly come to mind. We are reluctant to punish adolescent criminals as severely as adult criminals. We sometimes give people another chance because it would be too cruel to ruin their lives on account of a single mistake. We occasionally give people more than their fair share because we want to "cheer them up" or motivate them to do even better in the future. We even forgive our enemies.

Despite the fact that Sher and Friedman are correct to stress the interaction between justice and care, in fairness to Gilligan, we must recognize that she too has explored this interaction. Initially she suggested that, properly developed, justice and care slowly

> converge in the realization that just as inequality adversely affects both parties in an unequal relationship, so too violence is destructive for everyone involved. This dialogue between fairness and care not only provides a better understanding of relations between the sexes but also gives rise to a more comprehensive portrayal of adult work and family relationships.[43]

For reasons she does not specify, however, Gilligan has recently replaced her "convergence" theory with a "gestalt" theory.

Like an ambiguous drawing that may be seen either as a duck or as a rabbit, a moral drama may be framed either in terms of justice or in terms of care. Although these two perspectives cannot completely and finally converge, neither are they diametrically opposed polarities. Most individuals will find themselves interpreting a moral drama first from one of these perspectives and then from the other, but some individuals will be unable to alternate their viewpoint between the justice and care perspectives. An exclusive focus either on matters of justice or on matters of care is not without precedent, however, for try as they might, some individuals can see only the duck *or* the rabbit in an ambiguous "duck-rabbit" drawing.[44]

Like her past efforts to interrelate care and justice, Gilligan's most recent efforts have tended to fall on deaf ears. The majority of Gilligan's readers continue to hear her words as a claim that care is somehow both separate from and better than justice. Moreover, some of Gilligan's most careful readers believe that she is committed to the view that women, on account of their alleged capacity for caring, *are* more moral than men.

In an attempt to bolster this interpretation of Gilligan, Michelle M. Moody-Adams cites the following passage from one of Gilligan's relatively recent articles:

> . . . stereotypes of males as aggressive and females as nurturant, however distorting and however limited, have some empirical claim. the overwhelmingly male composition of the prison population and the extent to which women take care of young children cannot readily be dismissed as irrelevant to theories of morality or excluded from accounts of moral development. If there are no sex differences in empathy or moral reasoning, why are there sex differences in moral and immoral behavior?[45]

Gilligan's linkage of empirical evidence with moral claims heightens her critics' fear that she tends toward "biologism." As Moody-Adams pointedly asks, does Gilligan believe that because more men than women are in prison, women are more moral than men? If so, would she be equally eager to note that given the higher percentage of blacks than whites in prison, whites are more moral than blacks?[46] Do we really want to tie morality to genetics—to accept the sexism and racism inherent in such a view?

Criticism Four

Even if care and justice are, after all, very distinct approaches to morality, Gilligan may be wrong to argue that care is just as good an approach to morality as justice. Philosopher Bill Puka, for example, suggests that care bears more resemblance to nonmoral virtues, or psychological traits, than to bona fide moral virtues. He claims that we must take seriously Kohlberg's objections to any kind of "benevolence ethics," including Gilligan's ethics of care.[47] First, benevolence ethics valorizes a certain set of nonmoral values or psychological traits. It puts a premium on possessing a certain type of *personality:* specifically, a kindly and caring one. Second, benevolence ethics does not take seriously the existence of mean, nasty, cruel, hard-hearted, hateful, or abusive individuals. It provides little or no guidance to a benevolent person who is harmed by a malevolent person, for example. May the benevolent person resist evil actively, or must s/he turn the other cheek passively? Third, and finally, benevolence ethics demands too much in the way of self-sacrifice. It often instructs benevolent persons to give until they can give no more—that is, until their physical, psychological, and spiritual resources are entirely exhausted.

Gilligan's ethics of care is vulnerable to all three of these objections, but especially to the first. As Puka sees it, everything Gilligan writes about care in *In a Different Voice* suggests an interpretation of care according to which it is

> a preference for relating to others closely, for getting into each other's psychologies to share fears, concerns and vulnerabilities when confronting moral issues; (2) a preference for harmonious, non-competitive feelings and cooperative spirit in relating; (3) a commitment to making relationships last by working on them and nurturing them.[48]

But if this is care, it is little more than a capacity for *psychological* relatedness that will be actualized to a greater or lesser degree by a person depending on his/her proclivities. For Gilligan to elevate this psychological capacity into a moral imperative is for her to make individuals "responsible for feeling certain ways, for generating certain psychological reactions and putting them in action."[49] Yet, as things stand, men find it much more difficult to show their feelings than do women. Society still socializes men, but not women, to suppress their feelings. Thus, Puka concludes that in demanding more of men than of women, Gilligan's ethics of care discriminates against men in ways that Kohlberg's ethics of justice does not discriminate against women:

> Even in expecting both genders to combine care and justice, women are given the far easier task. To become more justice oriented women need only revise certain behavior, certain minimal treatment of others. But to become more caring, systematically de-sensitized males must somehow discover how to make compassion flow.[50]

Puka is certainly correct to insist that ought implies can. We cannot be morally required to do something that we do not have the physical and psychological capacities to perform. Still, in fairness to Gilligan, it is not clear that it is any easier for women to be just than it is for men to be caring. Consider the female welfare administrator who wants to give the women and children who come to her office what they really need to thrive, but whose hands are tied by bureaucratic regulations. As she sends these vulnerable people away with the inadequate amount of resources to which they are legally entitled, she will feel frustrated. As hard as it is to do *more* for people than one wants, it is just as hard to do *less* for people than one wants.

What is more, Puka's tendency to trivialize care and to valorize justice may simply signal how much he subscribes to traditional definitions of morality (see Pojman in Chapter 2). Because Kohlberg's ethics of justice fits those definitions better than Gilligan's ethics of care, Puka simply endorses Kohlberg's ethics without challenging the criteria that validate it. Certainly, he fails to take seriously the possibility that justice commits us to a morality that few women *or* men are prepared to practice.

In a forthcoming book on friendship, Friedman discusses how an excessive emphasis on justice can generate morally perplexing situations. To clarify the ways in which we can have too much of a good thing—in this instance, justice—Friedman refers to the passage in Kohlberg's Moral Stages where he summarizes eleven-year-old Jake's reactions to the Heinz case. Not only did researchers ask Jake whether it would be morally permissible (required) for Heinz to steal a drug to save his wife's life, they asked him whether it would be morally permissible (required) for him to do so for a stranger. At first, the boy answered "No," noting that Heinz and the stranger did not have a relationship strong enough to motivate such an act. Later, however, the boy altered his initial judgment, commenting, "But somehow it doesn't seem fair to say that. The stranger has his life and wants to live just as much as your wife; it isn't fair to say you should steal it for your wife but not for the stranger."[51]

As Friedman sees it, Jake's second response is technically correct. It is not *fair* for Heinz to steal for his wife but not for the stranger. Yet, there is more to morality than being fair to everyone in general. There is the matter of the special duties I owe to the people to whom I am intimately related—especially the people who depend on me for their material, psychological, and spiritual well-being.[52] These intimates have a right to *more* than an equal share of what I have to offer to humanity in general. And it is good that they do, for my sake as well as theirs; for if I were related to no one in particular, there would be no reason for me to meet one person's needs more or less concertedly than some other person's. I would be committed to spreading myself as "thinly" as possible in order to distribute myself as "fairly" as possible.

Yet another thinker who objects to the valorization of justice and the trivialization of care is Annette C. Baier. As she sees it, "'warmer,' more communitarian virtues and social ideals" need to supplement what the eighteenth-century philosopher David Hume termed the "cold jealous virtue of justice."[53] Baier observes that traditional ethics encourages individuals to seek their own good, their own way. Under such conditions, a "minimal formal common good," based on contracts that protect the self from the other, replaces a maximal substantive common good, based on the close relationships that exist in well-functioning families.[54] Supposedly, each person is a rational contractor who has the same right to life, liberty, and the pursuit of happiness as any other person. Provided that s/he knows what s/he wants and has the power to attain it freely, each rational contractor may pursue his/her goals singlemindedly, provided that s/he does not harm any other rational contractor in the process. Such a vision of human relationships is not only an impoverished one in Baier's estimation but also an unrealistic one, since so many human relationships are not contractual. Nevertheless, traditional ethics operates on the assumption that morality exists, first and foremost, to order relationships between so-called consenting adults:

It is a typical feature of the dominant moral theories and traditions, since Kant, or perhaps since Hobbes, that relationships between equals or those who are deemed equal in some important sense have been the relations that morality is concerned primarily to regulate. Relationships between those who are clearly unequal in power, such as parents and children, earlier and later generations in relation to one another, states and citizens, doctors and patients, the well and the ill, large states and small states, have had to be shunted to the bottom of the agenda, and then dealt with by some sort of "promotion" of the weaker so that an appearance of virtual equality is achieved.[55]

By deceiving ourselves that those weaker than ourselves are actually as strong as we are, however, we neglect to develop adequate moral guidelines for relations between stronger and weaker individuals. Moral realism begins with the perception that we, who began life as helpless infants, will spend the rest of it relating to individuals who are either more powerful or less powerful than we are.[56] Because our true equals are few and far between, we need moral rules that take account of this fact.

An ethics of care is not just an alternative ethics for "softies"—a second-rate morality for runners up in the struggle to be good and to do good. On the contrary, an ethics of care is just as necessary as an ethics of justice. Although Baier is not a moral monist who insists that caring is the only intrinsically valuable moral virtue—the ultimate root of morality—she refuses to reduce an ethics of care to "popular psychology," to some version of "I'm okay, you're okay, we're all okay because we're all connected somehow or another." For Baier, an ethics of care is no less required than an ethics of justice, since "Not all morally important relationships can or *should* be freely chosen."[57] Ethics is a matter of learning how to live excellently within the limits that our humanity imposes on us. We cannot escape, nor should we seek to escape, all of our biological ties—not if we wish to ensure "that each new generation is made appropriately welcome and prepared for their adult lives."[58]

Criticism Five

Even if Gilligan constructs a persuasive case about the distinctive natures and functions of justice and care, her argument that justice and care are gender correlated fails to convince one and all. Indeed, whenever I present the justice-care debate to my ethics students, they immediately bring up films such as *Three Men and a Baby*, in which the men supposedly deserve the Nobel Prize for basic child care, and *Mommie Dearest*, which portrays Joan Crawford as a vicious child abuser. They also refer to saints like Francis of Assisi who loved all vulnerable creatures, animal as well as human, and to public figures like Margaret Thatcher, former prime minister of Great Britain, known for her iron will and tough political stands. Finally, they relate stories about their dads, moms, siblings, and friends: dads who cry; moms who enforce rigid rules and regulations; brothers who are always ready to lend a hand; sisters who care only about their own privileges and successes; male friends who donate time and energy to the downtrodden; and female friends who support war, capital punishment, and the elimination of welfare programs.

Clearly, some women care little for others. Historian Linda Kerber, for example, calls attention to a disturbing book of essays on women in Weimar and Nazi Germany that details the ways in which German women deserted and even betrayed Jewish women.[59] Not all German women opposed the extermination of the Jews, and among those who did, relatively few publicly expressed their opposition.

Conversely, some men care much for others. At a recent men's conference in Boulder, Colorado, for example, one attendee said he left elementary school teaching because parents objected to his "practice of hugging" his third-grade students: "As men, we're encouraged to be more nurturing. But then when we nurture, people can't cope with it."[60] Reinforcing his friend's words, another attendee, who works as a guidance counselor and yoga instructor, commented: "Men want the same things that women want. . . . Men want to be loved, touched and respected, the same as women. We should appreciate these common threads between us, not just get caught up in all the conflict."[61]

Yet even if *empirical* observations and studies reveal that women do not have a monopoly on care any more than men have a monopoly on justice, Friedman maintains that our culture nonetheless conceives "specific moral ideals, values, virtues, and practices as the special projects or domains of specific genders."[62] "Genderized" moral conceptions guide our social expectations about how "normal" men and women should talk and act. Men should fight for truth, justice, and the American way. Women should care for their loved ones' physical and psychological needs. What Gilligan may have discovered, then, is something that exists as *value* rather than as *fact:*

> The moralization of gender is more a matter of how we *think* we reason than of how we actually reason, more a matter of the oral concerns we *attribute* to women and men than of true statistical differences between women's and men's moral reasoning. Gilligan's findings resonate with the experiences of many people because those experiences are shaped, in part, by cultural myths and stereotypes of gender which even feminist theorizing may not dispel. Thus, both women and men in our culture *expect* women and men to exhibit this moral dichotomy, and, on my hypothesis, it is this expectation which has shaped both Gilligan's observations and the plausibility which we attribute to them.[63]

We accept the surface truth of Gilligan's empirical findings because society trains us to see women as caring and men as just. Before we can study men and women as they truly are, then, we must remove the cultural lens that distorts our vision.

Gilligan herself unintentionally corroborates Friedman's belief that the alleged differences between men's and women's morality are more ideological than empirical. For example, one of her most recent studies on these alleged differences showed (1) thirty-one men and twenty-two women focused equally on justice and care; (2) thirty men and ten women focused exclusively, or primarily, on justice; and (3) twelve women but only one man focused exclusively, or primarily, on care.

Instead of underscoring the encouraging fact that *thirty-one* men spoke the language of care and justice *equally*,[64] however, Gilligan chose to emphasize the fact that only *one* man spoke the language of care *exclusively*—as if one must speak *only* the language of care to be truly moral. In her focus on care, Gilligan reveals an all-or-nothing perspective that may be as myopic as the perspective of those who focus on justice. If men must learn to care, perhaps women must learn to be just. Replacing one approach with the other is not the solution.

Criticism Six

Even if women are better carers than men (for whatever reasons), it may still be epistemically, ethically, or politically unwise to associate women with the value of care. To link women with caring is to promote the view that women care by nature. It is also to promote the view that because women can and have cared, they should always care no matter the cost to themselves.

In *Femininity and Domination*, Sandra Lee Bartky seeks to determine whether women's experience of feeding men's egos and tending men's wounds ultimately disempowers or empowers them. She notes that the kind of "emotional work" practiced by female flight attendants often leads "to self-estrangement, an inability to identify one's own emotional states, even to drug abuse or alcoholism."[65] To pay a person to be "relentlessly cheerful"[66]—to smile at even the most verbally abusive and unreasonably demanding passengers—means paying a person to feign a certain set of emotions. A person can pretend to be happy only so many times before that person forgets how it feels to be genuinely or authentically happy.

The kind of emotional work flight attendants do for passengers, however, may be far more alienating and disempowering than the kind of emotional work wives do for their husbands, for example. Bartky notes that many wives find the experience of caring for their husbands empowering. The better carer a wife is, the more able she may be to think of herself as an extraordinarily good person. Yet subjective feelings of empowerment are not the same as the objective reality of actually having power. Bartky explains how women's androcentric emotional work eventually *harms* women far more than it benefits them. Among the ways that women accord men status is through a variety of "bodily displays" including "the sympathetic cocking of the head; the forward inclination of the body; the frequent smiling; the urging, through appropriate vocalizations, that the man continue his recital, hence, that he may continue to commandeer the woman's time and attention."[67] Men do not accord women similar status, however, and because they do not, women's caregiving of men amounts to "a collective genuflection by women to men, an affirmation of male importance that is unrecipro-cated."[68]

In Bartky's estimation, the epistemic and ethical consequences of women's unreciprocated caregiving of men is most worrisome. The more emotional support a woman gives a man, the more she will tend to see things as he sees them. Indeed, to the extent that her viewpoint diverges from his, she will find it difficult to participate in his projects, share his friends, rejoice in his successes, and feel badly about his fail-ures. But women do not need yet another reason to doubt their own vi-sion of reality and version of the truth. Men's and women's interests are not identical in a patriarchal society, and it is important that women, who tend "to get the short end of the stick," realize this.

As bad as it is, from an epistemic point of view, to know the world only, or primarily, through someone else's eyes, especially someone who looks down on you, it is even worse, from an ethical point of view, to affirm someone else's morality no matter the goodness or badness of his/her values. Bartky points to Teresa Stangl, wife of Fritz Stangl, Kommandant of Treblinka. Despite the fact that her husband's mon-strous activities horrified her, she continued to "feed" and "tend" him dutifully, even lovingly. In doing so, however, she was playing "footloose and fancy free" with her own soul. Quoting the following passage from Jill Tweedie's *In the Name of Love,* Bartky observes that one cannot re-main silent about evil and expect to keep one's goodness entirely intact:

> Behind every great man is a woman, we say, but behind every monster there is a woman too, behind each of those countless men who stood astride their narrow worlds and crushed other human beings, causing them hideous suf-fering and pain. There she is in the shadows, a vague female silhouette, ten-derly wiping blood from their hands.[69]

Because horror perpetrated by a loved one is still horror, women need to analyze "the pitfalls and temptations of caregiving itself" before they embrace an ethics of care wholeheartedly.[70]

For reasons related to Bartky's general concerns about any and all ethics of care, Puka singles out Gilligan's ethics of care for specific criticism. He claims that care can be interpreted in two ways: (1) in

Gilligan's way, "as a general orientation toward moral problems (inter-personal problems) and a track of moral development,"[71] or (2) in his way, "as a sexist service orientation, prominent in the patriarchal social-ization, social conventions, and roles of many cultures."[72] Those who in-terpret care as Gilligan does will trace women's moral development through the three levels presented earlier in this chapter. In contrast, those who interpret care as Puka does will view these supposed levels of moral development largely as coping mechanisms or defensive strat-egies that women use in a patriarchal world structured to work against their best interests.

Puka develops a persuasive case for his view of care. First, he inter-prets Level One as those strategies of self-protection and self-concern that women use to avoid rejection or domination. "I'm out for myself" and "If I don't care about myself, no one else will" are statements likely to be uttered by a woman who feels that she has to privilege herself over other people simply because other people, especially men, are not likely to concern themselves about her.[73]

Second, Puka interprets Level Two, which often develops in reaction to the loneliness of Level One, as a resumption of the "conventional slavish approach" that women typically adopt in a patriarchal society.[74] Although Level Two is frequently described as altruistic, as if women always *freely* choose to put other people's needs and interests ahead of their own, in reality Level Two is simply another coping mechanism. Within a patriarchy, women learn that men will reward, or at least not punish, the women who faithfully serve them.

Third, and finally, Puka interprets Level Three as a coping mecha-nism that involves elements of self-protection as well as slavishness:

> Here a woman learns where she can exercise her strengths, interest, and commitments (within the male power structure) and where she would do better to comply (with that structure). A delicate contextual balance must be struck to be effective here.[75]

Insofar as a woman is rationally calculating her chances of surviving and possibly even thriving within a patriarchy, Level Three constitutes a de-gree of *cognitive* liberation for her. It does not, however, signal *personal* liberation for her. As long as society remains patriarchal, women will not be able to strike an appropriate and abiding balance between rights and responsibilities in their moral lives. On the contrary, women will tend to practice not so much the moral virtue of care as either its "vi-cious" excess of slavishness or its "vicious" defect of self-preservation.

CONCLUSIONS

In expressing concern about the dangers of care, Gilligan's critics echo Elizabeth Cady Stanton's nineteenth-century admonition that, given society's tendency to take advantage of women, it is vital that women make self-development rather than other-directed self-sacrifice their first priority.[76] Still, it is important not to overemphasize the problems associated with retrieving feminine or womanly virtues from the webs of patriarchy. Whatever weaknesses Gilligan's ethics of care may have, there are serious problems with women abandoning all of their nurturant activities. The world would be a much worse place tomorrow than it is today were women suddenly to stop meeting the physical and psychological needs of those who depend on them. Just because men and, yes, children have more or less routinely taken advantage of some women's willingness to serve them, does not mean that every woman's caring actions should be contemptuously dismissed as yet another instance of women's "pathological masochism," "fear of success," or "passivity."[77] Care is worth "rescuing" from the patriarchal structures that would misuse or abuse it. If it is to be rescued, however, we need to recognize the differences between what Sheila Mullett terms "distortions of caring" on the one hand and "undistorted caring" on the other.[78]

According to Mullett, a person cannot truly care for someone if she is economically, socially, and/or psychologically forced to do so.[79] Thus, genuine or fully authentic caring cannot occur under patriarchal conditions, that is, conditions characterized by male domination and female subordination. Only under conditions of sexual equality and freedom can women care for men without men in any way diminishing, disempowering, and/or disregarding them. Until such conditions are achieved, women must care cautiously, asking themselves whether the kind of caring in which they are engaged:

1. Fulfills the one caring

2. Calls upon the unique and particular individuality of the one caring

3. Is not produced by a person in a role because of gender, with one gender engaging in nurturing behavior and the other engaging in instrumental behavior

4. Is reciprocated with caring, and not merely with the satisfaction of seeing the ones cared for flourishing and pursuing other projects.

5. Takes place within the framework of consciousness-raising practice and conversation[80]

Care can be freely given only when the one caring is not taken for granted. As long as men *demand* and *expect* caring from women, both sexes will morally shrink: Neither men nor women will be able to authentically care.

In the next chapter, we will analyze Nel Noddings's attempts to reclaim care not only for women but also for men. Her success will depend on whether her vision of care tends to empower rather than disempower women. If Gilligan has persuaded us that, either as "fact" or as "value," women speak a different moral language than men do, perhaps Noddings can persuade us that this different language is one that women should continue to speak and men should start to learn.

NOTES

An earlier and somewhat different version of pages 80–102 was published in Rosemarie Tong, *Feminist Thought: A Comprehensive Introduction* (Boulder, Colo.: Westview Press, 1989), 161–168.
1. Mary Belenky, Blythe Clichy, Nancy Goldberger, and Jill Tarule, *Women's Way of Knowing* (New York: Basic Books, 1987).
2. Carol Gilligan, *In a Different Voice* (Cambridge, Mass.: Harvard University Press, 1982).
3. Carol Gilligan, "Moral Orientation and Moral Development," in Eva Feder Kittay and Diana T. Meyers, eds., *Women and Moral Theory* (Totowa, N.J.: Rowman & Littlefield, 1987), 25.
4. Ibid.
5. Carol Gilligan, *In a Different Voice* (Cambridge, Mass.: Harvard University Press, 1982), 7. [Quoting Freud.]
6. Ibid.
7. Ibid., 173.
8. Lawrence Kohlberg, "From Is to Ought: How to Commit the Naturalistic Fallacy and Get Away With It in the Study of Moral Development," in T. Mischel, ed., *Cognitive Development and Epistemology* (New York: Academic Press, 1971), 164–165.
9. Owen J. Flanagan, Jr., "Virtue, Sex, and Gender: Some Philosophical Reflections on the Moral Psychology Debate," *Ethics* 92, no. 3 (April 1982):499–512.
10. Gilligan, *In a Different Voice,* 173.
11. Ibid.
12. Ibid.
13. Ibid., 28.
14. Ibid.
15. Nancy Chodorow, *The Reproduction of Mothering* (Berkeley: University of California Press, 1978), 127.
16. Ibid., 104.
17. Gilligan, *In a Different Voice,* 76.
18. Ibid., 77.

19. Ibid.
20. Ibid., 81.
21. Ibid., 92.
22. Ibid., 73.
23. Ibid., 174.
24. Carol Gilligan, Janie Victoria Ward, and Jill McLean Taylor, eds., *Mapping the Moral Domain* (Cambridge, Mass.: Harvard University Press, 1988), ii.
25. Carol Gilligan, "Adolescent Development Reconsidered," in Gilligan, Ward, and Taylor, eds., *Mapping the Moral Domain*, xxii.
26. Ibid., viii.
27. Ibid., x.
28. Ibid., xi.
29. Ibid.
30. Ibid., 21.
31. I owe this last point to Claudia Card, professor of philosophy at the University of Wisconsin.
32. Elizabeth V. Spelman, "The Virtue of Feeling and the Feeling of Virtue," in Claudia Card, ed., *Feminist Ethics* (Kansas: University Press of Kansas, 1991), 211–220.
33. Catherine G. Greeno and Eleanor E. Maccoby, "How Different Is the Different Voice?" in "On *In a Different Voice:* An Interdisciplinary Forum," *Signs: Journal of Women in Culture and Society* 11, no. 2 (Winter 1986):312.
34. Lawrence Walker, "Sex Differences in the Development of Moral Reasoning: A Critical Review," *Child Development* 55, no. 3 (June 1984):677.
35. Carol Gilligan, "Reply by Carol Gilligan," in "On *In a Different Voice:* An Interdisciplinary Forum," 329.
36. George Sher, "Other Voices, Other Rooms? Women's Psychology and Moral Theory," in Kittay and Meyers, eds., *Women and Moral Theory*, 187–188.
37. William K. Frankena, *Ethics* (Englewood Cliffs, N.J.: Prentice-Hall, 1963), 42.
38. Marilyn Friedman, "Beyond Caring: The De-Moralization of Gender," in Marsha Hanen and Kai Nielsen, eds., *Science, Morality and Feminist Theory* (Calgary: University of Calgary Press, 1987), 109.
39. Sher, "Other Voices, Other Rooms? Women's Psychology and Moral Theory," 188.
40. Friedman, "Beyond Caring: The De-Moralization of Gender," 100.
41. Marilyn Frye, *The Politics of Reality* (Trumansburg, N.Y.: The Crossing Press, 1983), 9; Sandra Lee Bartky, "Feeding Egos and Tending Wounds: Deference and Disaffection in Women's Emotional Labor," in Sandra Lee Bartky, ed., *Femininity and Domination* (New York: Routledge, 1990), 99–119.
42. Friedman, "Beyond Caring: The De-Moralization of Gender," 101f.
43. Gilligan, *In a Different Voice*, 174.
44. Gilligan, "Moral Orientation and Moral Development," in Kittay and Meyers, eds., *Women and Moral Theory*, 25–26.
45. Carol Gilligan and Grant Wiggins, "The Origins of Morality in Early Childhood Relationships," in Jerome Kagan and Sharon Lamb, eds., *The Emergence of Morality in Young Children* (Chicago: University of Chicago Press, 1987), 279.

46. Michele M. Moody-Adams, "Gender and the Complexity of Moral Voices," in Card, ed., *Feminist Ethics,* 193–198.
47. Bill Puka, "Interpretive Experiments: Probing the Care-Justice Debate in Moral Development," *Human Development* 34 (1991):76.
48. Ibid., 77.
49. Ibid., 78.
50. Ibid.
51. Lawrence Kohlberg, Charles Levine, and Alexandra Hewer, *Moral Stages: A Current Reformulation and Response to Critics* (Basel, Switzerland: S. Karger, 1983), 92. [Quoted by Friedman.]
52. Marilyn Friedman, *What Are Friends For?* (Ithaca: Cornell University Press, 1992). (To be published.)
53. Annette C. Baier, "The Need for More than Justice," in Hanen and Nielsen, eds., *Science, Morality and Feminist Theory,* 43.
54. Ibid., 48.
55. Ibid., 52–53.
56. Ibid., 53.
57. Ibid., 54.
58. Ibid., 55.
59. Linda K. Kerber, "Some Cautionary Words for Historians," in "On *In a Different Voice:* An Interdisciplinary Forum," 309.
60. Dirk Johnson, "In Search of the Male Just Right for Today," *New York Times* (October 24, 1991):A8.
61. Ibid.
62. Friedman, *What Are Friends For?*
63. Ibid.
64. Gilligan, *Mapping the Moral Domain,* xix.
65. Bartky, *Femininity and Domination,* 105.
66. Ibid., 104.
67. Ibid., 109.
68. Ibid.
69. Ibid., 113.
70. Ibid., 118.
71. Bill Puka, "The Liberation of Caring: A Different Voice for Gilligan's 'Different Voice.'" *Hypatia* 5, no. 1 (Spring 1990):59.
72. Ibid., 60.
73. Ibid.
74. Ibid.
75. Ibid., 62.
76. Elizabeth Cady Stanton, *The Woman's Bible* (Salem, N.H.: Ayer Company, Reprint Ed. 1991), 131.
77. Barbara Houston, "Rescuing Womanly Virtues: Some Dangers of Moral Reclamation," in Hanen and Nielsen, eds., *Science, Morality and Feminist Theory,* 240.
78. Sheila Mullett, "Shifting Perspectives: A New Approach to Ethics," in Lorraine Code, Sheila Mullett, and Christine Overall, eds., *Feminist Perspectives* (Toronto: University of Toronto Press, 1989), 119.

79. It is important to note that oppressed people can authentically care for each other under oppressive conditions even if they cannot authentically care for their oppressors. In one of her studies of African-American return migrants to the rural South, for example, Carol Stack observed that these men and women tended to speak in the same moral voice: the voice of care. Stack speculates that under certain conditions such as those of economic deprivation and political oppression, close human relationships between those who are oppressed become the locus of moral behavior. Convinced that universal justice is not to be had in the public realm, families and friends bind themselves together into relational networks maintained by an ethics that stresses "concern for reciprocity, commitment to kin and community, and belief in the morality of responsibility." Even if the value of care is temporarily lost among certain segments of society, Stack gives us reason to hope that it will not be abandoned by all. In the end, care may not be the prerogative of any one gender, as some of Gilligan's critics insist, but of any group of people who understand that without specific others, the self is a tragically impoverished, even if gloriously autonomous, creature. (Carol Stack, "The Culture of Gender: Women and Men of Color," in "On *In a Different Voice:* An Interdisciplinary Forum," 324.)
80. Mullett, "Shifting Perspectives: A New Approach to Ethics," 119–120.

6

Nel Noddings's
Relational Ethics

EXPLANATIONS OF NODDINGS'S
RELATIONAL ETHICS

Like Gilligan, Nel Noddings's approach to ethics is "feminine." She observes that traditional ethics has favored theoretical as opposed to practical modes of reasoning and "masculine" as opposed to "feminine" values. Rather than using the interpretive style of reasoning that characterizes the humanities and social sciences, most traditional ethicists have instead used the deductive-nomological style of reasoning that characterizes math and the natural sciences. So focused have most traditional ethicists been on "principles and propositions" and "terms such as justification, fairness, and justice," that "human caring and the memory of caring and being cared for . . . have not received attention except as outcomes of ethical behavior."[1]

Noddings's assertion is remarkably similar to one of Gilligan's tentative suggestions in *Mapping the Moral Domain:* namely, that "care" is probably the foundation of ethics and "justice" its supplement or corrective. Noddings underscores the fact that, in its preoccupation with universals, traditional ethics has overlooked the particulars. Specifically, she comments that deontologists (especially Kantians) and utilitarians either neglect the kind of relationships that exist between intimates or analyze them in highly counterintuitive ways. For example, some utilitarians actually suggest that if parents can net more overall utility by depriving their child of a much-*wanted* birthday gift so that they can partially fund a much-*needed* operation for their disadvantaged neighbor's child, then it is their duty, as utilitarians, to do so.[2] To be sure, this somewhat atypical course of action may indeed be the morally preferable one. Yet it is not transparently clear that parents have a *duty* to deprive their child of a much-wanted gift, especially if the child will interpret their act as a sign of parental coldness. Insofar as parents are concerned, not all children are created equal. Their own count for more.

Whatever quarrels Noddings has with rationalistic ethics, however, she does not seek to substitute what she terms "eros, the feminine spirit" for what she terms "logos, the masculine spirit."[3] She does not argue that logos understood as logic or reasoning has no role to play in ethics. Rather, she argues that eros—understood as an attitude "rooted in receptivity, relatedness, and responsiveness"[4]—is an *alternative* and more basic approach to ethics than logos. As important as analyzing the concept of goodness is, Noddings suggests that ethics begins at the emotional level, with the *desire* to be a good person, rather than at the intellectual level, with an *analysis* of the concept of "goodness."

Among the features of traditional ethics that most disturbs Noddings is its tendency to undervalue caring, as if it were easy to truly care for people. Although Noddings concedes that women can speak the language of justice as well as men can, she insists that this language is not their native tongue. Women enter the moral realm through a "different door" than men do, and although women can construct hierarchies of principles and argue deductively, they are apt to regard such displays of reasoning as beside the point. When it comes to deciding whether to withhold further medical treatment from her dying child, a woman is not likely to approach this intensely personal decision as she would approach an extremely difficult math problem. As she struggles to discern what is in her child's best interest, she will prefer to consult her "feelings, needs, impressions, and . . . sense of personal ideal"[5] rather than some set of moral axioms and theorems. Her goal will be to identify herself as closely as possible to her dying child so that her decision will in fact be his/her decision.

Ethics, insists Noddings, is about particular relations, where a "relation" means "a set of ordered pairs generated by some rule that describes the affect—or subjective experience—of the members."[6] There are two parties in any relation: the first member is the "one-caring"; the second is the "cared-for." The one-caring is motivationally engrossed or "displaced" in the cared-for. S/he makes it a point to attend to the cared-for in deeds as well as in thoughts.[7] When all goes well, the cared-for actively *receives* the caring deeds of the one-caring, spontaneously sharing his/her aspirations, appraisals, and accomplishments with him/her. Caring is not simply a matter of feeling favorably disposed toward humankind in general, of being concerned about people with whom we have no concrete connections. There is a fundamental difference between the kind of care a mother has for her child and the kind of "care" a well-fed American adult has for a starving Somali child s/he has never met. Real care requires actual encounters with specific individuals; it cannot be accomplished through good intentions alone.

Noddings realizes that we will tend to care about our family members and friends more than anyone else. She recommends, however, that we move beyond our present circles of intimate connection by means of what she calls "chains." These chains, meant to deliver us from what would be a regrettable ethical incestuousness, apparently function in one of two ways: one "personal" and the other "formal."[8]

On the *personal* interpretation, we widen our circles by revealing ourselves to persons who are linked to individuals for whom we already care: for example, a spouse of a child, or a friend of a friend. On the *formal* interpretation, we widen our circles by virtue of some role we play. Noddings claims, for example, that teachers are linked to their future, as well as present, students. She seems to mean that right now there exist (or will exist) students in the world to whom teachers will eventually be related. We build caring through the strength of anticipated hypothetical relationships. Another group of persons to whom we could conceivably relate are strangers, that is, persons who lie outside both our formal and personal networks. Although we must be prepared to be linked or chained even to total strangers, Noddings concedes their demands are harder to meet. In fact, she confesses that the one-caring "would prefer that the stray cat not appear at the back door—or the stray teenager at the front."[9]

Unlike Gilligan, Noddings claims that an ethics of care is not only *different* from but ultimately *better* than an ethics of justice. As she sees it, we must reject rules and principles as major guides to ethical behavior and with them the accompanying notion of universalizability. For Noddings, relationships are not about universals but about particulars— about what makes each man or woman, boy or girl uniquely different. Noddings qualifies her rejection of universals and affirmation of particulars, however. She insists that she is not espousing relativism, since there is something properly "universal" about the "caring attitude" that underpins her ethics. A child's memories of caring are not memories peculiar to him or her alone. On the contrary, they are the kind of memories to which virtually all human beings have access. "Indeed, I am claiming that the impulse to act in behalf of the present other is itself innate. It lies latent in each of us, awaiting gradual development in a succession of caring relations."[10]

Because our memories of caring and being cared for can fade, Noddings believes that our natural tendency to care must be enhanced through education. We will recall that in Gilligan's first major book, *In a Different Voice,* she described what she perceived as the differences between men's and women's moral frameworks. Men speak the language of rights and women the language of responsibilities. She did not, however, specify what society should *do* about this state of affairs. She left her readers wondering whether men and women should become bilingual, learning to speak both the language of rights and the language of responsibilities, or whether it is permissible for society to maintain a sex-segrated linguistic scheme, provided that girls are regarded as no less capable of moral development than boys. In her second major book, *Mapping the Moral Domain,* Gilligan decided to answer her readers' residual questions, making it clear that the linguistic status quo should not be affirmed. She claimed that although educators currently teach the language of justice to girls as well as boys, they do not teach the language of care to boys as well as girls. Indeed, many of them do not even teach the language of care to girls anymore, forsaking it because of its supposed softness, sentimentality, and emotionality. Distressed by this bias against caring, Noddings, like Gilligan, insists that both men and women not only can but *must* learn how to care if they are ever to become moral.

As someone who believes that virtue can be taught, Noddings insists that an ethics of caring can be communicated just as effectively as an ethics of rules and principles can. Our initial experiences of care come easily, almost unconsciously. We act from a *natural* caring that impels us to help others because we *want* to:

> The relation of natural caring will be identified as the human condition that we, consciously or unconsciously, perceive as "good." It is that condition toward which we long and strive, and it is our longing for caring—to be in that special relation—that provides the motivation for us to be moral. We want to be moral in order to remain in the caring relation and to enhance the ideal of ourselves as one-caring.[11]

The little boy helps his exhausted mother fold the laundry simply because she is his mommy. He wants to be connected to her and to have her recognize him as mommy's helper. Later, when he is an adolescent, his memories both of caring *for* mommy and being cared for *by* mommy as a child flood over him "as a feeling—as an 'I must.'"[12] He chooses to be late for a party so that he can help his mother in "remembrance" of his little-boy "sentiments." The deliberateness of *ethical* caring replaces the spontaneity of *natural* caring.

It is interesting that Noddings does not describe moral development as the process of *replacing* natural caring with ethical caring. Although ethical caring requires efforts that natural caring does not, Noddings disagrees with Kant's view that ethical caring is somehow better than natural caring. We will recall that for Kant an action is not a morally worthy one unless its agent does it out of duty and not merely out of inclination. Kant even suggests that to the degree an action goes against our grain, to that same degree can we be certain that we are doing it because we *ought* to and not simply because we *want* to.[13]

In contrast to Kant, Noddings believes that our "oughts" build on our "wants": "An ethic built on caring strives to maintain the caring attitude and is thus dependent upon, and not superior to, natural caring."[14] Morality is not about affirming others' needs through the process of denying one's own interests. Rather, morality is about affirming one's own interests through the process of affirming others' needs. When we act morally (engage in ethical caring), we act to fulfill our "fundamental and natural desire to be and to remain related."[15] If we have any duty when our interests conflict with others' needs, it is not some duty to these others but our duty to ourselves to be moral—that is, to be and to remain related. We meet others' needs not because our natural inclination toward caring *impels* us to do so, nor because our rationality instructs us that we *must* do so (Kant), but because, on reflection, we *choose* to do so.

In addition to her book on caring, Noddings has written a book on evil. Although she makes it quite clear in *Caring* that men, as well as women, can and must be caring persons—that is, people who choose to do the right things because they are motivated by feelings such as love, affection, compassion, sympathy, and empathy—in *Women and Evil*, Noddings suggests that women resist evil better than men do. Indeed, Noddings believes women are more capable of withstanding evil than men are. Women root their conception of evil in what she terms the "mother model" of caring.[16] Evil consists in the kind of fundamental fears to which mothers respond—that is, the kind of pain, helplessness, and separation infants experience. Although none of these evils can ever be totally eliminated, and although a modicum of them are essential to growth, mothers fight against them. They put Band-Aids on scratches; they help their children with their impossible science projects and history reports; and they try to be there when their children go to sleep at night and get up in the morning.

Women's understanding of evil, therefore, is very concrete, whereas men's understanding of evil is very abstract. For women, an evil event is a bad event—something that harms someone; for men, an evil event is a rule-breaking event—a violation of God's commandments or the state's laws. Noddings finds particular fault with St. Augustine's theory of evil. First, Augustine claims that natural evils such as disease and death, fires and storms, and blizzards and famines are not really evil. Rather, they are simply contributing factors to a greater good that God will eventually disclose. Second, Augustine states that moral evils—that is, the deliberate harms people inflict on each other—are not God's doing. Because people have free will, they can choose to act against God's will. For this reason, they must be punished for their sins either in this life or the next, and if they fail to show proper contrition, they may even have to be punished eternally in the flames of hell. As Noddings sees it, however, no loving parent—and certainly no loving mother—could, in the name of justice, consign a child to pain without end. How, then, could an all-loving God do this to one of his creatures, let alone to many of them, and how could Augustine reach the conclusion not only that the blessed need feel no pity for the damned but that they should derive a certain smug sense of satisfaction from the realization that, in contrast to the damned, they are "good" enough to be saved?[17]

Noddings wants to replace the fathers' *idea* of evil as sin, guilt, impurity, and fault with the mothers' *experience* of evil as "that which harms or threatens harm."[18] Noddings insists that evil is not about disobeying authority figures. Rather, it is about experiencing, in a wide variety of ways, the kind of pain, separation, and helplessness we experienced shortly after birth. This new conception of evil, and its concomitant stress on relations, may make it easier for us to resist evil as we grow older. Noddings gives the fathers' abstract idea of evil a face we recognize.

For example, in her story *The Diary of a Good Neighbor*, Doris Lessing explores the evil experienced in old age. As Noddings interprets this novel, it is about women caring for women. In the story, Jane, a middle-aged, highly successful novelist and magazine editor, tries to alleviate the suffering of Maudie, a skinny, dirty, lower-class, ninety-year-old woman. A variety of female nurses and nurses aides assist Jane's efforts. In contrast to the male doctor who views Maudie as a "case," these women view Maudie as a unique individual who needs their help in fighting against the infirmities of old age. Noddings says that pain, separation, and helplessness do not constitute evil in and of themselves. Rather, evil is tolerating such suffering even when it does not lead to something good, or accepting it as somehow deserved. The women who take care of Maudie do not find "meaning" in her suffering, since it is not contributing to her recovery. Nor do they speak of God's will, as if Maudie's suffering were the price she must pay for her "sins." On the contrary,

> they work to relieve her pain, alleviate her loneliness, and preserve—as nearly as they can—her autonomy. To these women evil is the deliberate or negligent failure to combat these great natural catastrophes, and the willful induction or aggravation of these ills would surely be unregenerate evil.[19]

These women see evil in the concrete suffering of Maudie, not in the abstract concept of sin or fault.

Using the story of Maudie as a specific example of evil, Noddings proceeds to construct what amounts to a phenomenology of evil. She distinguishes among natural, cultural, and moral forms of evil. The pain of disease and death are *natural* evils, whereas poverty, racism, sexism, and war are *cultural* evils. In contrast to both natural and cultural evil, *moral* evil is "the deliberate infliction of physical or psychic pain—unless we can show convincingly that it is necessary for a desirable state in the one undergoing pain."[20] The way to fight all of these evils is to care: We must seek to preserve, rather than to break or neglect, our human relations.

To read *Women and Evil* together with *Caring* is to realize that Noddings is striving to develop a relational ethics, a type of ethics to which she believes many women are predisposed. Noddings admits that women's ability to think and act "relationally" arises from some of their negative as well as positive experiences. Maintaining their father-daughter, husband-wife, brother-sister, and son-mother relationships has often been a "matter of survival" for women.[21] Nevertheless, even though Noddings believes that women are much more than men's daughters, wives, sisters, and mothers, she worries that women "will lose the strengths of relational thinking"[22] as they begin to define themselves as independent selves. Human beings should not struggle to elude what they cannot ultimately escape, namely, the fact that not only women but men are ultimately defined in relational terms. Comments Noddings: "It is not just that *I* as a preformed continuous individual enter *into* relations; rather, the *I* of which we speak so easily is itself a relational entity. I really am defined by the set of relations into which my physical self has been thrown."[23]

To keep relationships healthy rather than pathological, Noddings claims that we must cultivate a set of relational virtues. One kind of relational virtue characterizes relationships in and of themselves. For example, the virtue of caring belongs to the *relationship* between people and not to the people themselves. A second kind of relational virtue, which characterizes *people themselves*, also enhances relationships between them. For example, honesty belongs to the persons involved in a relationship independent of their relationship to each other. Yet it certainly strengthens the quality of their relationship.

Noddings believes that traditional ethicists have underanalyzed both kinds of relational virtues. First, they have largely failed to specify the necessary and sufficient conditions for positive, as opposed to negative, forms of caring, friendship, and companionship. Second, they have presented virtues such as honesty, truthfulness, justice, courage and self-control in a highly abstract manner. Noddings insists that there is a difference between teaching honesty "in connection to principles" on the one hand and teaching honesty "in connection to persons and relations" on the other hand.[24] To be honest simply because "honesty is the best policy" is one matter, but to be honest because unless I am honest, I can never have a *deep* friendship is quite another. Lies and secrets distance people one from the other; appearances prevent us from getting to know and love each other for whom we really are.

So convinced is Noddings of her relational framework that she urges all teachers, especially ethicists, to adopt it both in and out of the classroom. As she sees it, most of our *individual* dilemmas are in fact *relational* dramas that require dialogue, not monologue. Seeking to make her point more concretely, Noddings argues that euthanasia, for example, should be interpreted relationally rather than individualistically. When it comes to an end-of-life decision, those who stress the value of individual autonomy focus almost exclusively on the dying patient's wishes. Does *s/he* want to die or not? If so, then all life-sustaining technologies must be withdrawn or withheld. If not, then all life-sustaining technologies must be applied and maintained. In contrast, those who stress the value of relational networks emphasize the ways in which a dying patient's suffering affects everyone who truly cares about him/her.

If one analyzes euthanasia relationally, says Noddings, it becomes clear that dying persons *alone* should not make the decision to stop living. Rather, they should consult their loved ones so that they can decide what is the best course of action for *all* of them, considered as a relational unit. Noddings concedes that some individuals may not wish to initiate such discussions for fear that their "loved ones" will want to get rid of them prematurely to save money, for example. However realistic this awful fear may be for some individuals, Noddings nonetheless maintains that, for the most part, dying persons' families and friends will rally around them. Together the group and the individual will be able to decide whether the moment to speak their final adieu has finally come.

Noddings is, of course, correct to insist that family members and friends should ordinarily be involved in a patient's treatment decisions. Yet such consultations should occur not because family members and friends should have an opportunity to badger and bully their loved one to do what they think is best but because they want to know what their loved one thinks is best. Noddings gives the impression, however, that if, for example, a patient's family members and friends would find his/her decision to die too distressing, then that patient is under some sort of obligation to go on living. But it strikes me, at least, as wrong to impose any such "obligation" on a patient. Although the cared-for may have an obligation to explain his/her decision to terminate (or continue) his/her treatment to the one(s)-caring, s/he is not under an obligation to go on living (or to die) simply to please the one(s)-caring. There are some things that the one-caring may not ask the cared-for to do. Relationships are important, but so is one's self. Any viable relational ethics must resist the tendency to make *the relationship* something the individual must serve at all costs to him/her. A self disconnected from others may be a solipsistic atom, but a self totally welded to others is no longer a self.

Relational ethics must also question Noddings's assumption that families, friends, and patients usually reach consensus when it comes to termination or continuation of treatment decisions. Even if *most* families, friends, and patients usually do reach consensus, some do not. Sometimes children compete with each other, trying to show their love for mom by begging her to go on living no matter what. Alternatively, sometimes parents are unable to let their child die, despite the fact that s/he can no longer withstand the painful ravages of disease. Noddings describes a very healthy relational network whose members pull together under crisis conditions. Most of us, however, are members of relational networks with several weak links. The deathbed scene can be a peaceful one, but it can also be a contentious one as families and friends play out old rivalries and as patients struggle to say their final good-byes to families and friends who will not listen to them. Under such strained and stressful conditions, the cared-for must determine whether his/her own needs outweigh those of the one(s)-caring. After all, if the one(s)-caring seek their own needs at the *expense* of the cared-for, the relationship ceases to be truly caring. The cared-for is on his/her own.

Noddings uses this same relational framework to discuss abortion, that is, the pregnant woman's decision to end her relationship with the fetus. The more abstract an analysis of abortion is—the more it is phrased in terms of the fetus's right to life versus the woman's right to privacy—the less likely it is to help a woman who must decide whether she should terminate her pregnancy. Noddings focuses on the moral shortcomings of what she regards as a typical philosophical "solution" to the problem of abortion—in this instance Michael Tooley's "solution." Tooley claims that abortion is morally permissible because (1) "an entity cannot have a right to life unless it is capable of having an interest in its own continued existence,"[25] and (2) "an entity is not capable of having an interest in its own continued existence unless it possesses, at some time, the concept of a continuing self, or subject of experiences and other mental states."[26] Because fetuses—especially early fetuses—have no concept of self, they have neither the interests nor the rights that flow from these interests. Therefore, it is not wrong to kill fetuses.

As logical as Tooley's argument is, Noddings doubts that a woman on the verge of aborting her fetus will take much comfort in the fact that her fetus has no "interests." Noddings suggests that we approach the abortion dilemma not with a language of rights but with a language of relations. We must question all of our values, including the ones that seem most basic to our identity: for example, the idea that competent adults are the paradigm for human personhood. According to traditional ethics, competent adults are special simply on account of their rationality. As Noddings sees it, however, human "specialness" is about something other than rationality. What makes someone special to us is not only the fact that s/he can reason well, or will one day be able to do so, but the fact that s/he both "call(s) forth our desire to care"[27] and can respond to our demonstrations of care.

This perspective, says Noddings, lets us address abortion in a new way. The reason why adult persons are permitted to abort fetuses—especially ones that are virtually indistinguishable from the eggs and sperm that together constitute them—is not because fetuses lack interests and/or rights but because they cannot respond to our caring in ways that are both "characteristic" of the human species and "valued by us."[28] Noddings believes that a woman who decides to have a first-trimester abortion should not feel any differently about the fate of her fetus than a woman who miscarries early on in her pregnancy. In both cases the appropriate emotional response is not the kind of intense grief adults feel when a young child dies but the kind of disappointment adults feel when a possibility evaporates. "We do not," claims Noddings, "hold funerals for lost embryos."[29] Until a fetus develops enough to respond to our caring, there is no true and actualized parent-child relationship.

Noddings does not agree that the fact that miscarriages are *unintentional*, whereas abortions are *intentional*, changes the significance of the fetus's death. Whether the fetus's death is unplanned or planned does not matter, since the early fetus does not have a "response-based claim"[30] on its parent(s). We should not seek to justify abortion by appealing to the principle of double effect, whereby what the pregnant woman seeks is the restoration of her body to its prepregnancy condition and not the death of the fetus—the regrettable side effect of removing the fetus from her body. If fetal extraction rather than fetal extinction were indeed the essential aim of abortion, the abortion controversy would end with the development of an artificial placenta. "Extracted fetuses" would simply be removed from their mothers' wombs and brought to term ex utero. Unfortunately, the assumption that grounds this line of reasoning is false. Most women who seek abortions do so not to avoid serving as fetal containers but to avoid becoming biological parents. More than anything, these women "do not want a person to exist who, by its genetic make-up, will have a response-based claim on them."[31] The availability of early abortion allows pregnant women to break with their fetuses before they can make significant claims on them. Choosing an abortion means choosing to end a relationship before it has fully begun.

In her discussion of poverty and war, Noddings continues to develop her relational ethics. She calls on us to resist the kind of dichotomous thinking that is at the root of all human conflicts. Too often we cast the evils of poverty into the black and white mold of the oppressors versus the oppressed. While some blame poverty on the sloth, genetic weakness, or "sins" of the poor, others blame it on the evil, indifference, and ruthless nature of the oppressors. In either case, the distorted nature of unreflected stereotypes offers only one half of the actual problem and one half of the possible solution.

It bothers Noddings that this type of "us" versus "them" thinking often leads the rich (or relatively rich) to condemn the poor, that is, to interpret the poor's hunger, disease, and isolation as somehow merited or deserved. So prevalent is our society's tendency to blame the victim that even organized religion adds its voice to the hue and cry directed against the unworthy poor. Saints in rags might hope for glory in heaven, but shopping-bag ladies and homeless men need not apply. The solution to this destructive state of affairs is not for the poor to rebel against the rich and to become rich themselves. Nor is it for the rich to become like the poor. Rather, the solution is for the rich and poor to come together and expose the lie embedded in the belief that poverty is a feature of the human condition that cannot be eliminated. Noddings calls on women to take the lead in bridging the gap that separates the oppressed poor from the oppressive rich since for centuries, women have lived "with both oppressors and oppressed in their own families."[32] Women mediate between the husbands who exploit them and the children who depend on them. Lacking political and economic power, women have learned how to "persuade, plead, appeal and sympathize, interpret, reward, and above all attribute the best possible motive consonant with reality to both parties to the dispute."[33] If anyone can bring the rich and the poor together, says Noddings, it is the same women whose survival and happiness have depended on reaching a loving compromise between weak and strong.

Like poverty, war is yet another evil whose roots Noddings traces to a worldview that warps traditional ethics. With Homer's *Iliad* begins the celebration of the warrior hero, a celebration that paradoxically couples Greek rationality and moderation on the one hand with irrationality and violence on the other. Rather than challenging the warrior hero and his deadly projects, Western philosophy tended to honor him. Indeed, even William James, who sought for war's "moral equivalent"—that is, for "something heroic that will speak to men as universally as war does"[34]— nonetheless praised the warrior's virtues: his boldness, energy, and valor. Wondering whether it is morally better to be a monk than a soldier, James initially opted for the military as opposed to the ascetic ideal. Only after he managed to reconceive the ascetic life in heroic, rather than "effeminate," terms did James manage to construct a convincing argument against war and on behalf of peace. Provided that the monk, like the soldier, goes about his business like a *man,* his path is the one to follow, since blood is not spilled on it senselessly. In order to feel good about himself, a man supposedly must strive to do his perceived duty no matter what the cost to himself or others. If a man is a warrior, he is to emulate the soldier who fought the hardest. If he is a monk, he is to emulate the martyr who suffered the most: "To reach the extremes by choice, whether of war or pacifism, of poverty or wealth, require[s] striving, and striving for extremes has been a mark of manhood."[35]

As Noddings sees it, war will not be discarded in favor of peace until concerted caring replaces "strenuous" striving aimed at *winning.* Only when the unappreciated art of relational ethics, of working to maintain connection, comes into its own will peace have a chance. It is not that women do not strive. They do. It is just that, when they strive, they do so not with the intention of vanquishing their external foes and/or internal demons once and for all but with the realistic intention of continuing on as best as they can:

> A woman knows that she can never win the battle against dust, that she will have to feed family members again and again (and that no meals are likely to go down in history), that she must tend the garden every year, and that she cannot overcome most of its enemies but must treat them with the sort of moderation that encourages harmony.[36]

She who knows that her loved ones' survival depends on her good relations even with those who oppose her also knows that bad relations—quintessentially, war—are not a genuine solution to the problems that underlie the "us versus them" dichotomy.

Caring does not give birth to rivals. Striving to be the best, the invidious competition hidden within the Greek idea of excellence, does not promote caring. On the contrary, the natural rivalry prevalent in our society quickly leads to enmity, and enmity leads to disaster. If we wish to avoid war, we must stop trying to be "Number One" and start trying to be part of a relational web.

Noddings realizes that we cannot *eliminate* all evil, since it stems foremost from a separation of ourselves from other human beings, from an objectification of those around us. We can only *reduce* evil by accepting and combating our own penchant for evil. Suppose, says Noddings, that your child was going to be killed in one hour unless you found her, and you had a man before you who knew where she was but would not tell you. Would you be capable of torturing the information out of him? Noddings admits that she, for one, would be up to this "challenge."[37] But if we are capable of torturing this man, of what other evils are we also capable?

For an answer to this disturbing question, Noddings turns to Simon Wiesenthal's story, *The Sunflower*. Here a young Jewish man, who turns out to be Simon himself, comes to the bedside of a dying Nazi, Karl. The Nazi, guilt-ridden and verging on death, beseeches the Jew, Simon, to forgive him. Simon wrestles with pity and repugnance and then leaves without saying a word. Simon invites his listeners/readers to plumb their own souls and answer the question "What would you have done in my place?" Haunted by the memory of his choice, Simon asks us to struggle with the limits and requirement of forgiveness.

As Noddings sees it, because Simon viewed himself *symbolically*, as a representative of the Jewish people, he could not see the situation that confronted him *relationally*, that is, as a situation involving one identifiable human being seeking forgiveness from another identifiable human being. "Seeing each other and ourselves as symbols," observes Noddings, "is . . . part of what sustains our capacity to inflict suffering."[38] Simon's rejection of the Nazi's pleas for forgiveness only compounded suffering and evil. Indeed, according to Noddings, Simon could only combat the evil in the world through a *genuine* forgiveness of the Nazi. If we forgive someone not because we empathize with his suffering but because some sort of God-imposed duty, for example, requires us to do so, our action is improperly motivated. We seek to maintain our relationship with God rather than with the human being before us, viewing him as a morally inferior version of ourselves. Had Simon forgiven Karl simply because it was his duty to do so, he would not have overcome the fundamental separation within himself that leads to evils such as that of Nazis torturing Jews. Karl sought absolution from *Simon*, and not from Jews in general, precisely because he wanted to establish a one-on-one relation with Simon: "He needed a genuine human response."[39] Even if Simon could only have yelled, wept, or screamed, a relation of sorts might have been established:

> Then gradually each might have seen the full horror of their situation. They both might have seen that the possibility of perpetrating unspeakable crimes lay in Simon as well as in Karl and that the possibility and thus the responsibility to resist lay also in both.[40]

Separation gives birth to the bastard child of evil, suggests Noddings.

When we anesthetize our souls to the cries of other human beings in pain—to men, women, and children who feel separate and helpless—we succumb to evil. Evil is not an abstract phenomenon; it is a concrete reality that takes at least one of the three following forms:

1. Inflicting pain (unless it can be *demonstrated* that doing so will or is at least likely to spare the victim greater pain in the future)

2. a. Inducing the pain of separation

   b. Neglecting relation so that the pain of separation follows or those separated are thereby dehumanized

3. a. Deliberately or carelessly causing helplessness

   b. Creating elaborate systems of mystification that contribute to the fear of helplessness or to its actual maintenance[41]

These actions, says Noddings, are evil. No higher or better "good" can ever justify our causing each other pain or rendering each other separate or helpless. Men must learn what women have known for some time, namely that "one's soul dies as soon as it detaches from the concrete persons who stretch out their hands in need or friendship."[42] Ethics is about overcoming pain, separation, and helplessness—a task that requires human beings to relate to each other as creatures whose goodness requires a sense of community.

Noddings's judgment of Simon, however, seems to place an undue burden on the one-caring. If the potential cared-for tortures, attacks, and abuses us, must we keep caring? Must Simon be held more morally accountable than the murderous Nazi? Why is it Simon's *responsibility* to relate to Karl, when throughout his participation in Nazi atrocities Karl refused to relate to the human beings before him? Surely Simon, awaiting death in the concentration camps, needed a "genuine human response" that he never received from his torturers. The Nazis and the SS men definitely numbed their souls to the cries of the men, women, and children they slaughtered. Should Jews, on their way to the gas ovens, have continued to seek a *relation* with their murderers? Must victims become martyrs, seeking relation over and over when all they receive in return is abuse?

Simon recounts one of his most vivid memories from his concentration camp days. On his way to a work assignment, Simon passes a graveyard of Nazi soldiers. A beautiful sunflower decorates each tomb. As he focuses on the yellow blossom, Simon realizes the crucial difference be-tween the fate of dead Nazis and dead Jews:

> Suddenly I envied the dead soldiers. Each had a sunflower to connect him with the living world, and butterflies to visit his grave. For me there would be no sunflower. I would be buried in a mass grave, where corpses would be piled on top of me. No sunflower would ever bring light into my darkness, and no butterflies would dance above my dreadful tomb.[43]

Noddings is right. Separation does give rise to evil. It is just that the Nazis rather than the Jews must bridge the chasm that separates them, assuming that the chasm is indeed bridgeable. In the end, the inhuman-ity of the Nazis blocks Simon's natural human response. Memories of Nazi torture prevent Simon from responding to Karl's suffering:

> Two men who had never known each other had been brought together for a few hours by Fate. One asks the other for help. But the other was himself helpless and able to do nothing for him. I stood up and looked in his direc-tion, at his folded hands. Between them there seemed to rest a sunflower.[44]

The image of the sunflower, of the difference between the destiny of torturer and tortured, comes between Simon and Karl. Simon's word-lessness may indeed be the appropriate response under the circum-stances—a resolution that Noddings apparently resists.

CRITICISMS OF NODDINGS'S RELATIONAL ETHICS

As we have just seen, a relational ethics based on caring is not unprob-lematic. Although some of the criticisms directed against Noddings echo those directed against Gilligan, others are quite distinct. What seems to weaken Noddings's ethics of caring are the facts that it (1) fo-cuses nearly exclusively on unequal relationships; (2) slights our duties to strangers; (3) confuses reciprocity with receptivity; and (4) contrib-utes to women's oppression.

Criticism One

As philosopher Sarah Lucia Hoagland sees it, if Noddings aims to de-velop an ethics that will elucidate the necessary and sufficient conditions for a morally good relationship, then there are at least four reasons why

Noddings should not use *unequal* relationships as the focus of her inquiry. First, the goal of practices such as parenting, teaching, and providing therapy "is to wean the cared-for of dependency."[45] The parent-child, teacher-student, and therapist-client relationships are meant to be transcended. As personified by the child, student, or client, the cared-for submits to the parent, teacher, or therapist, trusting that there is really a method in the "madness" of these authorities (drink this nasty penicillin, read this boring book, dredge up all your phobias). Repeatedly, Hoagland notes that dependency relationships are ethically problematic.[46] If the cared-for is to achieve full moral development, s/he must break these relationships of dependency as quickly as possible, a fact that makes them an unviable paradigm for what constitutes a morally good relationship. There is more to the moral life than being a follower; one must be a leader.

Second, Hoagland does not accept Noddings's assumption that it is at least morally permissible, and even morally required, for the one-caring to control the relationship with the cared-for. After all, the one-caring does not always know what is best for the cared-for. Sometimes the cared-for is in fact the best judge of his or her own good. Similarly, the cared-for is not the only one who should expect to be nurtured. The one-caring should also receive love and attention. Morally good relationships are not about the one-caring playing the role of "giver" and the cared-for playing the role of "taker." As long as this sort of role playing occurs, says Hoagland, we can be sure that the relationship being described is less than morally good.

Third, Hoagland rejects Noddings's assumption that inequalities in ability make a relationship an unequal one. What makes our friendship relationships equal is not the fact that our friends have precisely the same skills that we have—that they are as linguistically or mathematically talented as we are, for example. Rather, it is the fact that our friends have approximately the same amount of *power* as we have. A relationship is unequal to the extent that one of its members controls its dynamics. When we choose unequal relationships as the paradigm for an ethical system, we propagate, rather than overcome, problems of power since "we live in a society premised on dominance and subordination, and oppression emerges in many forms—from parental all the way to colonial relationships—when decisions are made 'for another's own good.'"[47] Any ethics based on the powerful "helping" the powerless is an ethics rooted in some people telling other people what to do and how to do it.

Fourth, and finally, Hoagland thinks that children, students, and clients should not be encouraged to blindly trust parents, teachers, and therapists. Teachers and therapists often join with parents to decide about a child's various abilities, aptitudes, and future prospects. The cared-for learns to trust a presumedly beneficent authority figure who knows virtually everything about her but about whom she knows virtually nothing. Such a model of blind trust makes the cared-for vulnerable in a hierarchical society where most people need to maintain the "upper hand" in their relationships. An ethics that would be moral must challenge the hierarchical ways of being, thinking, and acting that make some, but not other, people vulnerable.

Taking unequal relationships as paradigmatic for ethics, however, leaves open the risk of abuse. Insofar as unequal relationships are unequal, they may become paradigms for domination-submission. This is particularly true of parent-child relationships, observes Hoagland. In nearly one-third of American households, fathers (or stepfathers) rape their female children,[48] and mothers are just as likely to feel "resentment" as tenderness toward their children.[49] The parent-child relationship is far from being totally innocent and purely good. S/he with the power—that is, the one-caring—is often reluctant to relinquish her/his power over the cared-for and may, depending on the circumstances, be tempted to wield it arbitrarily and abusively.

Criticism Two

Much of Noddings's ethics of caring depends on actually caring for specific individuals. To care for someone is to be intimately involved in at least some of the details of his/her life; it is to have the same kind of concern for him/her that we have for our family members, personal friends, and, to a lesser extent, professional colleagues. Realizing that our familial, collegial, and friendship circles are relatively small, and that ethics is of more than tribal interest, we will recall that Noddings recommends that we stand ready to care for people who are *potential* members of our intimacy circles—for example, our children's spouses-to-be and our future students.

Among other things, what perplexes philosopher Claudia Card about Noddings is her concept of potential relationships. Card asks: "Does the existence of a potential relationship mean that *potentially* I have an ethical relationship with those who are presently strangers? Or does it mean that because of the potentiality, I have such a relationship *now*?"[50]

Certainly, it cannot mean that I have such a relationship now, for Noddings insists that relationships involve *actual* encounters between *real* individuals—not *hypothetical* encounters between one *real* individual and one *imaginary* individual. Therefore, it must mean that *potentially* I have such a relationship. If so, with which present strangers should I actualize my "relational potentiality"? Does Noddings provide us with any guidance about which strangers we should seek out as new friends or about how many?

Another problem Card has with Noddings is her distinction between "feminine" and "masculine" approaches to morality. Noddings characterizes a "feminine approach" to morality as that of "one attached" and a "masculine approach" as that of "one detached,"[51] adding that ethics is ultimately a matter of close attachments. As Card sees it, however, we are closely attached only to a tiny fraction of the world's people, and yet, given advances in communication networks and technology, we invariably affect not only this small percentage but also a multiplicity of people from whom we are profoundly "detached." Therefore, says Card, we require "an ethic that applies to our relations with people with whom we are connected *only by relations of cause and effect* as well as to our relation with those with whom we are connected by personal and potential encounters."[52] Such an ethic need not view universal principles as "masculine" impediments to particular relationships. On the contrary, principles such as "Honor thy parents" help to bridge many generational gaps, and principles such as "Love thy neighbor as thyself" help bring people together rather than drive them apart.

As wonderful a virtue as caring is, Card concludes that it is not the only intrinsically valuable moral virtue. Justice is also an intrinsically valuable moral virtue and even though ideas such as justice, impartiality, and objectivity can be misinterpreted in ways that encourage fathers, for example, to sacrifice their sons on the altar of some higher cause, properly interpreted, justice is necessary for our defense against the sexism, racism, ethnocentrism, homophobia, and xenophobia that plague our "poorly integrated, multicultural society."[53] Given the fact that so many social groups knowingly or negligently, willfully or unintentionally, fail to care about those whose sex, race, ethnicity, religion, or even size and shape differ from their own, justice must be treasured. We cannot have a caring society, suggests Card, until we have a just society, and our society is anything but one in which all persons are equally well treated. Justice must not be dismissed simply as the abstract, alien tool of the fathers, for it can be used to protect the weak as well as the strong. Justice often is correctly blind to particulars in order to prevent details of sex, race, and creed from determining whether we care for someone or not.[54]

Noddings takes Card's objections seriously, conceding that we need a concept of justice to clarify our obligations to those whom we cannot include in our circles or link on our chains of moral responsibility.[55] She insists, however, that this concept of justice cannot simply be the traditional one that tends "to bog down in endless abstract wrangling over procedural rules and definitions instead of listening and responding."[56] And indeed, anyone who has ever sat through a court trial, a legislative hearing, a faculty meeting, a union dispute, or the like understands Noddings's point only too well. Justice is no less impervious to human foibles than caring is.

Criticism Three

In addition to arguing that unequal relationships work against the cared-for's interests, Hoagland also argues that unequal relationships work against the one-caring's interests. Unequal relationships are, she says, unidirectional relationships of *agape*. In Noddings's view, reciprocity is the only thing needed for the solidification of a caring relationship. It is disturbing that this condition can be met simply by the cared-for acknowledging in some way or another that it "knows" that it is the object of the one-caring's attention. Thus, a baby need only smile to complete caring. Hoagland advises us, however, that a baby is not in a position to really *know* what it is that the one-caring has just given him/her. The mother-child relationship is, at least at its inception and for some time thereafter, an ethically diminished one.

Hoagland's point is that if Noddings wishes her ethics of care to function properly, she should not model it on a "dependency relationship that is ideally transitory."[57] After all, the relationship between a mother and an infant is not a truly caring relationship, since, as Card has observed, there is a major difference between *receptivity* and *reciprocity*. When a baby smiles at its mother, it is receiving her caring acts but not reciprocating her for them:

> Reciprocity, in the ordinary sense, refers to doing to or for another something that is either equivalent in value or in some sense, "the same thing" that the other did to or for oneself. That characterization can be rough and

abstract, as in returning a favor, where the favor returned differs from the original favor. However, in the ordinary sense, we do not say people have *reciprocated* when they have simply received and acknowledged what others have given. Receptivity *complements,* or *completes,* others' behavior but reciprocates it only if equivalent in value.[58]

However sweet a baby's fleeting smile may be, it is not equivalent in value to a mother's unending work.

Like Card, Hoagland has fundamental reservations about "the promotion of infant nonreciprocity-beyond-acknowledgement as a model for ethically relating to others."[59] Such a model does not communicate the kind of respect that is necessary for a morally good relationship. Unless I expect from my intimate what I demand from myself, and unless what I demand from myself is what my intimate expects from me, our relationship cannot be an entirely morally good one. Certainly, it cannot be an equal one. No matter what she says about the one-caring and the cared-for switching roles, the overall picture Noddings draws, says Hoagland, is that of the one-caring consistently giving and the cared-for consistently taking. In fact, Noddings even suggests that the obligation of the cared-for is not to attend to the needs and wants of the one-caring but simply to do his own thing:[60]

> The cared-for is free to be more fully himself in the caring relation. Indeed, this being himself, this willing and unselfconscious revealing of self, is his major contribution to the relation. This is his tribute to the one-caring.[61]

Such a "tribute" gives little to either party. A unidirectional mode of caring does little to teach the cared-for about the burdens of the one-caring, and it does even less to teach the one-caring about the legitimacy of her own needs and wants.

Criticism Four

Noddings's carers seem called to care under any and all circumstances, no matter the cost to themselves. Although Noddings protests that, in her estimation, it is moral for the one-caring to care for herself, Hoagland counters that the one-caring cares for herself only insomuch as this enables her to be a *better* carer. The one-caring's self-interest and self-concern are nothing more or less than disguised forms of other-directed care. I am permitted to care about myself only when such action is important to the other. If this is true, says Hoagland, "then I get my ethical identity from always being other-directed,"[62] and "being moral" becomes another term for "being exploited."

Hoagland cautions that there is more to the moral life than being responsive to other persons' needs and wants. The woman who would be moral must see herself as a self, for unless she can see herself as a unique individual as well as a member of one or more groups, she cannot "acknowledge difference," and the inability to acknowledge difference as a positive value is precisely what perpetuates racism, sexism, ageism, and all the other "isms" that impede genuine relation.[63] Noddings probably errs when she suggests that relationships are so important that "ethical diminishment" is almost always the consequence of breaking a relationship—even a destructive one. It may be morally permissible for an abused wife to leave her abusive husband, and even to kill him in self-defense, but she is not necessarily a better person for doing so.[64]

For Hoagland, it is not only morally permissible but morally required for women to withdraw from destructive relationships. Hoagland appropriates Noddings's term *ethical diminishment*[65] and uses it to describe staying in, rather than escaping from, unequal and destructive relations. In no way, shape, or form should the mother who withdraws from "the incestuous father" or the wife who withdraws from "the abusive husband," for example, feel "ethically diminished."[66] The naive view that "down deep he is a really great person who needs a good woman to save him" traps and destroys women. If a woman is told that leaving a husband who beats her or rapes her child compromises her moral ideals, that woman's guilt, coupled with her fear of reprisal, may deprive her of the moral courage to leave him. Hoagland refuses to say anything at all negative about women who leave abusive relationships:

> I must be able to assess any relationship for abuse/oppression and withdraw if I find it to be so. I feel no guilt, I have grown, I have learned something. I understand my part in the relationship. I separate. I will not be there again. Far from diminishing my ethical self, I am enhancing it.[67]

Perhaps it is appropriate here to turn to other critics who share Hoagland's concerns about Noddings. For example, Card believes that Noddings makes unreasonable moral demands on all people but especially on women. We will recall that, for Noddings, it is theoretically possible for any two existent people in the universe to enter into a caring relationship. All that precludes their doing so is time and space.

Nevertheless, even if time and space will not permit the one-caring to care for all human beings, time and space may afford the one-caring more opportunities to care than she can comfortably sustain. Is there, then, any way for the one-caring to decide that she is morally justified in rejecting a possibility for a new friendship, for example?

Noddings's answer to this question is not entirely reassuring. She claims that we have an "absolute obligation" to care for someone if we have a "present relation" with that person either in actuality or in potentiality.[68] Anytime we are in a position to care for someone with whom we either have or could have a relationship, we must choose, then, whether to accept or reject the "I must" of ethical caring. To be sure, concedes Noddings, we do not have an *absolute* obligation to care for each and every one of these actual and possible cared-for(s) *equally*. We are permitted to spend more time on those relationships that show signs of "growth . . . including the potential for increased reciprocity and, perhaps, mutuality."[69] Therefore, if a *future* relationship is very likely to remain one-sided or extremely lop-sided, we are permitted to assign a low priority to it, devoting most of our energies to our more promising relationships. Similarly, if a *past* relationship no longer has any potential for growth, reciprocity, and actuality, we are permitted to end the relationship, though apparently not without some moral regrets.

We can appreciate critic Barbara Houston's concern here. Given that the "ethical ideal" of exploited and victimized people has largely "been shaped in terms of self-sacrifice,"[70] it should not surprise us, for example, when women see nonexistent "potential" in a relationship or blame themselves for not being able to actualize whatever potential there may be in an extremely troubled relationship, like that between a sexually molested daughter and her father. We can also appreciate Card's negative reaction to Noddings's observation that women who, in one way or another, get out of bad relationships with men act under a "diminished ethical ideal." As Card sees it, when excessive physical as well as psychological abuse characterizes a relationship, there is nothing "ethically diminished" about the woman who chooses to get out of it. "I should have thought," says Card, "that the richness of our ethical ideals *enabled* us to reject bad relationships and freed us up for ethically fuller ones."[71]

Ultimately, Noddings's critics fault her ethics of caring for demanding *agape,* or self-sacrificial love. To Noddings's defense that her ethics is not agapeistic, since it does not issue a *command* to love, Hoagland replies that *agape* has to do with the *direction* of love, not with a *command* to love:

In direct contrast to eros, which is self-centered, agape is other-centered. The caring of agape always moves away from itself and extends itself unconditionally. Certainly Nel Noddings's analysis is that caring moves away from itself. However, I would add that since there are no expectations of the cared-for beyond being acknowledged by the one-caring, since my ethical self can emerge only through caring for others, since withdrawal constitutes a diminished ideal, and since there is allegedly no evaluation in receiving the other, one-caring extends itself virtually unconditionally.[72]

Talk of such unconditional, other-directed love evokes the image of the proverbial black southern mammy, who not only obeyed but supposedly *loved* her master/oppressor. If "motivational displacement is one consequence of enslavement,"[73] then Hoagland is right to state that Noddings's analysis implies that "the care of one-caring is successful if the son of a slave owner grows up under the one-caring of the mammy to become a master."[74]

To these objections, Noddings replies that there is a difference between *caring* for others on the one hand and *self-destruction* on the other. Simple common sense dictates that "if caring is to be maintained, clearly, the one-caring must be maintained."[75] Still, there are a variety of ways to support the one-caring; some methods will permit her to preserve her ethical ideal "undiminished," to remain in a very troubled relationship. Noddings observes that even though abusive husbands are to blame for the abuse they heap on their wives, not every abusive relationship has to terminate with a divorce decree, a prison sentence of the abuser, or an act of preemptive self-defense. Provided that enough of the right kind of third parties intervene, some abusive relationships may be salvaged:

> Women in abusive relations need others to support them—to care for them. One of the best forms of support would be to surround the abusive husband with loving models who would not tolerate abuse in their presence and would strongly disapprove of it whenever it occurred in their absence. Such models could support and re-educate the women as well, helping her to understand her own self-worth. Too often, everyone withdraws from both the abuser and the sufferer.[76]

Underneath Noddings's words lurks her desire to overcome evil—to ultimately reconcile the "abuser" and the "sufferer," as she struggled to reconcile Karl and Simon, sunflower or not. Although Noddings permits a battered wife to withdraw from her spouse "where physical withdrawal is necessary for [her] self-protection," one senses that she wants even this sad story to end "happily" with the couple reunited in marital bliss.[77] In this connection, it may be useful to recall that terrifying section of Fyodor Dostoyevski's *The Brothers Karamazov* in which Ivan shrieks that he does not want to dwell in any kind of "heaven" in which a cruelly murdered child, his mother, and his murderer embrace in a cosmic hug of reconciliation.[78] Dostoyevski indicates that some things are so evil that they must not be forgiven. There is a final limit on caring.

Apparently, Noddings resists not only Dostoyevski's verdict but also Hoagland's assessment that far from being diminished, the ethical self is enhanced by withdrawing from relationships in which a partner is guilty of evil, that is, of gross wrongdoing or wrong-thinking.[79] As we noted above, Noddings argues that rather than self-righteously withdrawing ourselves from evil, we should try to do something to "alleviate" it. Rather than leaving the wrongdoer "to find companionship and support among like-thinkers,"[80] we should "saturate" him/her with our presence.[81] The "great reconciliation" seems to remain a constant possibility for Noddings—a possibility that her critics, like Simon and Ivan, find morally unsatisfactory.

NOTES

1. Nel Noddings, *Caring: A Feminine Approach to Ethics and Moral Education* (Berkeley, Calif.: University of California Press, 1984), 1.
2. Susan Sherwin makes a similar point in "A Feminist Approach to Ethics," *Dalhousie Review* 64, no. 4 (Winter 1984–1985).
3. Noddings, *Caring*, 1.
4. Ibid., 2.
5. Ibid., 3.
6. Ibid., 3-4.
7. Ibid., 9 and Chapter 2.
8. Ibid., 47.
9. Ibid.
10. Ibid., 83.
11. Ibid., 5.
12. Ibid., 79.
13. Ibid., 80.
14. Ibid.
15. Ibid., 83.
16. Nel Noddings, *Women and Evil* (Berkeley, Calif.: University of California Press, 1989), 112.
17. Ibid., 19.
18. Ibid., 91.

19. Ibid., 96.
20. Ibid., 120–121.
21. Ibid., 236.
22. Ibid.
23. Ibid., 237.
24. Ibid., 238.
25. Ibid., 144.
26. Ibid.
27. Ibid., 151.
28. Ibid.
29. Ibid., 143.
30. Ibid., 152.
31. Ibid.
32. Ibid., 167.
33. Ibid., 167–168.
34. Ibid., 179.
35. Ibid., 181.
36. Ibid., 182.
37. Ibid., 206.
38. Ibid., 211.
39. Ibid., 213.
40. Ibid.
41. Ibid., 221-222.
42. Ibid., 222.
43. Simon Wiesenthal, *The Sunflower* (New York: Schocken Books, 1976), 20.
44. Ibid., 58.
45. Sarah Lucia Hoagland, "Some Thoughts about *Caring*," in Claudia Card, ed., *Feminist Ethics* (Lawrence, Kans.: University Press of Kansas, 1991), 250.
46. Ibid., 251.
47. Ibid.
48. Ibid., 252.
49. Ibid., 253.
50. Claudia Card, "Caring and Evil," *Hypatia* 5, no. 1 (Spring 1990):103.
51. Ibid., 104.
52. Ibid., 105, her emphasis.
53. Ibid.
54. Ibid.
55. Nel Noddings, "A Response," *Hypatia* 5, no. 1 (Spring 1990):122.
56. Ibid.
57. Sarah Lucia Hoagland, "Some Concerns about Nel Noddings' *Caring*," *Hypatia* 5, no. 1 (Spring 1990): 110.
58. Card, "Caring and Evil," 106.
59. Hoagland, "Some Thoughts about *Caring*," 254.
60. Ibid.
61. Noddings, *Caring*, 73.

62. Hoagland, "Some Thoughts about *Caring*," 255.

63. Ibid., 256.

64. Ibid., 114.

65. I owe this point to Claudia Card, professor of philosophy at the University of Wisconsin. It was she who called my attention to Hoagland's use of Nodding's expression.

66. Hoagland, "Some Thoughts about *Caring*," 256.

67. Ibid.

68. Noddings, *Caring*, 86.

69. Ibid.

70. Barbara Houston, "Caring and Exploitation," *Hypatia* 5, no. 1 (Spring 1990):118.

71. Card, "Caring and Evil," 106.

72. Hoagland, "Some Thoughts about *Caring*," 257.

73. Ibid., 258.

74. Ibid.

75. Noddings, *Caring*, 100.

76. Noddings, "A Response," 125.

77. Ibid.

78. Fyodor Dostoyevski, *The Brothers Karamazov* (New York: Signet Classics, 1980).

79. Hoagland, "Some Concerns about Nel Noddings' *Caring*," 111.

80. Noddings, "A Response," 124.

81. Card, "Caring and Evil," 103.

7

Maternal Ethics

Despite the fact that some feminists express serious reservations about using the parent-child relationship or the mother-infant relationship as the basis for feminine, let alone feminist, ethics, other feminists (besides Noddings) claim that the concepts, metaphors, and images associated with the practice of parenting (more specifically, mothering) are precisely the ones to use. To decide whether a "maternal" approach to ethics is in women's best interests, however, we must first identify the necessary and sufficient conditions of motherhood. Does the term *mother* denote simply a female who gives birth to a child who is genetically and gestationally related to her? Or does it instead denote any person, male or female, who rears a child in a maternal manner—that is, in a caring, nurturant, and attentive manner?

As difficult as it is to determine whether mothers are born or made, it is even harder to explain the precise connection between the practice of mothering (or parenting) on the one hand and the development of a new approach to ethics on the other. Dorothy Dinnerstein reminds us that the image of the mother is not altogether benign. She points out that "Mother" is the source of pain as well as pleasure for the infant, who is never certain whether "Mother" will meet his/her physical and psychological needs. As a result of this uncertainty, the infant grows up feeling very ambivalent toward mother figures (women) and what they represent (the unreliability and unpredictability of the material/physical universe). Not wanting to reexperience utter dependence on an all-powerful force, men seek to control both women and nature, to exert power over them. Concomitantly, fearing the power of the mother within themselves, women seek to be controlled by men.[1]

Dinnerstein's emphasis on "Mother's" dark side signals an important cautionary note. As Joyce Trebilcot points out, under patriarchy, mothering can be oppressive in the following ways:

Women are required to give birth only to children of their own race; mothers are required to make children conform to gender roles according to biological sex; mothers are expected to transmit the values of the dominant culture, whatever they may be, to their children, and more generally, to teach their children to be obedient participants in hierarchy; and women are expected not only to reproduce patriarchy in children but also to care for the men who create and maintain it.[2]

Given all the limits that fathers impose on mothers, any recommendation that the mother-child relationship should serve as the paradigm for *all* ethical relationships must be carefully assessed.

Yet even if mothering is constricting under patriarchy, it may be liberating outside of it. This hope has inspired feminists such as Sara Ruddick, Virginia Held, and Caroline Whitbeck to argue that mothers not only can, but *must,* raise their children without burdening them with the "isms"—racism, classism, and sexism—that perpetuate human oppression. Because each of these thinkers has a distinctive conception of mothers and mothering, we need to emphasize the points that separate them as well as the ones that join them. Thus, my aims in this chapter are to ascertain (1) the degree to which a maternal ethics is "feminine," "feminist," or both; (2) the degree to which mothers are biological entities, cultural constructs, or both; (3) the degree to which the practice of mothering can or should be reduced to the practice of parenting; and, finally, (4) the degree to which conceiving of one's self as a mother (or a parent) motivates one to be a better person than one would be otherwise.

SARA RUDDICK ON "MATERNAL THINKING"

Sara Ruddick identifies the ways in which mothering is both cultural and biological, that is, an activity that men as well as women *can* do, even though, as a result of their historic experiences, women now do it better. Ruddick observes that although biology destined women to bear children, it did not destine women to rear them. Nevertheless, because of a complex interaction between women's childbearing capacities and society's childrearing needs, childrearing became women's work. As a result, most women, though by no means all women, developed what Ruddick terms "maternal practice."[3]

Ruddick claims we should not trivialize maternal practice. Like any human practice, it requires special abilities and particular ways of thinking and acting:

The agents of maternal practice, acting in response to demands of their children, acquire a conceptual scheme—a vocabulary and logic of connections—through which they order and express the facts and values of their practice. . . . There is a unity of reflection, judgement, and emotion. This unity I call "maternal thinking."[4]

Ruddick rejects the notion that maternal thinking is merely an emotional, irrational display of love that comes naturally to women; instead she presents it as a type of learned thought. Like all modes of human thinking, maternal thinking has its own logic and interests; specifically, the preservation, growth, and acceptability of one's children.[5]

Although philosopher Alasdair MacIntyre's analysis of a practice differs from that of Ruddick, it still offers a useful point of departure in any sustained discussion of maternal thinking. According to MacIntyre, a practice is a cooperative human activity that has its own standards of excellence. These practices include everything from professional activities like healing, defending/prosecuting, buying/selling, and teaching on the one hand, to personal activities like parenting (MacIntyre's substitute for maternal practice) on the other.

As MacIntyre sees it, no practice can flourish unless its practitioners acknowledge and strive for the goods or satisfactions that the community judges to be "essential" to it. For example, the practice of parenting cannot flourish unless parents *want* to be the "best" parents possible, that is, the kind of parents whom society regards as "excellent."

To enter into a practice is to accept the authority of those standards and the inadequacy of my own performance as judged by them. It is to subject my own attitudes, choices, preferences and tastes to the standards which currently and partially define the practice.[6]

Within the pursuit of any practice, we discover the *good* intrinsic to that kind of life. Concomitantly, once we devote ourselves to a practice, we discover and follow the best standards of excellence *available* (standards may change).

The transformative process of becoming an excellent practitioner of any cooperative activity like parenting is, in MacIntyre's opinion, personally demanding. Indeed, anyone engaged in a human practice knows how hard it is to do what one has chosen to do well. We cannot persevere in this process without the kind of virtues that push us forward on those days we would prefer to fall behind:

We have to learn to recognize what is due to whom; we have to be prepared to take whatever self-endangering risks are demanded along the way; and we have to listen carefully to what we are told about our own inadequacies and to reply with the same carefulness for the facts. In other words we have to accept as necessary components of any practice with internal goods and standards of excellence the virtues of justice, courage and honesty.[7]

Unless practitioners are virtuous, a practice will wither, and the values internal to it will disappear.

As *necessary* as virtuous practitioners are for a practice's survival, MacIntyre does not claim that they are *sufficient*. In fact, he maintains that practices and their practitioners cannot act alone. They need institutions—that is, economic, social, and cultural support systems.[8] Although we tend to identify practices like teaching, business, and medicine with institutions like colleges, corporations, and hospitals, we should not do so. Practices are characteristically concerned with so-called internal goods like satisfaction in a job well done, and they are held together by the sealing cement of human cooperation. In contrast, institutions are necessarily concerned with so-called external goods like money, power, and status, and they are energized by the fragmentary fires of human competition. Yet, provided that "the ideals and creativity of the practice" do not succumb to "the acquisitiveness of the institution,"[9] practitioners need not automatically reject all forms of institutional support. It is simply too hard for practitioners to do without institutions in an ever more complex, interrelated, and interdependent world.

Ruddick's analysis of a practice clearly differs from MacIntyre's. Ruddick denies, for example, that the way to achieve the good(s) internal to maternal practice is through compliance with the accumulated wisdom of humankind—especially if humankind turns out to be *mankind*. For a woman to submit her own "attitudes, choices, preferences and tastes" to prevailing standards may, after all, be a large mistake; for as Adrienne Rich notes, our culture conflates the *practice of mothering* with the *institution of motherhood*.[10] A variety of authorities, most of them men, tell women how to mother, blaming them for whatever goes wrong in their children's lives.

Under patriarchy men want sons, often for the wrong reasons: "as heirs, field-hands, cannon-fodder, feeders of machinery, images and extensions of themselves; their immortality."[11] What is worse, husbands sometimes demand that their wives raise their sons to be "real men," that is, tough, strong, fighting men. Rich happily recollects a vacation she spent alone with her two sons, ignoring her husband's childrearing rules. She and her boys ate the wrong food at the wrong time. They stayed up past their proper bedtime. They wore the wrong clothes. They giggled at silly jokes. Through all of these trespasses, they enjoyed themselves enormously. Rich concludes that if mothers were permitted to make—and not simply break—the childrearing rules, they would readily achieve the good(s) internal to maternal practice.

Ruddick's analysis of a practice also differs from MacIntyre's in that she disagrees with him that honesty, courage, and justice are the three virtues individually necessary and jointly sufficient for the flourishing of any and all human practices. Each human practice has its own set of virtues, insists Ruddick. For example, mothers must cultivate a multitude of very specific virtues in order to meet the three fundamental goals of maternal practice: namely, the preservation, growth, and social acceptability of children.[12]

Preserving the life of a child is the "constitutive maternal act."[13] Infants are totally vulnerable. They simply will not survive unless their caretakers feed, clothe, and shelter them. Ruddick gives the example of Julie, an exhausted young mother with a very demanding infant. Having reached her physical and psychological limits, Julie pictures herself killing her baby daughter. Horrified by her own thought, Julie spends the night riding a city bus, her baby in her arms. She reasons that, as long as they remain in the public eye, her baby will be safe.[14]

Ruddick tells Julie's story to stress how difficult it is for a mother to meet her child's material needs. Not every mother grows so run-down and desperate that she has to take steps to ensure that she will not slaughter her child. However, even under relatively ideal circumstances, most mothers do have days when they wish they were not mothers. In order to be able to "preserve" their children on these "bad days," women who would be mothers must cultivate three enabling virtues: the intellectual virtue of scrutiny and the moral virtues of humility and cheerfulness.

Scrutinizing eyes scan for the kinds of events that could seriously harm a child. Whereas some mothers perceive nonexistent dangers everywhere, others are oblivious to the real dangers that threaten their children's very lives. Children will not die from their first face-scratching or knee-scraping, but they will die if they are left to fend for themselves. Although children are not as fragile as "goldfish," neither are they as hardy as "roaches" or "weeds."[15] Scrutinizing eyes must learn when to peer and when to shut.

Closely related to the intellectual virtue of scrutiny are the interrelated moral virtues of humility and cheerfulness, without which mothers cannot lovingly preserve their children. Humility is a way of "preserving and controlling" children in an "exhausting, uncontrollable world."[16] It avoids both the *excess* of dominating a child and the *defect* of being dominated by a child.

Ruddick observes that two kinds of mothers lack humility: (1) arrogant mothers who seek to keep their children safe from the "world" itself and (2) servile mothers who insist that they lack the strength, power, and/or intelligence to resist the evils that threaten to engulf their children. Luckily, the virtue of cheerfulness can help both arrogant and servile mothers become humble mothers—that is, the kind of mothers who realize that even if their powers of preservative love are limited, they are *powers* nonetheless. Because cheerfulness also has its excesses and defects, however, mothers need to guard against hopelessness and despair on the one hand and "cheery denial" on the other.[17] They should fill their children's heads neither with images of the Big Bad Wolf nor with visions of the Sugar Plum Fairy, but with portraits of fallible and imperfect human beings trying to make the "best" of things. Cheerfulness is indeed riding "the bus up and down the nighttime city streets, keeping yourself and your baby safe even though you've imagined murdering her."[18]

The second dimension of Ruddick's maternal practice is *fostering* children's growth. Whatever fostering a child's growth may mean, it does not mean the act of imposing an already written script on one's child. It is wrong for a mother to hand her child a book entitled *The Tale of the Perfect Child,* insisting that s/he enact in the scenes of his/her own *imperfect* life the scenes of the "perfect child's" *perfect* life. On the contrary, mothers should tell "maternal stories"—that is, realistic, compassionate, and delightful stories[19] that permit their children to incorporate the bad as well as the good moments of their lives into their autobiographies. A mother should weave a story about her daughter's stubbornness (realism), for example, that enables both of them to understand *why* she became stubborn (compassion) and how she either has transformed (present delight) or could transform (future delight) that stubbornness into proper self-determination. Mothers should help their children grow not only in physical size and mental intelligence but in self-awareness of their relative strengths and weaknesses.

The third and final dimension of Ruddick's maternal practice is *training*. For the most part, maternal practitioners work hard to socialize their children—to help them become committed and concerned citizens as opposed to members of either armed gangs or opium dens. On occasion, however, maternal practitioners will demur from this task. They will refuse to "fit" their children's vulnerable bodies into military uniforms, or diet them into designer jeans, or dress them for success in the so-called "dog-eat-dog" world. In a patriarchal society—that is, an overly competitive, hierarchical, and individualistic society—maternal practitioners (especially young ones) may find themselves caught between the external demands of patriarchy on the one hand and their own inner conviction that these external demands are not necessarily humanizing ones on the other. If a mother trains her son to "dress for success," he may become both the chief executive officer of a large firm and a very mean-spirited human being. In contrast, if she refuses to teach her son the lessons of conformity, he may become both a very nice guy and someone whom patriarchy labels "a loser." What maternal practitioners must decide, then, is whether their personal values or those of the larger society should guide their child-training practices. Here Ruddick adds the interesting point that maternal practitioners should not make this decision by themselves; they should make it together with their children. If children follow their mothers' instructions unquestioningly or blindly, their "training" will never be completed.[20] External compliance with someone else's values is an inadequate substitute for choosing one's own values and living in conformity to them.

Clearly, maternal practice is a complex activity. What Ruddick terms "attentive love"[21] links together the preservation, fostering of growth, and training of children. This metavirtue, which is at once cognitive and affective, rational and emotional, enables mothers to "really look"[22] at their children and not be shocked, horrified, or appalled by what they see. Indeed, among the several characteristics that distinguish maternal thinkers from nonmaternal thinkers is their utter realism. Mothers who love their children inattentively let their fantasies blind them.[23] They do not see their children as they actually are. Rather they see their children as they could perhaps be: the fulfillment of their dreams. In contrast to these mothers, mothers who love their children attentively accept their children for whom they are, working within their physical and psychological limits.

Ruddick's ultimate goal is not simply to develop a phenomenology of maternal practice. Rather, she wants to demonstrate that anyone, male or female, who engages in maternal practice will come to think like a mother. As it happens, most of the people who have traditionally engaged in maternal practice have been women. Because women have been excluded from the public realm until relatively recently, *maternal* thinking has not been prevalent in government, medicine, law, business, the church, and the academy. Instead a very *nonmaternal* kind of thinking has dominated the public realm—the kind of thinking that leads to ecological disorder, to social injustice, and especially to war. People who do not *think* like mothers, suggests Ruddick, do not *see* like mothers. They do not make a connection, for example, between war in the abstract and war in the concrete. For them, war is about winning, defending one's way of life, and establishing one's position of power. For a maternal thinker, war is about destroying that boy or girl whom one has spent years preserving, nurturing, and training: a unique human person who cannot be replaced. In sum, for a maternal thinker, war is about death—about canceling out the "product(s)" of maternal practice.

Ruddick does not claim that all women are pacifists, however. She concedes that "maternal peacefulness" is a myth,[24] since mothers do not always think and act in maternal ways. The scene in the film *The Battle of Algiers* that most haunts me, for example, is one in which several Algerian women shed their veils in order to dress in the style of French women. They then put bombs in their shopping bags, and holding their own children in their arms, they elude the suspicion of the French police as they cross over from the Algerian into the French section of town. After all, they look so harmless—the epitome of French motherhood! Having escaped detection, these Algerian women then proceed to plant their bombs in an open cafe where large numbers of French men, women, and *children* are drinking espresso or licking ice-cream cones. The camera focuses on the French children's happy faces and on the Algerian women's stonelike faces. The message is a chilling one: For the "cause" of Algerian liberation, Algerian women must be prepared to kill not only "guilty" adults but "innocent" children, indiscernible from their own precious children.

Despite scenes like the one I have just described, Ruddick nevertheless insists that the *logic* of maternal thinking is such that were mothers to *follow it to its conclusion,* they would be forced, if only in the name of consistency and coherence, to commit themselves to the work of peace. Were mothers to closely examine and compare the goals of maternal practice with those of war, they would see an irreversible and undeniable contradiction. Maternal practice may be about loyalty and protectionism, but it is also about love, nurturance, and preservation. War uses loyalty and protectionism as excuses to sacrifice the once-preserved child on the altars of the state. Such a realization inches, if it does not actually catapult, mothers in the direction of peace.

As a first "conceptual-political bridge,"[25] linking women and peace, Ruddick offers a *women's politics of resistance*. When confronted with policies that undermine, frustrate, or otherwise impede their maternal activities—when they discover, for example, that the government is stockpiling nuclear weapons or letting major corporations pollute the environment—women may feel moved to protest, picket, and even riot against such life-threatening policies. Although rebellious women often fight alongside sympathetic men, they sometimes fight alone, *as women*, deliberately exploiting their "culture's symbols of femininity":

> Women who bring to the public plazas of a police state pictures of their loved ones, like women who put pillowcases, toys and other artifacts of attachment against the barbed wire fences of missile bases, translate the symbols of mothers into political speech.[26]

Only a thoroughly unsocialized police officer or soldier will be able to overcome the human sentiments that pictures of "mother love" typically evoke. Women who resist are not above manipulating men's emotions, "woman-handling" them toward peaceful ends.

Conceding that the word *mother* evokes for many feminists sentimentality, even as the word *peacemaker* suggests servility, Ruddick nonetheless proposes a *feminist politics* as a second way to join together women and peace. A feminist politics supports women, fighting against all forms of discrimination. Feminists work for women's economic, psychological, and sexual liberation, thereby rendering the lives of *all* women—including mothers—easier. Perhaps most important, a feminist politics makes women think about the solidarity between women. The resistance of a women's politics joins with the consciousness-raising of a feminist politics to bring women together against war.

VIRGINIA HELD ON "MOTHERING PERSONS"

Virginia Held approaches maternal practice from a somewhat different perspective than Ruddick does. She suggests that because women have spent so much of their time mothering, they should develop moral theories that fit the kind of relationships and activities that characterize the *private* rather than the *public* domain.

. . . the moral approaches most suitable for the courtroom are not those most suitable for political bargaining; the moral approaches suitable for economic activity are not those suitable for relations within the family, and so on.[27]

In addition to recognizing the differences between "private" and "public" morality, men and women should attach equal value to them. Traditional ethicists simply assumed that bona fide moral issues took root in one sphere only, the public sphere. But only a myopic view of moral experience can possibly justify such an assumption. For it to count as a *moral* experience, an experience need not unfold in a bustling marketplace, or in a contentious courtroom, or in a harried hospital emergency room. What makes an experience "moral" is not *where* it occurs but *how* it occurs. If moral experience is "the experience of consciously choosing, of voluntarily accepting or rejecting, of willingly approving or disapproving, of living with these choices, and above all of acting and of living with these actions and their outcomes,"[28] then such an experience can as easily happen in one's bedroom or nursery as in one's boardroom or office. Therefore, any adequate moral theory must address filial, parental, spousal, and friendship relations as well as physician-patient, lawyer-client, and seller-buyer relations. In the grand scheme of moral concerns, women's traditional struggles and strivings count as much as men's.

Although Held knows that not all women live in the private realm, and although she does not believe that all women are determined by nature to have a distinctive set of moral experiences, she does claim that a sizable gap still exists between women's and men's moral experience. It concerns her that traditional ethics not only discounts *women's* morality but presents what amounts to *men's* morality as *human persons'* morality. Were traditional ethics really gender-neutral, however, it would not favor paradigms—for example, the contract model described in Chapter 4—that speak much more to men's experience than to women's. Women's relationships to their helpless infants, aging parents, ailing siblings, and distraught friends—relationships between persons who are not really each other's equals—do not fit the model for transactions between equally informed and equally powerful adults. The way in which two bankers negotiate a business deal is not to be compared to the way in which a mother "negotiates" a bedtime with her child. If any model fits relationships between unequals, says Held, it is the relationship between children and mothers—or more precisely—between children and *mothering persons*.[29]

Held insists that human mothering is not nearly as "natural" as animal mothering. She claims that too often, the assumption is made that "what human mothers do within the family belongs to the 'natural' rather than to the 'distinctively human' domain."[30] Nothing could be further from the truth. Bearing as well as rearing a child is a *human* enterprise; it is a matter of conscious choice rather than blind instinct. Unlike animal mothers, human mothers do not *instinctively* reproduce and maintain the species. Rather, they *deliberately* create new human persons by giving life to minds as well as bodies, and this may be the most human of all experiences.

Traditional ethicists view *contractual* relations as the primary model for human interaction, justifying a human relationship as moral to the degree that it serves the separate interests of individual rational contractors. Yet life is about more than conflict, competition, and controversy—about getting what one wants. It is, as mothering persons know, also about cooperation, consensus, and community—about meeting other people's needs. Held speculates that were the relationship between a mothering person and a child, rather than the relationship between two rational contractors, the paradigm for good human relationships, society might look very different.

Held concedes, however, that the kind of relationships that exist between mothering persons and children can be just as oppressive—indeed, even *more* oppressive—than the relationships that exist between two rational contractors. For example, it is sometimes harder to recognize abuses of power in a father-son relationship than in an employer-employee relationship.[31] A father's subtle pressure that his artistic son give up the theater and go to law school may not be as evident an abuse of power as the executive who steals his assistant's ideas and presents them as his own, but both situations exploit and undercut the autonomy of the two relatively powerless agents involved.

Held also admits that, in their attempt to celebrate the positive features of maternal ethics, some maternal thinkers unnecessarily reject the valuable features of traditional ethics. Just because a maternal ethics can handle issues that exceed the "moral minimum" of taking everyone's rights seriously does not mean that it should dispense with this "moral minimum."[32] Mothering persons must be fair as well as compassionate; rational as well as emotional; able to make generalizations about human relations as well as to articulate their unique features. A maternal thinker who says that no two human relationships are *ever* alike invites moral chaos. Like principles, relationships can be qualified as good, better, or best (bad, worse, or worst), and that which is subject to *qualification* is also subject to *evaluation*.[33] In the same way that we can ask what makes a principle good or bad, we can ask what makes a relationship good or bad.

Unlike some maternal thinkers, Held believes that men as well as women can be mothering persons. Just because men cannot bear children does not mean that they cannot rear children. Men as well as women can, indeed should, appropriate the moral outlook of those who care for others. Leaving caregiving to women alone produces boys with personalities "in which the inclination toward combat is overdeveloped and the capacity to feel for others is stunted."[34] Because bellicose, unfeeling *boys* usually mature into bellicose, unfeeling *men* in positions of power, Held claims that human survival may depend on our ability to reorganize the way we parent. Equal parenting, based on men's and women's "equal respect" for each other's "equal rights to choose how to live their lives,"[35] must become the order of the day.

Held argues that from a child's point of view, it does not matter who provides the clothes and who changes the diapers as long as both are forthcoming. Parents should sit down and decide what their child needs and then divide up the duties between themselves. Achieving an equitable division of labor is not an easy task, however, since parents will be tempted to fall back on the traditional gender roles society has imposed on men and women. Although Held does not claim that all gender differences in parental tasks are inherently oppressive, she warns that parental tasks should not be divided according to the skills a man and woman had when they first married, as these may stem from years of sex-role socialization. As much as possible, a man and a woman should try to perform the same parental tasks, departing from this nontraditional style of parenting only if there are "good reasons, and not merely customs and social pressures"[36] for doing so.

Despite the fact that Held believes that men as well as women can mother, she still indicates that there may be a *qualitative* difference between female mothering and male mothering. The fact that women can *bear* children as well as *rear* children may signal that "women are responsible for the existence of new persons in ways far more fundamental than are men."[37] Women need men to begin a pregnancy, but they do not need men to end a pregnancy. Through abortion or suicide, women can say a definite "no" to life.

By stressing women's ultimate responsibility for bringing (or not bringing) new persons into existence, Held does not wish to negate her previous point that fathers as well as mothers are obligated to rear children. Because men participate in the creation of life, they should participate in its maintenance. Nevertheless, men's direct role in procreation lasts but a few moments, whereas women's lasts for nine months. The experiences of pregnancy make women especially aware of their procreative role. For example, when a pregnant woman eats, she can focus on the fact that she is, as the old saying goes, "eating for two." If she fails to eat a healthy diet, both she and the fetus will suffer. Likewise, when a pregnant woman finally gives birth, she can say to herself, "Through this pain, I bring life into this world." These kinds of experiences are ones that a man can never have. The well-being of the fetus his sperm helped create depends on him only indirectly, and he will probably never be called to physically suffer for his son or daughter as much as his wife (or lover) did on the day she gave birth to their child.

Even if the daily toil of bringing up a child will eventually take a greater toll on a parent than the "momentary" suffering of giving birth, Held asserts that we should not trivialize the birthing act as if it had no effect whatsoever on subsequent parent-child relationships. In suggesting that biological experiences may influence "the attitudes of the mother and father toward the 'worth' or 'value' of a particular child,"[38] Held wants to explore the relationship between the kind of *feelings* women and men have for their children on the one hand and the kind of *obligations* they have to them on the other. If ethicists assume that "natural" male tendencies play a role in determining men's moral rights and responsibilities, then they should make the same assumption about "natural" female tendencies:

> Traditional moral theories often suppose it is legitimate for individuals to maximize self-interest, or satisfy their preferences, within certain constraints based on the equal rights of others. If it can be shown that the tendency to want to pursue individual self-interest is a stronger tendency among men than among women, this would certainly be relevant to an evaluation of such a theory. And if it could be shown that a tendency to value children and a desire to foster the developing capabilities of the particular others for whom we care is a stronger tendency among women than among men, this too would be relevant in evaluating moral theories.[39]

The fact that Gilligan and Noddings shudder at the biblical account of Abraham, who was willing to kill his son, Isaac, in order to honor God's command, is to be expected. Women who birth children—who preserve, nurture, and train them—are not likely to believe that obeying a command, even a command of God, is more valuable than preserving the very lives of these children. To be sure, from the standpoint of traditional ethics, a mother's refusal to subordinate the concrete life of *her* child to the abstract commands of duty or higher law indicates her underdevelopment as a moral agent. Yet, in an age where a blindness to interconnection has led to the destruction of the environment and a perilous buildup of the nuclear arsenal, a focus on connection rather than individualistic rights may indeed not only suggest a higher morality but offer a saving grace in an increasingly chaotic world.[40]

CAROLINE WHITBECK ON "THE MATERNAL INSTINCT"

In the past, Caroline Whitbeck has offered an interpretation of mothering that, more than Ruddick's or Held's, emphasizes the *biological* facts of motherhood. In fact, Whitbeck suggests that women's "maternal instinct" causes them to notice things about their babies that men do not.[41] Specifically, a mother often feels as vulnerable as an infant throughout her pregnancy, but especially during labor. It is her helplessness—in the sense of losing control of her body during pregnancy, of suffering pain during labor, of feeling weak during the postpartum period—that enables a mother to understand just how dependent her infant is on her.[42] No matter how hard a father tries, he can never experience either a mother's or an infant's helplessness. All he can do is to intellectualize about this experience, sympathizing with it the best he can.

Despite the fact that Whitbeck concedes that men can learn how to mother their children and that women can choose not to mother their children, she nonetheless believes that men's and women's different biological *experiences* typically affect the *intensity* of their respective attachments to their offspring. The bodily experiences that women have simply because they are women tend "to *enhance* those feelings, attitudes, and fantasies which induce people generally to care for their infants."[43] To the degree that human beings are mind-body unities rather than mind-body dualities, a mother's physical experiences will affect the way she thinks about her children.

CRITICISMS OF MATERNAL ETHICS

Early on in *Maternal Thinking*, Ruddick notes that critics are likely to fault her emphasis on mothers for three reasons:

1. an unwarranted idealization of mothers;

2. an unnecessary exclusion of men and nonbiological mothers from maternal work; and

3. an insensitivity to the differences that exist among mothers some of whom must mother under extremely oppressive circumstances.[44]

To a greater or lesser extent, critics have leveled precisely these charges, as well as the charge that the mother-child relationship is anything but the proper paradigm for moral relationships, against Held and Whitbeck, as well as Ruddick. Unless these maternal thinkers are able to affirm biological mothering without suggesting that a person needs to experience something like the "helplessness" of pregnancy, labor, and birthing in order to become deeply moral—that is, connected to other people—the critics' case against maternal approaches to ethics will be fairly decisive.

Criticism One

Critics complain that Held, Ruddick, and Whitbeck glorify mothers, idealizing them as flawless human beings. Although a cursory reading of any of these thinkers may give the initial impression that mothers are saints and heroines who know, love, and serve their children perfectly, a careful reading usually yields a more balanced view of mothers. In particular, Ruddick pays as much attention to women's weaknesses as to their strengths. Her portrait of motherhood is not of the Hallmark card or Norman Rockwell variety. On the contrary, it is of the "school of hard knocks" variety. Political, economic, social, and cultural factors can as easily hinder as help a woman to mother her children properly. In addition, the number, age, personalities, and moods of a woman's children join with a woman's health, career, and stamina in determining whether she will have an easier or harder time preserving, nurturing, and training her children.[45] Some mothers will succeed in these tasks. Others will fail. Instead of preserving their children, they will abuse them; instead of nurturing their children, they will crush their spirits; and instead of training their children to be their best selves, they will squeeze them into whatever procrustean bed society has made for them. Far from idealizing mothers, it seems that Ruddick is actually providing one of the few *realistic* assessments of mothers currently available.

Criticism Two

The criticism that maternal ethics results in an unnecessary exclusion of men and nonbiological mothers from maternal work is a very serious one for several reasons. First, to even suggest that the elements of maternal practice—preserving, nurturing, and training—are biologically linked or sex-rooted is to suggest something that is potentially dangerous to women's liberation.[46] Connecting maternal ways of thinking and acting with women's characteristic thought and action patterns risks reintroducing traditional gender roles just when women are beginning to make significant strides educationally, professionally, and politically. Maternal thinkers tempt society to send women out of the workplace and back to the kitchen when they claim that, because of their biological experiences, women mother *best*. After all, men might question, if women mother best, should not they do so exclusively?

Second, to claim that women excel at mothering deters men from shouldering their childrearing responsibilities and from learning how to mother as well as women do. As we noted previously, Chodorow argues that sexual equality is a matter of men and women being not only "dual career" but "dual parent." Dual parenting is a structural adjustment that would permit women and men to develop those parts of their psyches that are currently underdeveloped and, therefore, to raise male and female children equally capable of adequately mothering the next generation of children. Specifically, dual parenting would have at least three positive results. First, the equal presence of the father as well as the mother in a child's life would diffuse the intensity of the mother-child relationship. Second, a mother who has a meaningful life outside the home is not so likely to view her child as her raison d'être—the be-all and end-all of her existence, without whom she has no meaning. Third, a boy raised partly by a father would not develop fears of maternal power or "expectations of women's unique self-sacrificing qualities."[47] Girls and boys would grow up expecting men as well as women to be loving and women as well as men to be autonomous. Boys would no longer have to reject feminine feelings of nurturance as unworthy of real men, and girls would no longer have to reject masculine feelings of self-assertion as unbecoming of real women.

One man who has written a particularly detailed and reflective defense of the need to stress *social* over *biological* mothering is philosopher Paul Lauritzen. He believes that feminine and feminist approaches to ethics have traditionally "oscillated" between "romantic" ideas about women's moral superiority and "rationalist" ideas about women's moral equality with men.[48] He thinks, however, that "romanticism" is currently in the ascendance:

> Once again feminists are claiming that women have a distinctive moral sensibility; once again feminine virtues are being celebrated, and once again it is claimed that women's experience bears witness to the values of intimacy and compassion absent in the competitive and dominant male work world.[49]

Lauritzen claims that there are two versions of late twentieth-century feminist romanticism: (1) a nonproblematic one that relies primarily on the experiences of *childrearing* as the source of maternal ethics and (2) a problematic one that relies primarily on the experiences of *childbearing*.

Lauritzen believes that Held and Ruddick emphasize childrearing experiences and how these experiences create a unique outlook on the world that shapes the identity of both parent and child. Because women typically rear children, women (but not men) develop "a set of priorities, commitments, attitudes, virtues, and beliefs"[50] that enable them not only to survive but even to thrive as childrearers. If it is indeed the case that this set of values leads to an ethics that is better than traditional ethics, then all human beings, as well as biological mothers, should have the opportunity to espouse it. In order to become proficient in maternal ethics, however, men and childless women need to spend time with children and/or other groups of people who are as vulnerable as children. Held and Ruddick do not claim that only biological mothers can or should be nurturing.[51] Instead they claim "that persons should be caring and compassionate and they should be so whether they are mothers or corporate executives, men or women."[52] This kind of "romanticism," observes Lauritzen, is a welcome corrective to the kind of rationalism that encourages women to be just as competitive and cutthroat as men.

To the degree that Lauritzen affirms a maternal ethics based on child*rearing* experiences, he disaffirms maternal ethics based on child*bearing* experiences. He interprets Whitbeck, for example, as arguing that unless a person actually experiences pregnancy, labor, childbirth, postpartum depression, and lactation, s/he cannot think maternally. Because the ability to think maternally is a necessary, if not also sufficient, condition for maternal ethics, *only* biological mothers can practice maternal ethics. However, if only childbearers have the capacity to truly care for children and for other vulnerable people such as the aged and infirm, then nature holds biological mothers accountable to a higher ethical standard than men and childless women. If only women/ mothers/biological mothers *can* care, then only they are *required* to care. Men/fathers/biological fathers are excused from this moral responsibility.

To be sure, Lauritzen may be misrepresenting Whitbeck, who admits, for example, "that different socialization experiences and individual differences in temperament may more than make up for the sex differences."[53] Whatever advantage a biological mother's experiences give her in initially relating to her infant, this "edge" may be quickly dulled if she immediately hands her infant over to a nanny in order to resume an all-consuming job as a corporate executive. Similarly, whatever advantage a father initially lacks in relating to his infant, this "edge" may be quickly sharpened if he regularly feeds, bathes, clothes, and plays with his son or daughter. Yet, despite these important concessions, Whitbeck still seems unconvinced that a father can ever *learn* how to mother *as well* as a biological mother. In her estimation, culture and society can do only so much to temper the effects of nature and biology:

> . . . it may be disquieting to consider that bodily differences between men and women, together with the social arrangements regarding infant care, may produce quite different conceptual structures, ways of living, and experiences of the human condition for the majority of males and females. For many women it is more comforting to think that an adequate dose of exhortation and encouragement would suffice to bring men to the point of being able to dedicate themselves to parenting and to mutual relationships to the same extent that women do. It may be a hard and somewhat terrifying possibility that a chasm may separate our own thought from that of the masculist culture.[54]

Encouraging husbands and lovers to co-parent may be helpful, but as long as women's and men's physical experiences differ, Whitbeck thinks that their psychological experiences will probably continue to differ. Cultural and social forces—be they patriarchal or nonpatriarchal—cannot completely compel "nature" and "biology" to do their bidding.

In the past, Whitbeck has suggested that not willing men like Lauritzen but loving daughters like her own are the only persons with the capacity to learn how to mother *as well as* biological mothers. The mother-daughter relationship is so "deeply physical and emotional"—so symbiotic—that it "prepare(s) the way for all future attachments, sexual and nonsexual."[55] Even if a woman cannot/does not/will not give birth, she can supposedly experience the birthing process *vicariously* through her mother. To the degree that a daughter is physically and psychologically identified with her mother—the woman who gave birth to her—she will be able to think and act maternally. Because the mother-son relationship is not as symbiotic as the mother-daughter relationship, sons will not be able to think and act as maternally as daughters do. Thus, critics maintain that this fact, *if it is a fact,* precludes any chance of the "equal parenting" movement ever succeeding. Try as they might, men will never be as good as women are at "mothering."

For all her reservations about the quality of male as opposed to female mothering, Whitbeck does not express serious concerns about letting men into the nursery—in fact, she seems generally well-disposed to their presence. Yet, given the predilection of many men to sexually abuse young children, especially young girls, it may be ill-advised to place men in positions of total and unsupervised control over young children. In addition, given the ways in which our society socializes men to be violent, are we ready to entrust a beloved, but whiny, two-year-old to his short-tempered father's care? Will such a father, like Ruddick's Julie, ride the city bus all night long to prevent himself from harming his child? Or, in a worst-case scenario, will he simply beat the child until it stops crying?

Criticism Three

Critics of maternal ethics complain that the maternal thinkers who populate the pages of books on mothering are almost always white, heterosexual, and middle class. Conceding that maternal thinkers have not always acknowledged the differences that exist among women, Ruddick has recently focused her attention on Hispanic and African-American mothers as well as on white mothers. Whether Ruddick and other maternal thinkers will be able to say anything at all *in general* about mothers and mothering after they take into account women's diverse experiences as mothers is, of course, an open question. Nevertheless, there is good reason to believe that maternal ethics will be strengthened as opposed to weakened after it is corrected for socioeconomic, religious, racial, and ethnic differences. Attention to difference is rarely invidious to any intellectual project.

Criticism Four

The claim that the mother-child relationship is an inappropriate paradigm for ethical relationships is the most serious challenge against maternal ethics. Critic Jean Grimshaw believes that at least three factors weaken the paradigmatic strength of the mother-child relationship.

First, parents are responsible for their children's physical and psychological well-being, but children are not responsible for their parents' physical and psychological well-being—at least minor children have no such filial duty. Second, parents are permitted—indeed sometimes required—to tell their children what to do, but not vice versa. Third, parents are expected to behave better than their children. Indeed, mom and dad are expected to "tolerate, accept, and try not to be hurt by behavior that would be quite intolerable or a cause for anger in most adult relationships."[56]

Given these three asymmetries, modeling adult relationships on the mother-child relationship seems like a prescription for disaster. The features that tend to make a mother-child relationship work are precisely the ones that are quite likely to damage or destroy a relationship between two adults.[57] For an adult relationship to work, both parties must be responsible for each other; neither must presume to know the other's "good" better than s/he herself/himself knows it; and both must "behave" equally well, since the small manipulations, name calling, and temper tantrums parents accept from children are not ones that one adult will accept from another adult.

Grimshaw's main critique of maternal thinking is that it is not necessarily the product of the task of mothering *children:*

> Insofar . . . as women give priority in their lives to the maintaining of relationships with others, and to attention to and care for others, such capacities should not be seen just as maternal. In fact, I think such priorities need explaining as a response to the material circumstances of life and as a resource developed in the face of deprivation and oppression rather than just as a result of the development of self in early infancy and childhood.[58]

Women think "maternally" for bad reasons as well as for good ones. Some women develop such virtues as care, responsiveness, attentive love, and resilient good humor in order to create and maintain strong female friendships from which they derive support. However, other women develop these same virtues simply to please the men on whom they are utterly dependent or to cater to the children on whom their identities depend. Rather than looking to unequal mother-child relationships to decide whether their maternal "virtues" are really virtues, women should compare and contrast their equal and unequal relationships. What women will discover in Grimshaw's estimation is that relationships between equals are ones of mutual respect and consideration, whereas relationships between unequals are almost always ones of either *benign* or *malign* domination and submission.

CONCLUSIONS

Grimshaw's reservations about using the mother-child relationship as a moral paradigm for all of one's relationships are small compared to those of philosopher Jeffner Allen. As Allen sees it, biological motherhood causes women to be viewed as "breeders," confining them to the kind of genital sexuality that is oriented toward procreation.[59] Allen insists that motherhood has nothing to do with female virtue and everything to do with female oppression. Women will be neither free nor truly virtuous, says Allen, until they "evacuate" motherhood.[60]

Allen believes that as long as women continue to have children, patriarchy will be reproduced over and over again. She asks women to stop having children so that "women's repetitive *reproduction* of patriarchy" may at last be replaced by the "genuine, creative, *production*" of women.[61] Were women to decide not to have any children for the next twenty years, says Allen, "the possibilities for developing new modes of thought and existence would be almost unimaginable."[62]

Allen's evacuation of motherhood is an ideologically promising notion. Perhaps women would be able to build a new, nonpatriarchal world after a twenty-year boycott on motherhood. Leaving behind their ties (or chains) to motherhood, they could fully explore new possibilities, new ways of being. Women would no longer need the mother-child relationship to serve as the moral paradigm for all of their relationships. On the contrary, friendship relationships between women would play this role. Without the dangers of exploitation by men, women could finally develop an ethics of care that would degenerate neither into servility, nor into abusive power plays.

Allen may be right; if any relationships have the potential for goodness, it may be the relationships between women in a nonpatriarchal society. Yet, the fact remains that many women are neither ready, willing, nor able to evacuate motherhood. Although Allen would disagree, there may be ways, short of the evacuation of motherhood, for women to achieve a wholeness that is neither necessarily enhanced nor diminished by their decision to have or not have children. What is more, even if thinking need not be "maternal" in order to be ethical, there is much that both women and men can learn from children about the requirements of the moral life.

NOTES

1. Dorothy Dinnerstein, *The Mermaid and the Minotaur* (New York: Harper Colophon Books, 1976).
2. Joyce Trebilcot, "Introduction," in Joyce Trebilcot, ed., *Mothering: Essays in Feminist Theory* (Totowa, N.J.: Rowman & Allanheld, 1984), 1.
3. Sara Ruddick, "Maternal Thinking," in Trebilcot, ed., *Mothering: Essays in Feminist Theory*, 214.
4. Ibid.
5. Ibid., 215.
6. Alasdair MacIntyre, *After Virtue* (Notre Dame, Ind.: University of Notre Dame Press, 1981), 177.
7. Ibid., 178.
8. Ibid., 181.
9. Ibid.
10. Adrienne Rich, *Of Woman Born* (New York: W. W. Norton, 1979), 174.
11. Ibid., 57.
12. Sara Ruddick, *Maternal Thinking: Toward a Politics of Peace* (Boston, Mass.: Beacon Press, 1989), 17.
13. Ibid., 19.
14. Ibid., 67.
15. Ibid., 71.
16. Ibid., 73.
17. Ibid., 75.
18. Ibid., 74.
19. Ibid., 98.
20. Ibid., 118.
21. Ibid., 123.
22. Ruddick, "Maternal Thinking," 214.
23. Ruddick, *Maternal Thinking*, 120–122.
24. Ibid., 221.
25. Ibid.
26. Ibid., 229.
27. Virginia Held, "Feminism and Moral Theory," in Eva Kittay and Diana Meyers, eds., *Women and Moral Theory* (Savage, Md.: Rowman & Littlefield, 1987), 112.
28. Ibid., 112–113.
29. Ibid., 114–115.
30. Ibid., 115.
31. Ibid., 116–117.
32. Ibid., 119.
33. Ibid., 120.
34. Virginia Held, "The Obligations of Mothers and Fathers," in Joyce Trebilcot, ed., *Mothering: Essays in Feminist Theory*, 7.
35. Ibid., 11.
36. Ibid., 18.

37. Held, "Feminism and Moral Theory," 121.

38. Ibid., 124.

39. Ibid., 125.

40. Ibid., 126.

41. Caroline Whitbeck, "The Maternal Instinct," in Joyce Trebilcot, ed., *Mothering: Essays in Feminist Theory*, 188.

42. Ibid., 190.

43. Ibid., 191 (my emphasis).

44. Ruddick, *Maternal Thinking*, 26–27.

45. Ibid., 36.

46. Patricia Ward Scaltsas, "Do Feminist Ethics Counter Feminist Aims?" in Eve Browning Cole and Susan Coultrap-McQuin, eds., *Exploration in Feminist Ethics* (Bloomington: Indiana University Press, 1992), 23.

47. Nancy Chodorow, *The Reproduction of Mothering* (Berkeley: University of California Press, 1978), 32.

48. Paul Lauritzen, "A Feminist Ethic and the New Romanticism—Mothering as a Model of Moral Relations," *Hypatia* 4 (Summer 1989):30.

49. Ibid.

50. Ibid., 37.

51. Ibid., 41.

52. Ibid., 41–42.

53. Whitbeck, "The Maternal Instinct," 191.

54. Ibid., 196.

55. Ibid., 197.

56. Jean Grimshaw, *Philosophy and Feminist Thinking* (Minneapolis: University of Minnesota Press, 1986), 251.

57. Ibid.

58. Ibid., 252.

59. Jeffner Allen, "Motherhood: The Annihilation of Women," in Joyce Trebilcot, ed., *Mothering: Essays in Feminist Theory*, 310.

60. Ibid.

61. Ibid., 326.

62. Ibid.

8

Feminist Approaches to Ethics

So far we have discussed two feminine approaches to ethics: Carol Gilligan's and Nel Noddings's. Both of these thinkers focus on women's "lost" values and on women's purported predisposition to care. Gilligan's and Noddings's morality stresses people's *responsibilities* to a variety of caring communities rather than their *rights* as autonomous individuals. One's relationships matter as much as, if not more than, one's personal ambitions, aspirations, and aims. They also believe that an ethics that emphasizes caring is just as good as, if not better than, one that emphasizes justice; being kind is as important as being fair. Yet in addition to many "feminine" twists, a few "feminist" turns characterize Gilligan's and Noddings's approaches to ethics. For example, insofar as Gilligan insists that her Level Three stage of moral development affirms neither the self over the other nor the other over the self,[1] it is feminist, for feminists do not want anyone's interests to be relentlessly subordinated to anyone else's interests, as if only some persons are truly worthy of care. Similarly, to the degree that Noddings admits that "ethical diminishment"[2] is sometimes the lesser of two evils (the greater evil being the sacrifice of an abused person to his/her abuser), it too is feminist. No one is morally required to stay in an abusive relationship simply to spare the abuser's feelings or to give him/her every conceivable opportunity to reform. For feminists, giving has its limits, and Noddings struggles to deal with those limits in what she often concedes is a less than ideal world.

In addition to Gilligan's and Noddings's feminine ethics of caring, we have also considered three maternal approaches to ethics that bridge some of the remaining gaps between feminine and feminist approaches to ethics. Held's, Ruddick's, and Whitbeck's respective works are *femi-*

nine insofar as they celebrate the psychological traits and moral virtues that society associates with women who mother. Yet, to the degree that their articles and books criticize "feminine" traits and virtues as possibly contributing to women's oppression, they are feminist. For example, in her discussions of the "feminine" virtues of humility and cheerfulness, Ruddick distinguishes between some of the liberating and oppressive aspects of the mother-child relationship. True humility is not about servility—about a mother being a "slave" to her child. Rather, it is about a mother knowing when "enough is enough." Humble mothers realize that they neither can nor should use every moment of their day frantically trying to make sure that their children have the best of everything.[3]

Likewise, true cheerfulness is not about a mother masking over her misery or desperation. On the contrary, it is an antidote to the fury that a mother sometimes feels, faced as she is with her children's foibles.[4] Cheerful mothers realize that some situations are so much out of their control that laughter is a better response than tears. Far from being a prescription for women's oppression, then, Ruddick's maternal approach to ethics seems like a promising cure for what has been ailing women for centuries. She encourages mothers to accept their weaknesses as well as their strengths, taking care to develop those traits of character that will enable them neither to dominate others nor to be dominated by them.

Given that some feminine and maternal approaches to ethics have feminist aspects and that most of the thinkers who are developing feminine and/or maternal approaches to ethics regard themselves as feminists, it is challenging to specify what makes an approach to ethics "feminist" as opposed to "feminine" and/or "maternal." Clearly, it is not the ontological and epistemological assumptions of feminist approaches to ethics that distinguish them from their related counterparts, for, as philosopher Susan Sherwin has noted, feminist ethics

> can agree with Gilligan (1982) that the morally relevant features of any decision-making situation include the agents' responsibilities to specific persons, including themselves. It also shares with feminine ethics a recognition of the significance of rooting ethical discussion in specific contexts and thus rejecting traditional ethical theory's commitment to purely abstract reasoning. . . . In addition, feminist ethics shares with feminine ethics a rejection of the paradigm of moral subjects as autonomous, rational, independent, and virtually indistinguishable from one another; it seems clear that an ontology that considers only isolated, fully developed beings is not adequate for ethics (Whitbeck 1984).[5]

Likewise, the focus of feminist approaches to ethics does not make them stand out. Feminine, maternal, and feminist approaches to ethics are all women-centered; they all speak primarily to women about women's moral experiences. Rather, feminist approaches to ethics are distinctive because they, far more than their feminine and/or maternal counterparts, are political. Because feminists are committed to "eliminating the subordination of women—and of other oppressed persons— in all of its manifestations,"[6] a feminist approach to ethics asks questions about *power*—that is, about domination and subordination—even before it asks questions about good and evil, care and justice, or mothers and fathers.

Admittedly, many traditional philosophers will be scandalized by the suggestion that a feminist approach to ethics is fundamentally political—that is, that its ultimate aim is to identify and eliminate oppressive imbalances of power between people. Yet, if people are not each other's equals in fact as well as in theory, any approach to ethics is bound to fail. After all, oppressors cannot treat those whom they oppress with the same respect and consideration they treat their peers.

Feminists are interested, to be sure, in a very specific dyad of oppression—namely, the relationship that has historically existed between dominant men and submissive women. Committed to the destruction of those patriarchal structures that maintain gender asymmetry, feminists systematically challenge traditional ethics for its contribution to women's oppression. To the objection that it is wrong to attend to women's interests more than men's, feminists reply that they are simply acknowledging women's interests as much as traditional ethicists have unconsciously acknowledged men's interests. Because many traditional ethicists have tended to conflate human beings' interests with those of biological males, they have sometimes excused, or even justified, men's oppression of women and children. Feminists seek to balance the moral scale, throwing all their weight in with women to correct centuries of patriarchal oppression. Sometimes an extreme, all-or-nothing approach is the best way to shock people out of what amounts to a moral stupor—a sleepy inattentiveness to women's concerns.

Perhaps the greater challenge in distinguishing primarily feminist approaches to ethics from primarily feminine and/or maternal approaches to ethics is deciding whose work to analyze. Because feminist ethics is such a rich field, it is tempting to say something about every feminist approach that has been developed to date. However, a realistic assessment of my own energy, time, and talent—as well as respect and admiration for their work—has led me to focus on Alison M. Jaggar's, Sheila Mullett's, Susan Sherwin's, and Annette Baier's feminist approaches to ethics. More than the work of some other equally significant and interesting feminist ethicists, their work permits me to return to a claim that I made in Chapter 1: namely, that there is a relationship between having a feminist consciousness on the one hand and developing a feminist approach to ethics on the other. Unless an ethicist's goal is to liberate women from the social, economic, cultural, and, yes, biological factors that limit women's capacity for goodness, his/her approach to ethics will not be feminist.

ALISON JAGGAR ON SPECIFYING THE CONDITIONS FOR A FEMINIST APPROACH TO ETHICS

Succinctly articulating the necessary and sufficient conditions for a feminist approach to ethics is a difficult assignment but one that philosopher Alison Jaggar has willingly accepted. She argues that traditional ethics is not nearly as interested in matters "feminine" or "feminist" as it is in matters "masculine" or "masculinist." As a result of this pervasive bias, traditional ethics has failed women in at least five ways.[7] First, it has shown little concern for women's interests as opposed to men's interests. Indeed, traditional ethics has actually encouraged women to develop "virtues" that serve men's needs, wants, and desires. To the degree that a woman is patient, obedient, long-suffering, and otherwise cheerfully compliant, to that same degree is she likely to make a man's life heaven on earth. It matters not that these "virtues" also make it difficult for a woman to identify and assert the importance of her own aspirations, ambitions, and expectations.

In addition to urging women to practice the "virtues" of passivity, traditional ethics has militated against women's interests in other, equally serious ways. Jaggar notes, for example, that some traditional ethicists have described a pregnant woman as little more than a fetal container, as if her life counted for virtually nothing as compared to the life of the fetus within her womb.[8] In some traditional approaches to ethics, even a woman's desire for an education becomes a mere means to the end of better serving her man. We will recall that Jean-Jacques Rousseau's Sophie studied the pleasing arts of music and manners to make herself a worthy "complement" for Emile. Such downplayings of women's interests teach women that they have no *important* interests, that their interests are footnotes or afterthoughts to those of men. In fact, some men even make it a *virtue* for a woman to neglect herself: "Oh, she won't mind if she has to change her plans for us. She's a good sport!"

In addition to neglecting women's interests, traditional ethics has neglected women in a second way. As Jaggar sees it, traditional ethicists have not found the so-called private or domestic realm—the world of cooking, cleaning, and child care—philosophically interesting. As a result, they have not often raised moral questions about women's issues. For example, traditional ethicists have not written much about women's "double day," that is, about whether it is *fair* that working wives do more in the way of housework than their working husbands. Likewise, traditional ethicists have not written much about the sexual abuse of women and girls outside the confines of their homes, let alone within them. Articles on marital rape, date rape, and incest either remain unwritten or are written from a defensive point of view. Given that most traditional ethicists have probably witnessed a man abusing a woman on one occasion or another, we must wonder why they have not identified violence directed against women as an ethical problem worthy of extended comment. We must also ask whether an ethics that fails or refuses to examine the multiple ways in which men systematically harm women constitutes a satisfactory ethics for *any* human being, irrespective of sex.

To claim that some issues are women's issues is not, however, to claim that these issues are necessarily "female." For example, it is not the inevitable consequence of women's *nature* that women, but not men, tend to worry more about their families' problems than their nation's woes; rather, it is "the result of women's culturally assigned confinement to and/or responsibility for"[9] what is generally termed "the home." Moreover, given that men and women typically live and/or work together, *women's* issues often become *men's* issues. Even if culture constructs men to worry about the grand scheme of things, most husbands still fret about Billy's poor grades as much as their wives do. Nevertheless, even if many women's issues are also men's issues, they tend to affect women more directly and sometimes more disastrously than men. For example, given that poverty is being "feminized,"[10] women may justifiably argue that government decisions to allocate more money to military budgets than to welfare subsidies discriminate against them. Ethicists cannot afford to proceed on the assumption that what is good for the gander is also good for the goose.

Jaggar also alludes to a third, particularly serious, deficiency of traditional ethics. Denying that women are moral agents means denying that women's ethical insights are valuable. Ever since the time of Aristotle, noted philosophers have claimed that women are capable of only a very limited kind of moral thought and action. In this connection, we will recall the claim that men are more morally developed than women because they score higher on Kohlberg's scale of moral development. As we noted, however, men's "high" scores do not constitute conclusive proof that they, but not also women, are autonomous moral agents. The possibility always remains that scales like Kohlberg's are deaf to women's different moral voice.

A fourth and further problem with traditional ethics, to which Jaggar correctly calls our attention, is its tendency to celebrate allegedly masculine traits like "independence, autonomy, intellect, will, wariness, hierarchy, domination, culture, transcendence, product, asceticism, war and death"[11] on the one hand and to depreciate allegedly feminine traits like "interdependence, community, connection, sharing, emotion, body, trust, absence of hierarchy, nature, immanence, process, joy, peace and life"[12] on the other. Because there is no apparent reason to value the former traits more than the latter ones, Jaggar suspects that "male bias"[13] has led traditional ethicists (most of them men) to value the traits that culture has assigned to men.[14] But the mere fact that one's group is linked to certain traits does not make those traits morally better than the traits to which another group is linked—a point so obvious that it is difficult to believe that traditional ethicists missed it.

A fifth and final charge that Jaggar levels against traditional ethics is that it devalues women's moral experience. As we saw in Chapter 4, traditional ethics has favored "masculine" ways of thinking that focus on rules, universality, impartiality, and reason over "feminine" ways of thinking that focus on relationships, particularity, partiality, and emotion. Because men have written the "Great Books" of traditional ethics, women might be tempted to reject any and all "masculine" values as ones that cannot possibly serve the interests of women. But so-called "feminine" values do not necessarily or always serve women's interests any better than so-called "masculine" values. As Jaggar observes:

Whether the feminine is construed as empirical characteristic, social ideal, or symbolic association, it has been constructed inevitably in circumstances of male domination, and its value for feminism is likely, therefore, to be very questionable. In some cases, it is arguable that feminists would do better to appropriate what may have been constructed as the masculine aspects of Western ethics rather than the feminine ones.[15]

Jaggar's fear is that, in their eagerness to affirm the "feminine," those who are developing feminine approaches to ethics may not always appreciate how dangerous it is to claim that feminine values are better than masculine ones. "Bad boys" may be only too happy to let "good girls" prove their superior virtue to them, claiming that the more a woman sacrifices for "her man," the better woman she is.

Acutely aware of the five ways in which traditional ethics has disfavored women, Jaggar urges feminists to develop approaches to ethics that begin "from the conviction that the subordination of women is morally wrong and that the moral experience of women is as worthy of respect as that of men."[16] From this kind of thoughtful beginning, feminists can move on to the kind of action that is incumbent on them. A person develops a feminist approach to ethics not only by criticizing practices that oppress women but also by imagining "morally desirable" alternatives to them and offering "morally justifiable" ways to resist them.[17] In sum, a person develops a feminist approach to ethics by trying to live the words s/he writes.

Jaggar's commitment to bridging the gap between thought and action is clear in her summary of the *necessary* conditions for a feminist approach to ethics. No matter what else an approach to ethics does or does not do, in order to be "feminist" it must (1) proceed on the assumption that women and men do not share precisely the same situation in life; (2) offer action guides "that will tend to subvert rather than reinforce the present systematic subordination of women";[18] (3) provide strategies for dealing with issues that arise in private or domestic life; and (4) "take the moral experience of all women seriously, though not, of course, uncritically."[19] Women should not focus first and foremost on making the world a happier place for *everyone*. Rather, their primary aim should be to make the world a better place for *women*. In Jaggar's estimation, women's supportive thoughts, kind words, and benign actions are not enough. A feminist approach to ethics entails women resisting and overcoming their continuing oppression under patriarchy.

If Jaggar's minimum conditions for a feminist approach to ethics are indeed necessary, then it becomes apparent why some *feminine* approaches to ethics fall short of being *feminist* approaches to ethics. For example, although the nineteenth-century thinker Catherine Beecher illuminated the contours of the domestic realm very well indeed, and although she took women's moral experience "seriously" enough, it is not clear that she took it "critically" enough. We will recall Beecher's tendency to overestimate women's capacity for "self-sacrificial benevolence" (see Chapter 3). Moreover, in constructing a world in which men and women live in separate, though purportedly equally valuable spheres, it could be argued that Beecher served to "reinforce" rather than to "subvert" women's subordination to men. Likewise, similar points could be raised and, as we have seen, have been raised against Gilligan and Noddings, as well as a variety of maternal thinkers. To the degree that these thinkers celebrate feminine "virtues" that tend to increase rather than decrease women's oppression, to that same degree do their writings warrant scrutiny. Caring actions, maternal feelings, and intimate relationships are not ethically unproblematic. On the contrary, such actions, feelings, and relationships may actually impede women's moral development insofar as they encourage women to become or remain subordinate to men or, for that matter, to children.

SHEILA MULLETT ON SHIFTING MORAL PERSPECTIVES

Although she does not deliberately set out to do so, philosopher Sheila Mullett meets Jaggar's minimal requirements for a feminist ethics. Mullett maintains that in order to develop a feminist approach to ethics, a thinker must first develop a feminist consciousness. She observes, however, that it is quite difficult for thinkers to become feminists "within a dominant culture that is essentially hostile, or at least unreceptive,"[20] to feminist views. Indeed, many women are so caught up in the patriarchal patterns of behavior that limit them that they become desensitized to the pain routinely inflicted on them. To overcome the moral numbness and moral callousness that serve to oppress them, these women must open their eyes to their own oppression. Feminist consciousness begins with moral sensitivity, proceeds to a moment of profound ontological shock, and ends in praxis, says Mullett.[21] More than simply a state of mind, feminist consciousness is a commitment to action.

When a woman becomes morally sensitive, she focuses on the violence done to women; she feels the pain that women feel when they are harassed, raped, and battered. Similarly, when a woman is ontologically shocked, she undergoes something akin to a religious conversion experience. In the same way that the world metamorphoses for the unbeliever turned believer, the world changes dramatically for the oppressed woman turned feminist. Suddenly, her eyes are open to realities to which she was previously blind, and she sees the damage done to women as something she must stop. No longer is she able to view sexual harassment as sexual attraction, pornography as sexual fantasy, or rape as consensual sexual intercourse. On the contrary, she sees only how women are being harmed and how they could instead be benefited. It is this new vision that impels a woman to action, or praxis. Together with other women who see what she sees, a feminist determines to *do* something to ameliorate women's lot.

What Mullett says about the relationship between moral sensitivity, ontological shock, and praxis resonates considerably with what so-called "prescriptivists" have said about the relationship between moral *belief* on the one hand and moral *action* on the other. One noted prescriptivist, R. M. Hare, claims that if a moral judgment is "prescriptive," it *entails* an imperative. In other words, if a proposition p entails another proposition q, I cannot (consistently) assert or accept p and deny or reject q. For example, if I say, "You ought not to war because war is evil," I cannot deny or reject the imperative "Don't war." Hare maintains that denying or rejecting an imperative is failing to act on it in any way whatsoever. Thus, the thesis that moral judgments are prescriptive implies that if I accept the moral judgment that I ought to do x, then I am committed to doing x—at least, I am committed to keep on trying to do x. Conversely, if I do not do x, or if I never even try to do x, then I probably don't mean what I say when I say, "I ought to do x."[22]

To be sure, Mullett does not use the language of propositions and entailments. Yet, she does say that when women become conscious of women's pain, their attitude is not one of "a passive acceptance of misery but a commitment to 'reformulating our actions and thought.'"[23] A feminist who knows *emotionally* as well as *rationally* that women suffer wants to do something to mitigate women's suffering—if not by actually giving aid to a battered woman or by participating in a "Take Back the Night" march against pornography, for example, then by comforting and supporting a friend who has been raped or abused. A feminist's first steps to action may need to be small ones, for her ability to resist and overcome women's oppression will not necessarily equal her willingness to do so. But be this as it may, the fact of her coming to consciousness constitutes the greatest step she will ever take. Provided that a feminist "will" is really present, a feminist "way" will ordinarily emerge after feminist awareness dawns.

Whether or not Mullett's approach is "prescriptive," she differs from Hare in her belief that feminists' actions should be *collective* rather than *individualistic*. There is no way that I, myself, can end my own suffering, let alone women's suffering. Unless other women help me in my personal struggles and vice versa, we will remain individually defeated in our mutual isolation. Whereas a traditional prescriptivist will present the moral agent as making his or her separate moral peace, Mullett presents the moral agent "as constructing a moral perspective within the context of a collective endeavor to transform existing social arrangements."[24] No one moral agent has the whole moral situation in view when she joins with other moral agents to remedy the pains they have been feeling/thinking. On the contrary, it is only when people actually work together that she and they come to understand precisely what has been ailing all of them. Feminist praxis is collective.

Realizing that "feminist consciousness" will remain an abstraction unless she can show how it functions, Mullett provides an example: namely, Susan Sherwin's work on in vitro fertilization (IVF). Traditional bioethicists have tended to discuss in vitro fertilization with no special focus on women. For example, utilitarian arguments, which stress the overall "good" of reproductive technology in offering infertile couples "choice," often ignore both why infertile women are willing to risk almost anything to have a genetic child and which kind of infertile women have enough knowledge, power, and/or money to make this "choice."[25] By enabling even infertile women to fulfill their "natural" role as biological mothers, however, reproductive technology may be contributing to women's continuing oppression rather than their liberation. Now that technology can make her a mother, how can an infertile woman say "no" to her quintessential role—to that which is supposed to fulfill her?[26] Only an irrational—no, a *bad* woman—would choose to spend her money, time, and effort on something other than a child.[27]

In contrast to traditional analyses of in vitro fertilization, Sherwin's analysis is characterized by each one of the three elements of women-focused moral sensitivity, ontological shock, and praxis. To begin with, Sherwin is *morally sensitive* to the fact that a woman's decision to enter an IVF program may not always be an entirely free one. Heavy social pressures lead many infertile women, and even some fertile women with infertile husbands, to IVF clinics. Often women crave babies to whom they are genetically related because they do not want to disappoint their husbands, and/or because they do not have any life goals other than rearing a family, and/or because they do not have access to children to whom they are not genetically related.[28]

Additionally, even when women do not bear the financial costs of in vitro fertilization, they certainly bear most, if not all, of its physical and psychological burdens. The process of in vitro fertilization strains women's bodies. They are the ones who must submit to a regimen of hormone therapy and, if necessary, to some relatively painful, as well as risky, surgeries. They are the ones who must learn to order their lives around the rhythm of their ovaries, coming to terms with the fact that each time an embryo is transferred into their uterus, it may or may not implant. Women's anxiety and frustration cannot help but grow with each failed IVF attempt and with each additional cash outlay (two cycles of IVF treatment, the standard regimen, cost approximately $9,376 in 1986).[29]

In addition to being morally sensitive to the problems of women who use in vitro fertilization, Sherwin is *ontologically shocked* by the way in which their treatment is managed. She is profoundly aware not only of how "bad" things are for infertile women but also how "good" things could be for them. In a world still characterized by male domination and female subordination, feminists must wonder whether in vitro fertilization is actually in infertile women's best interests. It is conceivable, after all, that many infertile women could be just as happy, if not happier, without children "of their own," or children at all. It is also conceivable that if society spent more money to reduce the causes of infertility, especially sexually transmitted diseases and toxic workplaces, the number of infertile women would decrease drastically.[30]

Yet, despite her grave reservations about in vitro fertilization, Sherwin does not favor a ban on it, both because some infertile women do freely choose it and because some people eagerly welcome any excuse to restrict women's reproductive rights. Given that certain segments of society still wish to deprive women of access to such reproduction-controlling technologies as contraception, sterilization, and especially abortion, now does not seem the time to encourage women to deny *themselves* access to such reproduction-aiding technologies as artificial insemination by donor and in vitro fertilization. The ground in which women's right to privacy is rooted is already crumbling beneath women's feet; feminists do not want, however inadvertently, to contribute to the erosion. Even if some women choose in vitro fertilization not because it is best for them but because it is best for someone else, at least no court of law is blocking their mistake.

Finally, Sherwin's analysis of in vitro fertilization reveals the dimension of praxis. She insists that if in vitro fertilization is going to serve women's interests, then *women* have to decide if they want to use it, for how long, when, and under what conditions. Among the things that concern Sherwin and other feminists about in vitro fertilization is that the women who use it do not always appreciate how *their* desire to have a genetically related child can put *other* women at risk. For example, some variations on in vitro fertilization like surrogate embryo transfer (SET), or lavage, pose special risks. In this flushing technique, a fertile donor woman is inseminated with the sperm of an infertile woman's partner. If she conceives, the embryo is flushed from her womb into the womb of the infertile woman. In North America, the results of twenty-nine SETs were twelve embryos but only two successful pregnancies. In addition, one donor woman had a life-threatening ectopic pregnancy that required surgical removal, and another donor woman had a normal (but unwanted) pregnancy that spontaneously aborted.[31] Clearly, in choosing for herself, a woman sometimes chooses for other women. Thus, feminist praxis imposes a new burden on women's choices. The woman who would be feminist does not have the luxury of acting simply on her own best interests. Rather, she must act on her own best interests, as amended by the best interests of other women.

SUSAN SHERWIN ON POLITICIZING MORALITY AND MORALIZING POLITICS

Sherwin's analysis of in vitro fertilization serves as a transition to her general approach to feminist ethics. Like Jaggar, Sherwin believes that a feminist approach to ethics differs from feminine and maternal approaches to ethics because it is more political than either of these two approaches. Although a feminist approach to ethics may affirm the same values and virtues a feminine approach does, it will not do so uncritically. Women must be wary of women's "values" and "virtues" to the degree that they are unliberating by-products of life in a sexist culture. Whatever positive features the virtue of care has, for example, it may still be a virtue that subordinates women to men. Vulnerable people know that they cannot afford to alienate the affections of those who have power over them. The powerless are especially motivated to accommodate the powerful—"to be sensitive to the emotional pulse of others, to see things in relational terms, and to be pleasing and compliant."[32] Similarly, whatever the moral advantages of maternal thinking may be, it is still a mode of thought produced in a certain kind of family structure—namely, a Western, middle-class, heterosexual family. Insofar as this *structure* oppresses women, the maternal mode of thought produced within it is likely to oppress women. By choosing to specialize, as it were, in motherhood and caring, women tend to legitimate patriarchal attempts to make mothering women's *prime* duty. Women must win the right *not* to mother—the right for equality in public and private life—before they can safely develop a maternal ethics.

A feminist approach to ethics does not focus only on *women's* oppression, however. As Sherwin sees it, because feminists are sensitive to patterns of male domination and female subordination, they are also attuned to patterns of domination and subordination that are classist and/or racist. Although a feminist approach to ethics usually begins with a question like "How does this policy, this state of affairs, oppress *women* in particular?" it sometimes ends with a question like "How does this policy, this state of affairs, oppress vulnerable *people* in general?" Having posed the question "How do current health care insurance schemes oppress women?" for example, many feminist ethicists tend to move on to the question "How do current health-care insurance schemes oppress severely impaired newborns, the chronically ill, the elderly, homosexual AIDS victims, and the poor?" Often, it takes an oppressed group—in this instance, women—to recognize the oppression of another oppressed group and to seek remedies for it.

Clearly, the aim of feminist ethicists is not to prove that women's oppression is the worst form of oppression imaginable; rather, it is to identify and eliminate the *kind* of oppression that women have traditionally experienced. Whatever one thinks of feminists Catharine MacKinnon and Andrea Dworkin's definition of pornography, for example, it invites women to link their oppression to the oppression other groups experience. Pornography is "the graphic sexually explicit subordination"[33] not only of women but also of men, children, or transsexuals who are used "in the place of women."[34] A picture "celebrating" homosexual rape can be just as pornographic—just as oppressive—as a picture "celebrating" heterosexual rape. Thus, many feminist ethicists willingly write about gay men's oppression, for example, finding in it many mirror images of women's oppression.

Another feature of Sherwin's feminist approach to ethics, which is common to most other feminist approaches to ethics, is her refusal to envision it as a theory to end all theories. To the degree that feminist epistemology rejects universal truth as a desirable goal for human knowledge, or that feminist ontology rejects the totally self-sufficient individual as a desirable goal for human relationships, a feminist approach to ethics rejects absolute goodness as a desirable goal for human action. It does not aim to articulate its version of the principle of utility or the categorical imperative, proclaiming it as *the* rock-bottom foundation of morality for all human beings, be they female or male, the oppressed or the oppressors. On the contrary, a feminist approach to ethics aims to provide oppressed women—and also other oppressed groups—with moral action guides suited to their particular historical situation. These flexible norms aim to help oppressed women liberate themselves from those who would dominate them, for unless a person is free, she cannot be moral. Because liberation is not an overnight process or a miracle that can be worked at will, most feminist approaches to ethics tend to be incremental. To the degree that a woman, usually with the help of other women, frees herself from the constraints that limit her ability to do the most moral thing anyone can do—namely, to help structure a world in which relationships of domination and subordination do not exist—to that same degree, she becomes a moral agent. Morality's imperatives are as different as the women to whom they speak. Each woman is like Joan of Arc. She must decide whether her "voices" are leading her out of the captive land or further into it.

As Sherwin sees it, however, it is not enough for a feminist approach to ethics to encourage women to assess the moral validity of the different voices that speak to them. On the contrary, a feminist approach to ethics must provide women with a rationale for determining whether a "voice" is singing gibberish or articulating a meaningful message. Even if feminists tend to reject what is ordinarily labeled "moral absolutism," they are not prepared to embrace the kind of "moral relativism" that permits anything and everything, including the oppression of women or other oppressed groups.

In broaching the topic of relativism versus absolutism in feminist approaches to ethics, Sherwin confronts an issue that feminists cannot afford to ignore. She notes that feminists tend toward relativism—understood as the theory that ethical judgments are applicable only to the time and place in which they arise. Supposedly, they regard it as less oppressive than absolutism—understood as the theory that ethical judgments are applicable to all times and all places. Yet, feminists, who rightly flee from the oppressiveness of an absolutism that refuses to recognize difference, may also wrongly flee from the universality of an absolutism that permits them to say, "Oppression is always wrong." Only if feminists can say that something is wrong can they justifiably try to make it right. A relativist critic is an oxymoron. If your decisions are as good as mine, then how can I possibly criticize you, or you me? We two are perfect; there is simply no need for either one or both of us to change our minds and/or course of action. Socially speaking, moral relativism costs us the possibility of moral progress—of a better tomorrow.

Even if it permits them to be relativists in *philosophical theory*, feminists' vision of a better world—that is, of a nonpatriarchal world—does not permit them to be relativists in *political practice*. For example, many feminists are prepared to condemn as universally wrong such practices as pornography, sexual harassment, rape, and woman-battery despite the "ambivalent acceptance" of at least some of these practices "within the community at large"[35] and even by some feminists. Proof of dissension within the ranks comes with noting the existence of such disparate groups as Women Against Violent Pornography (WAVP) and the Feminist Anti-Censorship Taskforce (FACT). Nor has it gone unnoticed that such popular women's magazines as *Ladies' Home Journal* print articles about pornography that are captioned "Today it's a billion-dollar business. But the uneasy question remains: 'Is its portrayal of women sexy—or sick?'"[36] Yet, if there is not always feminist consensus, let alone general community consensus, on the wrongness of a practice like pornography, on what basis do some feminists (who claim that they are not absolutists) morally condemn it?

In an attempt to elucidate just how difficult it is for feminists to steer a course between the Scylla of absolutism on the one hand and the Charybdis of relativism on the other, Sherwin focuses on the widespread practice of female genital mutilation in many African and Middle Eastern countries. She considers that more than 84 million women now living have undergone this painful, frequently unsanitary, often harmful surgical procedure. Among the justifications for genital mutilation are "custom, religion, family honor, cleanliness, aesthetics, initiation, assurance of virginity, promotion of social and political cohesion, enhancement of fertility, improvement of male sexual pleasure, and prevention of female promiscuity."[37] Despite the fact that large numbers of women as well as men endorse this practice, Sherwin still insists that it is wrong. In proclaiming the wrongness of genital mutilation, however, Sherwin remains wary of absolutism. Too often, moral absolutism has been used to support cultural dominance. Oppressors make the leap from "There is a truth" to "I *know* that truth, but you do not." In their desire to show proper respect for cultural diversity, however, feminists must be careful not to pull the moral carpet out from under themselves.[38] Surely, some actions are so egregiously wrong—for example, rape—that feminists must be willing to take the risk of saying "Rape is *wrong*" even if some culture or another happens to endorse rape. In taking this risk, however, feminists must be able to articulate why they are making an exception to their general rule of respect for difference.[39]

Sherwin concedes that it is easier to be a *traditional* relativist than a *feminist* relativist. Whereas the traditional relativist is willing to live with the fact that he cannot condemn a practice such as genital mutilation (or, I suppose, even rape) if the majority of a population accepts it, the feminist relativist is not. Sherwin agrees with traditional relativists "that we do not have access to anything more foundational than community standards in ethics,"[40] but she also insists that some communities are morally worse than other communities. A community that structures its relations in terms of patterns of domination and subordination is simply morally worse than one that does not. Unless feminists are assured that a community is worthy of moral trust—that it is one in which no group of people is systematically exploited, manipulated, or otherwise dominated by other people—feminists believe that they are not obligated to tolerate, let alone respect, its standards.

Before feminists decide to trust a community's standards, they must make some baseline judgments about its moral methodology. If the community's standards are the result of a truly democratic conversation, then Sherwin believes those standards ought to be tolerated, indeed respected, by feminists. So, for example, if it turns out that *all* segments of a society are truly in favor of female genital mutilation— that no affected group has been forced to support this practice as the result of "coercion, exploitation, ignorance, deception, or even indifference"[41]—then it is a nonoppressive practice. However, in Sherwin's estimation, it is doubtful that *all* the segments of the societies that practice genital mutilation truly favor it. Indeed, there is increasing evidence that support for genital mutilation is waning even in those nations that have traditionally practiced it. For example, over a decade ago, then Kenyan President Daniel Moi condemned female genital mutilation. Like many other people in his government, he had become convinced that female genital mutilation harms women and children physically and psychologically and that since no developing country can afford to harm its own human resources, it was in everyone's best interests to stop the practice.[42]

Conceding that it is not always easy to determine whether a community is oppressive or nonoppressive—or just how nonoppressive a community must be before feminists can trust its moral judgments— Sherwin seeks additional guidance for feminists. In her estimation, philosopher David Wong's nontraditional (but still nonfeminist) version of moral relativism can help feminists determine which of two sides in a moral controversy they may justifiably take.

Wong believes that two equally justified, equally true, opposed moral positions can exist side by side. The individuals who espouse these two separate positions, however, should not interfere with each other's ends unless such interference would be "acceptable to them were they fully rational and informed of all relevant circumstances."[43] In order to clarify his meaning, Wong gives the example of abortion. As he sees it, people fight endlessly over abortion, but neither the anti-abortion nor the prochoice camps can convert the other side. Both positions are grounded in reflective, well-established moral systems. Both positions, therefore, are probably morally justified. Wong invokes his own "justification principle" to declare that since no fully rational and informed person is willing to accept active interference with his/her ends, both the conservatives and the liberals should confine themselves to verbal volleying.[44] Both sides should simply respect the moral convictions of the other and curtail activities that make it impossible, or nearly impossible, for the other side to follow its own ethical lights.

What is wrong with Wong's otherwise helpful position on relativism, says Sherwin, is that it accepts the conservatives' and liberals' respective moral systems as equally well established without asking certain crucial questions; namely, how did the systems come to be, whose interests do they foster, and whose interests do they impede?[45] These are the kinds of questions that feminists tend to ask. The answers to them reveal not only that the conservative position favors fetuses' and men's interests over women's interests but also that the conservative goal of stopping abortion limits liberals in ways that the liberal goal of safe, affordable, and accessible abortion does not limit conservatives.

The conservatives would block liberals from doing something they believe is right—having an abortion because one is not ready, willing, and/or able to be a parent; yet, the liberals would not stop the conservatives from doing what they believe is right—not having an abortion. The bumper sticker "Don't like abortion? Don't have one!" comes close to making Sherwin's distinction succinctly. To the degree that conservative abortion policies block liberals in a way that liberal abortion policies do not block conservatives, feminists may actively interfere with conservatives on the grounds that their abortion policies are less "democratic" than those of liberals:

A feminist moral relativism demands that we consider who controls moral decision-making within a community and what effect that control has on the least privileged members of that community. Both at home and abroad, it gives us grounds to criticize the practices that a majority believes acceptable if those practices are a result of oppressive power differentials. It will not, however, always tell us precisely what is the morally right thing to do, because there is no single set of moral truths we can decipher. Feminist moral relativism remains absolutist on the question of the moral wrong of oppression but is relativist on other moral matters; in this way, it is better able to incorporate feminist moral sensibilities.[46]

Apparently, not all differences are created equal.

However promising the future of feminist relativism may be, at present it cannot escape all of its absolutistic tendencies. Feminist moral relativists want to respect difference, but they reserve the right to judge *which* differences between individuals and/or groups must be respected and which ones must not. Yet, can morality be mixed and matched in this way? What does it mean to be an absolutist with respect to the matter of oppression and a relativist on other matters? Are we to slice oppression off from the rest of morality? If so, does this suggest that oppression is ultimately a "political" matter only indirectly related to "moral" matters? Feminist moral relativism, practiced within the confines of "good" communities—that is, nonoppressive, democratic ones—may be both an appealing and an incoherent view.

ANNETTE BAIER ON TRUSTING MORE AND CONTRACTING LESS

Jaggar's, Mullett's, and Sherwin's writings generate the conclusion that in order to count as "feminist," an approach to ethics must focus on and challenge the power relations within patriarchal society. Feminist ethicists tend to work outside the patriarchal power structure. There they are free to seek new paradigms for good human relationships—paradigms not based on the idea that in a human relationship someone must be the controller, the taker, and the dominant one, and someone else the controller, the giver, and the subordinate one. Philosopher Annette C. Baier offers us the paradigm of appropriately trusting[47] relationships as the model for good human relationships in general.

Although Baier believes that "appropriate trust" includes both men's ethics of obligation and women's "ethics of love,"[48] she concedes that it is easier to understand the relationship between trust, love, and feeling than the relationship between trust, obligation, and reason. Still, appropriate trust "nicely mediates between reason and feeling, those tired old candidates for moral authority, since to trust is neither quite to believe something about the trusted, nor necessarily to feel any emotion toward them—but to have a belief-informed and action-influencing attitude."[49] Trust and love are indeed two sides of the same moral coin. Unless people trust each other, they will have enormous difficulty loving each other. Lack of trust is probably behind most divorces and the erosion of most friendships. Yet trust is also closely connected to obligation in the sense that "to recognize a set of obligations is to trust some group of persons to instill them, to demand that they be met, possibly to levy sanctions if they are not, and this is to trust persons with significant coercive power over others."[50]

With the invocation of the idea of "coercive power," Baier transforms what could have been interpreted as a feminine approach to ethics into a feminist approach to ethics. She asks the crucial questions, What is trust? Whom can we trust with coercive power? Ourselves? Others? No one? Why should we trust anyone? Traditional ethics has tended to look at moral obligations from the point of view of those with the power: the coercers, or controllers. Rather than assuming that *the* moral problem is dealing with rule-makers who abuse their coercive power, traditional ethics has focused on punishing rule-breakers: the renegers, the defaulters, the liars. In contrast, a feminist approach to ethics tends to look at moral obligations from the point of view of those without the power: those who have to trust the rule-makers, the people with power, not to harm them. "To trust," says Baier, "is to make oneself or let oneself be more vulnerable than one might have been to harm from others—to give them an opportunity to harm one, in the confidence that they will not take it, because they have no good reason to."[51]

In an attempt to show why "trust" relationships rather than "contractual" relations are the proper moral paradigm for good human relationships, Baier claims that the essence of trust is "reliance" on another person's "good will," knowing full well that the other person's "good will" is not absolutely dependable.[52] My spouse can betray me; my friends can desert me; my parents can abandon me; my colleagues can undermine me; and so on. Realizing that trust entails risks, we must ask ourselves why we willingly make ourselves vulnerable. Baier answers that we need to trust others because we are not self-sufficient. Without the help of others, the kind of things and persons we value would never be created;

certainly, they could never be sustained. Not only do art, music, theater, literature, science, political debate, and economic exchange require more than one person for their existence and maintenance, so too do "life, health, reputation, our offspring and their well-being."[53]

Baier proceeds to construct a phenomenology of trust by describing *what* values we entrust to *whom*. Trust is a "three-place predicate (A trusts B with valued thing C)."[54] To appreciate the variety of forms trust can take, we need to look at the variety of ways in which B disappoints A and/or in which A retaliates against B, for example. The more carefully articulated and specified a relationship is, the easier it is to tell when trust has been violated. For example, if I promise to deliver your child's birthday cake on time and I fail to do so because I oversleep, you will probably conclude that I am untrustworthy. However, most of our relationships are considerably less articulated and specified than those between cake-buyers and cake-deliverers. A wife trusts her husband, for example, to have her best interests at heart. Such trust permits considerable discretion. It will be difficult for the wife to decide when her husband has seriously, perhaps irrevocably, destroyed the trust between them and when he has only temporarily threatened it. There is, after all, a major difference between one's husband flirting with a waitress and one's husband having a year-long extramarital affair with one's best friend. When trust is irrevocably destroyed, the relationship dies with it, but when trust is merely threatened, "some tact and willingness to forgive on the part of the truster and some willingness on the part of the trusted both to be forgiven and to forgive unfair criticism"[55] may yet save the relationship.

Baier emphasizes that because traditional ethicists have assumed that most human relationships are contractual relationships between two or more perfectly equal and rational persons, their analyses of trust have been few and far between. Trust is about keeping promises. We should trust promise-keepers and distrust promise-breakers. Yet most of our relationships are anything but perfectly equal and rational. In fact, if we really want to understand the necessary and sufficient conditions for trust, we should look to the kind of total trust an infant has in his/her parents, says Baier. Such trust is "primitive and basic."[56] Like it or not, an infant is "totally dependent on the good will of the parent, totally incapable of looking after anything he cares about without parental help or against parental will."[57] Although Baier concedes that, from the moment they are born, some infants seem profoundly mistrustful of everyone, including their parents, she still insists that

Surviving infants will usually have shown some trust, enough to accept offered nourishment, enough not to attempt to prevent such close approach.
The ultra-Hobbist child who fears or rejects the mother's breast, as if fearing poison from that source, can be taken as displaying innate distrust, and
such newborns must be the exception in a surviving species.[58]

Because trust ordinarily exists in our infancy and persists throughout
our childhood, we need to explain not the beginnings of trust but "the
ceasings to trust, the transfers of trust, the restriction or enlargements
in the fields of what is trusted, when, and to whom, rather than any
abrupt switches from distrust to trust."[59]

In his account of a contractual promise, David Hume argues that it is
"an artificially contrived and secured case of mutual trust."[60] The fact
that we can "will" ourselves into a contractual relationship makes it an
exception to the kind of noncontractual relationships that rule in our
everyday lives. Whereas infants *do not choose* to trust those on whom
they depend, adults sometimes *do choose* to trust certain individuals
with their possessions, their jobs, their loved ones, and even their own
lives. For infants entering a parent-child relationship, trustful actions
precede trustful thoughts; for adults entering a contractual relationship,
trustful thoughts precede trustful actions.

Baier observes that traditional philosophers have not been interested
in "infant trust," that is, in the kind of natural and nonvoluntary trust
that exists between unequals, especially intimates. Instead, they have
been interested in the kind of artificial and voluntary trust that has
tended to characterize "relations between more or less free and equal
adult strangers, say, the members of an all male club, with membership
rules and rules for dealing with rule breakers and where the form of cooperation was restricted to insuring that each member could read his
Times in peace and have no one step on his gouty toes."[61] Traditional
philosophy's preoccupation with adult contractors, or promise-makers
(historically male), has had the consequence, then, of relegating not
only children but women to the margins of morality.

Because Baier's approach to trust is a feminist one, she focuses on
the *power* differentials that affect human relationships either positively
or negatively. We must know when not to trust as well as when to trust.
Although we cannot construct a moral network if we are always looking
over our shoulders for someone to stab us in the back, we should not
ignore the scrape of the knife between our shoulder blades either. Too
much trust is as dangerous as too little trust:

We should not assume that promiscuous trustworthiness is any more a virtue than is undiscriminating distrust. It is appropriate trustworthiness, appropriate trustingness, appropriate encouragement to trust, which will be virtues, as will be judicious untrustworthiness, selective refusal to trust, discriminating discouragement of trust.[62]

Because women's oppression has in large measure depended on women's—but not men's—trustworthiness, women must cultivate the virtues of appropriate distrust as well as appropriate trust. Although Baier does not say much about what constitutes appropriate distrust, her admonition recalls those feminists who have faulted feminine approaches to ethics for stressing the pleasures more than the perils of women's caring too much. Even as an untempered ethic of care invites exploitation, so too does a morality based on trust risk deception in patriarchal society. Until men learn to be carers, women cannot safely embrace the role of one-caring, and until women gain equal status with men, women cannot assume that men always tell them the truth. If justice seasons care, distrust must season trust.

CRITICISMS OF FEMINIST ETHICS

Although feminist approaches to ethics avoid many of the problems that plague feminine approaches to ethics, they are not impervious to challenge. As I see it, there are at least three possible challenges to bring against feminist ethics: (1) feminist ethics is *sexist* because it attends only to women's morality; (2) feminist ethics is *not feminist* because it shares many features in common with other nontraditional approaches to ethics; and (3) feminist ethics is *not ethics*, but politics, because it focuses on issues of power.

Criticism One

In an article on feminist directions in medical ethics, Virginia L. Warren ponders what a sexist ethics might be like. She suggests that such an ethics—and she has a male-biased sexist ethics in mind—would be prone to several distortions. First, a sexist ethics would ask its moral questions and develop its answers to them from a "male perspective."[63] Warren notes, for example, that the autonomy-paternalism debate in medical ethics generally focuses on authority issues. *Who* decides whether a still-recovering patient should be sent home to defray large costs to the hospital? The patient or the physician? The debate focuses so much on the authority question that the traditional ethicist fails to ask *who* will bear the burden of caring for the not quite well patient when s/he comes home. Most likely a woman—not a man—will assume this burden.

Second, a sexist ethics "would never appear sexist"[64]—that is, more interested in men's than in women's issues. On the contrary, it would disguise itself as neutral. As Warren sees it, however, even if traditional approaches to ethics were *genuinely* neutral—which, in her opinion, they are not—they would remain decidedly unappealing. Not everyone believes that a moral system that strives to ignore the particularities of persons is superior to one that does not. Since "ought" implies "can," many distinctive things about a person's socioeconomic background, racial heritage, or sexual preference may serve to increase or decrease his/her blameworthiness as a moral agent. What is more, not attending to a person's gender, for example, sometimes leads to treating men and women exactly the same—providing them with the same kind of education, for example—when their intellectual and/or emotional needs may be genuinely different. To teach women in precisely the same way that one teaches men, without taking into account the fact that women have been socialized in ways that men have not, does not give women an education equal to men's. Rather, it requires them, in many instances, to think like men in order to succeed.

Third, a sexist ethics would keep women on the "defensive"[65] by focusing on issues likely to make women appear in an unfavorable light. Warren observes that traditional ethicists fixate on topics such as abortion (which pits women against their fetuses) and preferential hiring (which pits women [and minorities] against white men). If it is true, as some psychologists have argued, that "talking out one's anger tends to make one *more* angry at a person, rather than less,"[66] focusing on such confrontational topics as abortion and preferential hiring would serve to confirm rather than disconfirm negative images of women.

As critics of feminist approaches to ethics see it, a sexist ethics is wrong whether the objects of its sexism are women or men. If it is wrong to use a "male" perspective in developing an approach to ethics, it is equally wrong to use a "female" perspective. Likewise, if it is wrong to disguise male values as human values, it is wrong to disguise female values as human values. Either gender-free moral values exist or they do not. If they do exist, they belong equally to men and women. Finally, if it is wrong to keep women on the moral defensive, it is also wrong to keep men on the moral defensive by focusing discussion on issues such as men's violence against women, for example.

Defenders of feminist approaches to ethics deny that they are sexist in the ways that traditional approaches to ethics are. Alison Jaggar points out that feminist approaches to ethics have sometimes been misrepresented as a "simple inversion"[67] of the five most frequently raised feminist challenges to traditional ethics we discussed above: namely, its (1) "lack of concern for women's interests; (2) neglect of 'women's issues'; (3) denial of women's moral agency; (4) depreciation of 'feminine' values; and (5) devaluation of women's moral experience."[68] As Jaggar sees it, just because feminists fault traditional approaches to ethics for not being concerned about women's interests does not mean that they wish to ignore men's interests. On the contrary, most feminists would be "morally outraged"[69] by any such suggestion. They would insist that ethics is concerned about everyone's interests.

Moreover, they would insist that when traditional ethics neglected such "women's issues" as "the availability or otherwise of child care and abortion,"[70] it actually neglected not only *women's* but *men's* issues. Childbearing and childrearing practices and policies affect men's as well as women's lives. Jaggar also insists that just because feminists wish to stress the point that women are moral agents capable of developing bona fide ethical approaches does not mean that feminists believe that women are "moral experts whose moral authority is beyond question."[71] Neither does it mean that feminists believe that each and every "feminine" value is superior to each and every "masculine" value or that all women, just because they are women, share precisely the same set of moral experiences.

Feminist approaches to ethics are less susceptible to sexism than traditional approaches to ethics for another reason, however. They do not attempt to be neutral. They specify whose interests they are considering and why, and they gladly admit their "biases" to their critics. As many feminists see it, by exposing their personal perspectives to their critics, they open themselves up for criticism voluntarily. It is easier, after all, to criticize a person or group that reveals its heartfelt thoughts to others than it is to criticize some sort of impartial, objective, neutral spectator whose very *lack of humanity*—of specificity and particularity—serves to ward off any and all criticisms. Just because an approach to ethics is gendered does not mean it is sexist. An approach to ethics becomes sexist only when it systematically excludes the interests, identities, issues, and values of one or the other of the two sexes.

Criticism Two

Some critics complain that feminist ethics sounds too much like communitarian ethics, which also emphasizes the importance of community for individuals' well-being. Both approaches, after all, reject the ontological and epistemological assumptions that privilege a separate, atomistic self over a connected and relational self. In fact, some critics insist that there is no real difference between these two approaches to ethics. Conceding that both feminists and communitarians object "to how the individual is privileged over the needs and interests of the community in the essentially liberal conception of social contract theories,"[72] Sherwin emphasizes that the communitarian understanding of the self-other relationship is ultimately very different from the feminist understanding of this relationship.

Communitarian theories insist that impartialism burdens the self and does not leave enough time to pursue the needs of specific relationships. If we must treat everyone with equal respect, consideration, and moral attention, how can we justify spending time on our own personal goals or with our loved ones? Impartiality may undercut community by making us shortchange the very ties that supposedly create and maintain community. Yet, despite the fact that the communitarian message about human relationships seems feminist on the surface, its deeper structure may be nonfeminist. Not all women find family life meaningful. Indeed, some women find its rituals, routines, and requirements impediments to their self-development. What distinguishes a feminist approach to ethics, then, from a communitarian approach is its total commitment to overcoming men's domination, oppression, and exploitation of women.[73] As wonderful as community ties can be, they must be severed if it turns out that they are either strangling women or tying them up in knots.

Criticism Three

To the extent that feminist approaches to ethics are indeed feminist—that is, focused on female subordination and male domination—critics claim that they are not so much *ethical* approaches as *political* agendas. Of course, the split between ethics and politics is a product of the same worldview that split the mind from the body, reason from the emotions, and the self from the other, and so it is not clear whether feminists should feel badly when told that they are blending ethics and politics.

In ancient times, ethics and politics were virtually indistinguishable. There were no distinctively political institutions to reconcile with ethical beliefs, practices, and standards. The formula for the good person was the formula for the good society. For example, in Plato's *Republic,* an isomorphic relationship exists between the virtues of the individual (wisdom, courage, temperance, and justice) and the virtues of the city. If all individual souls are rightly ordered, then society is rightly ordered, and vice versa. Plato's ideal state is a society that has no political problems as we know them. Similarly, Aristotle's world is an amalgam of ethical and political considerations. For him, ethics and politics are two aspects of a single path leading to human good. When Aristotle claims that human beings are political animals, he means that the distinctively human life—the life that marks us off from beasts and gods—is a life lived among fellow citizens, partners in virtue and friends in action. Such a life cannot be lived, however, in a society that fails to exercise practical reasoning because of an excessive, or even exclusive, reliance on technical reasoning; for the aim of technical reasoning is to control things and persons, while the aim of practical reasoning is to liberate persons, to let them engage in those activities that will serve their best interests.

In marked contrast to the classical tradition stands the modern tradition. The good of the community becomes separate from that of the individual; politics comes to be understood as the process through which each person seeks to secure his or her own particular good—to do his or her "own thing." Even as the individual splits from the community, ethics splits off from politics; then technical reasoning eclipses practical reasoning. As a result, politics is increasingly viewed as hostile to ethics—as a matter of invidious power plays.

To say that feminist approaches to ethics are "political" in the modern sense of the term, then, is to say something decidedly negative. It gives the impression that women are fighting against men to gain control over them—to have their own way, no matter what. But to say that feminist approaches to ethics are "political" in the classical sense of the term is to say something quite different. It is to say that feminists pay attention to issues of power because in so doing they liberate themselves and others. Politics is indispensable to ethics in the sense that only an empowered person has the capacity to *self-reflectively* make this a better world. Only free persons can be moral persons.

CONCLUSIONS

Clearly, feminist approaches to ethics have a different set of goals than feminine and maternal approaches to ethics. Whereas feminine and maternal approaches tend to focus more on retrieving women's "feminine" values from the netherworld of patriarchal neglect, feminist approaches tend to focus on criticizing these values to determine whether they add to or subtract from women's oppression. A feminist approach to ethics is always interested in issues of power—specifically, male domination and female subordination—and it always seeks to provide women with action guides that will lead to women's liberation from oppression, suppression, and repression.

As difficult as it is to distinguish feminine and maternal approaches to ethics from feminist ones, it may be even more difficult to explain what distinguishes a lesbian approach to ethics from a feminist one. In the next chapter, we will seek to explore the relationships between feminine, maternal, feminist, and lesbian approaches to ethics, noting that many lesbian approaches to ethics differ in fundamental ways from feminist as well as feminine and maternal approaches to ethics. Like feminist ethicists, most lesbian ethicists believe that feminine and also maternal approaches to ethics come dangerously close to reinforcing women-oppressing ideas. In particular, lesbian ethicists reject the icon of the self-sacrificing mother as a fitting paradigm for moral relationships in a patriarchal, oppressive society, embracing instead the image of the daughter and/or the Amazon. But lesbian ethicists do not confine their words of criticism to "feminine" and "maternal" thinkers. On the contrary, many lesbian ethicists believe that *feminist* ethicists do not go far enough in their critique of traditional approaches to ethics. Because most feminist ethicists tend to affirm some relationships with men, they have accommodated men's as well as women's "good" in their ethical approaches. In contrast, because most lesbian ethicists do not think that it is *their* responsibility to develop a universally applicable ethics, they make many controversial claims, including the claim that what is good for lesbians is not necessarily good for heterosexual women—let alone men.

What we will notice in the next chapter is that if it was difficult to justify to traditional ethicists a "politicized" feminist ethics, it will be even more difficult to justify a "separatist" lesbian ethics to them. How particular may the focus of an ethics get before it is no longer an ethics? Are feminist and lesbian approaches to ethics challenging the very *meaning* of ethics? If so, should we fear or welcome this transformation?

NOTES

1. Carol Gilligan, *In a Different Voice* (Cambridge, Mass.: Harvard University Press, 1982), 92.
2. Nel Noddings, *Caring: A Feminine Approach to Ethics and Moral Education* (Berkeley: University of California Press, 1984), 89–96.
3. Sara Ruddick, *Maternal Thinking: Towards a Politics of Peace* (Boston, Mass.: Beacon Press, 1989), 72–73.
4. Ibid., 74–75.
5. Susan Sherwin, *No Longer Patient: Feminist Ethics and Health Care* (Philadelphia: Temple University Press, 1992), 52–53.
6. Ibid., 54.
7. Alison M. Jaggar, "Feminist Ethics," in Lawrence Becker with Charlotte Becker, eds., *Encyclopedia of Ethics* (New York: Garland, 1992), 363–364.
8. Ibid., 363.
9. Alison M. Jaggar, "Feminist Ethics: Projects, Problems, Prospects," in Claudia Card, ed., *Feminist Ethics* (Lawrence, Kans.: University of Kansas Press, 1991), 85.
10. Barbara Ehrenreich and Frances Fox Piven, "The Feminization of Poverty," *Dissent* (Spring 1984), 162–170.
11. Jaggar, "Feminist Ethics," 364.
12. Ibid.
13. Jaggar, "Feminist Ethics: Projects, Problems, Prospects," 90.
14. Ibid., 88.
15. Ibid., 90.
16. Jaggar, "Feminist Ethics," 361.
17. Ibid.
18. Ibid., 366.
19. Ibid., 367.
20. Sheila Mullett, "Shifting Perspectives: A New Approach to Ethics," in Lorraine Code, Sheila Mullett, and Christine Overall, eds., *Feminist Perspectives: Philosophical Essays on Method and Morals* (Toronto: University of Toronto Press, 1988), 109.
21. Ibid., 114.
22. R. M. Hare, *The Language of Morals* (New York: Oxford University Press, 1964), 1–16, 155–158.
23. Mullett, "Shifting Perspectives: A New Approach to Ethics," 115.
24. Ibid., 116.
25. U.S. Congress, Office of Technology Assessment, *Infertility: Medical and Social Choices,* OTA-BA-358 (Washington, D.C.: U.S. Government Printing Office, May 1988), 205–207.
26. Sherwin, *No Longer Patient: Feminist Ethics and Health Care,* 133–134.
27. Ibid.
28. Mullett, "Shifting Perspectives: A New Approach to Ethics," 117.
29. Richard T. Hull, ed., *Ethical Issues in the New Reproductive Technologies* (Belmont, Calif.: Wadsworth, 1990), 92.
30. Sherwin, *No Longer Patient: Feminist Ethics and Health Care,* 135.

31. Robyn Rowland, "A Child at Any Price," *Women's Studies International Forum* 8, no. 6 (Great Britain: Pergamon Press, 1985), 540.

32. Sherwin, *No Longer Patient: Feminist Ethics and Health Care*, 50.

33. Catharine A. MacKinnon and Andrea Dworkin, Minneapolis, Minn., Ordinance amending Chs. 139 and 141, Minneapolis Code of Ordinances Relating to Civil Rights (December 30, 1983).

34. Ibid.

35. Sherwin, *No Longer Patient: Feminist Ethics and Health Care*, 60.

36. Kathryn Casey, "Women and Pornography," *Ladies' Home Journal* 109, no. 8 (August 1992):117, 175–177.

37. Sherwin, *No Longer Patient: Feminist Ethics and Health Care*, 62.

38. Ibid., 65.

39. Ibid., 62.

40. Ibid., 67.

41. Ibid., 69.

42. Leonard J. Kouba and Judith Muasher, "Female Circumcision in Africa: An Overview," *African Studies Review* 28, no. 1 (March 1985):105–109.

43. Sherwin, *No Longer Patient: Feminist Ethics and Health Care*, 71.

44. Ibid.

45. Ibid.

46. Ibid., 75.

47. Annette C. Baier, "What Do Women Want in a Moral Theory?" *Nous* (March 1985):57.

48. Ibid.

49. Ibid.

50. Ibid.

51. Ibid., 60–61.

52. Annette Baier, "Trust and Antitrust," *Ethics* 96 (January 1986):235.

53. Ibid.

54. Ibid.

55. Ibid., 238.

56. Ibid., 245.

57. Ibid., 241.

58. Ibid.

59. Ibid., 245.

60. Ibid.

61. Ibid., 248.

62. Baier, "What Do Women Want in a Moral Theory?" 61.

63. Virginia L. Warren, Ph.D., "Feminist Directions in Medical Ethics," *Health Care Ethics Committee Forum: An Interprofessional Journal on Healthcare Institutions' Ethical and Legal Issues* 4, no. 1 (1992):20.

64. Ibid.

65. Ibid., 21.

66. Ibid., 22.

67. Jaggar, "Feminist Ethics," 364.
68. Ibid., 363–364.
69. Ibid., 365.
70. Ibid.
71. Ibid.
72. Sherwin, *No Longer Patient: Feminist Ethics and Health Care,* 54.
73. Ibid.

9

Lesbian
Approaches to Ethics

To the degree that feminist approaches to ethics focus on issues of power, they are more political in character than feminine and maternal approaches to ethics. If a practice, rule, or virtue contributes to female subordination and male domination, feminists will label it "harmful," "wrong," or "immoral." To be sure, critics of feminist approaches to ethics believe that there is something fundamentally misguided about a "political" approach to ethics that specifically attends to *women's* issues, interests, and virtues. Because these critics dismiss the claim that traditional approaches to ethics have presented *male* moral concerns as *human* moral concerns, they reject the explanation that a feminist focus on women's morality is a compensatory mechanism, not a privileging mechanism. As a result, they view feminist approaches to ethics as an outright attempt to discredit, discount, or otherwise disregard men's moral concerns. Rather than conceding that feminist approaches to ethics might lead to a more inclusive moral vision—that is, one that accommodates male and female moral concerns equally—these critics prefer to dismiss feminist approaches to ethics as partisan politics.

Like feminist approaches to ethics, lesbian approaches are subject to the charge of "female bias." Because lesbian ethics is typically defined as "ethical inquiry with the object of defining conditions of well-being for women-loving women,"[1] and because their standpoints are ordinarily identified as "those of feminist women whose primary, passionate, connections are with women,"[2] critics complain that lesbian ethics is even more narrow in its scope than feminist ethics. Indeed, they insist that whereas feminist approaches to ethics focus on *all* women's moral concerns to exclude men, lesbian approaches to ethics focus on *some* women's moral concerns to exclude heterosexual women as well as men.

In this chapter, we will examine Mary Daly's, Janice Raymond's, and Sarah Lucia Hoagland's lesbian approaches to ethics to determine whether their moral vision is, in fact, "exclusionary" in any pejorative sense of the term. Although other lesbian ethicists such as Andrea Dworkin, Adrienne Rich, Joanna Russ, Julia Penelope (Stanley), Susan Griffin, Marilyn Frye, Jeffner Allen, Joyce Trebilcot, Jacqueline Zita, and Maria Lugones[3] have developed equally interesting lesbian approaches to ethics, Daly's, Raymond's, and Hoagland's works constitute a representative introduction to lesbian thought. By focusing solely on women-loving women's moral concerns, these three writers challenge the very nature and function of morality. Not only do they suggest that an ethics does not have to speak to everyone in order to be an ethics, they proclaim that freedom, rather than goodness, is lesbians' ultimate moral concern.

MARY DALY ON TRANSVALUATING MORAL VALUE

In *Gyn/ecology: The Metaethics of Radical Feminism,* Mary Daly transcends the limits of traditional ethics and even of many feminine, maternal, and feminist approaches to ethics. Her work is not written to appease the patriarchs but to heal the women.

> The Journey of this book, therefore, is . . . for the Lesbian Imagination in All Women. It is for the Hag/Crone/Spinster in every *living* woman. It is for each individual Journeyer to decide/expand the scope of this imagination within her. It is she, and she alone, who can determine how far, and in what way, she will/can travel.[4]

Daly's work speaks to the "Female Self" in all women, whether they sexually define themselves in terms of women or not. The path to female consciousness is a long one. Each woman makes her own progress as she struggles to escape patriarchy. Lesbianism is much more than a definition of one's sexual orientation or sexual preference. It is a way of life, of thinking; it is woman-centered existence. As Daly sees it, to be moral a woman must escape from the patriarchy that refuses to acknowledge her true identity. She must "spin" free of everything the patriarchs have said about her, including what they have said about her "goodness"/"evilness."

Daly concedes that it is difficult for a woman to escape patriarchy—especially its conceptual scheme. The woman who would be a "Spinster"—that is, a woman "who has chosen her Self, who defines her Self, by choice, neither in relation to children nor to men, who is Self-identi-fied"[5]—must forget about traditional ethics. Instead she must question the very concepts of "good" and "evil" that have guided ethics to date. Daly's metaethics—that is, her reflections on the conceptual building blocks of any and all ethical systems—bears no resemblance to tradi-tional metaethics, which she describes as "masturbatory meditations by ethicists upon their own emissions."[6] Daly's metaethics focuses pre-cisely on what these meditations have supposedly omitted/"emitted"—namely, women's well-being and freedom.

In exhorting women to come to life (a resurrection of sorts), Daly calls on spinsters to free themselves not only from socioeconomic and political oppression but also from linguistic repression. Daly urges women to reject the language and meanings that ground all traditional approaches to ethics and also those feminine approaches to ethics that embrace the value of care unreflectively. Whereas Christians extol the life/martyrdom/death of saints in *hagiography,* Daly celebrates the life/ creation/spinning of Hags in *hag-ography.* To patriarchs, Hags are scary demonesses, nightmares, evil spirits. To Spinsters, Hags are examples of "strength, courage and wisdom."[7] Christian martyrs die in masochis-tic ways (hardly a good role model for women), but Hags live, create, spin, and soar. As Daly sees it, Spinsters recognize that it is good, not bad, to be *haggard,* for as originally defined, the word *haggard* meant "an intractable person, especially: a woman reluctant to yield to woo-ing."[8] Haggard women are blessed among women because they refuse to assume the bonds of marriage and motherhood, preferring to create their own Selves.

Self-creation is women's primary moral responsibility, but women who fail to create themselves should not be blamed for their failure. The patriarchs use labels such as *sick, selfish,* or *sexless*[9] to strike fear into the hearts of women who would be Spinsters—especially women who would be Hags. If a woman does not see "the totality of the Lie which is patriarchy,"[10] she will react to the imposition of these labels "by becoming mindlessly 'moral,' murderously 'selfish,' moronically 'sexy.'"[11] She will, in short, do everything she can to become and stay "good"—that is, pleasing to the patriarchs. Only if other women who have already seen the "Lie" raise her consciousness will she be able in-stead to please her self.

Self-creation is an arduous task requiring women to forge their own moral pathways. Nevertheless, Daly believes that women can use some of the lessons of traditional ethics for their own purposes. She points to the work of St. Thomas Aquinas, the medieval theologian, who defined the passions as "*movements* of a faculty known as the 'sensitive appetite,' which tends toward the good and shrinks from the evil as perceived by the senses."[12] There are, said the saint, six basic passions: love, desire, and joy, which move people toward whatever is good; and hate, aversion, and sorrow, which move people toward whatever is evil. In addition, there are five other passions—hope, despair, fear, daring, and anger—which help people struggle to acquire whatever is good and/or to avoid whatever is evil. As Daly sees it, the advantage of St. Thomas's analysis is that women can use it as a tool to *name* the causes and objects of their feelings. Love, desire, joy, hate, aversion, sorrow, hope, despair, fear, daring, and anger are "movements, verbs . . . e-motions connecting one's psyche with others and with the external world."[13]

In contrast to the real passions listed above, Daly identifies two groups of pseudopassions: what she terms "plastic passions" and "potted passions."[14] Unlike real passions, plastic passions do not serve to connect and integrate women; on the contrary, they make women feel disconnected and fragmented. Because plastic passions lack specific causes and/or objects, they tend to generate "free-floating feelings"[15] in women. Because all of these amorphous feelings are negative—guilt, anxiety, depression, hostility, bitterness, resentment, frustration, boredom, resignation, and fulfillment—their overall effect is to make women miserable.

Although women always feel these plastic passions, they cannot always name them. For example, when Betty Friedan wrote *The Feminine Mystique*, she wanted to name the problem middle-class American housewives had but could not articulate. Eventually, she decided that these "happy" housewives were dying of "fulfillment." From Daly's perspective, Friedan's diagnosis is right on target: a "fulfilled" woman is a "finished" woman.[16] She has no potential to actualize. She is over and done with: "a stuffed container, her condition being comparable to that of a wild animal that has been shot and stuffed."[17] In contrast to fulfilled women, feminists are unfulfilled; they are dynamic, always-on-the-go, human persons who can name the source of their passion. They are the kind of women who refuse to go on guilt trips or to confess sins they never committed.

Another poor substitute for real passions, the potted passions, are, in Daly's estimation, "less than they should be."[18] They are the bonsai trees in the forest of virtue. Because bonsai trees look like real trees— that is, trees that grow naturally rather than artificially—some people believe that bonsai trees *are* real trees, only smaller. Analogously, because bonsai virtues—that is, potted passions—look like real virtues, some women believe that they *are* real virtues, only smaller. Unfortunately, potted passions lead women astray, directing them to love the wrong people or to be angry at the wrong people. They cause daughters, for example, to blame their woes on their mothers, as if their fathers, sons, and/or husbands were in no way responsible for their plight.

Of all the plastic and potted passions that poison women, Daly believes that guilt inflicts the most harm on them. Guilt erodes women's moral core; it undermines women's real passions, their "Pure Lust,"[19] and it causes women either to betray and abandon each other or to expect too much in the way of support from each other. When a woman abandons another woman who needs her, for example, it is usually not that she intends to hurt that other woman. Rather, it is that she intends to avoid the guilt she will feel if she chooses to minister to a woman rather than to a man; for in this culture men come first. The "original sin" of being born female, says Daly, is women's "birthwrong" of no self-esteem,[20] and until women learn to esteem themselves, the only passions they will feel are the potted and plastic ones—the ones that keep them loyal to men.

Daly wants women to become genuinely virtuous so that they can become truly passionate. Given her penchant (and talent) for coining new words, one would think that Daly would be particularly eager to rename the word *virtue.* Surprisingly, she prefers to retain this word—perhaps for old times' sake. Daly concedes, however, the problematic nature of women using the patriarchal word *virtue* to denote the good habits they should cultivate. When Virgins—that is, "never captured: UNSUBDUED women"[21]—begin to "exhume [virtue] from the graveyards of phallic ethics,"[22] they will discover that it "reeks of reversals"[23] and that it can be used to oppress women. Moreover, they will discover that the "virtues" patriarchy has assigned them are not their *Virgin* virtues—that is, their real virtues. Men have stolen women's Virgin virtues, their original graces, and claimed them as their own. The *female* "virtues" of "obedience, humility, patience, long-suffering, purity"[24]—of "vanity, frivolity, triviality, weakness, etc."[25]—are not women's true virtues. On the contrary, women's true virtues are the supposedly *male* virtues of "emotional strength and independence, forcefulness, dynamism, decisiveness, coolness, objectivity, assertiveness, courage, integrity, vitality, intensity, depth of character, grooviness, etc."[26] When Virgins begin to reclaim their true virtues back from men, however, men will describe

them as aggressive, strident, hard-hearted, mean-spirited—as full of
"*vice*. . . . meaning 'moral depravity or corruption. . . . WICKEDNESS.'"[27]
Virgins must not take such name calling to heart, for it is one of the
patriarchs' "deadliest devices,"[28] intended to make women feel badly
about themselves. Thus, Virgins' best path to resistance is to wear labels like *vicious* as badges of honor.

Daly reinterprets many traditional virtues, among them the *intellectual* virtue of prudence and the *moral* virtues of justice, courage, and
temperance. Traditional ethicists define prudence as "practical wisdom," or "right reason about things to be done."[29] Supposedly, prudence enables a person to find the mean or point of moral balance between immoral excess on the one hand and immoral defect on the
other—for example, courage is the mean between the excess of foolhar-
diness and the defect of cowardice. So habituated is the prudent person
to doing the right thing at the right time, that s/he is able to do so spontaneously, without even thinking about it.

What disturbs Daly about the traditional presentation of prudence,
however, is precisely its celebration of the ability to act virtuously in a
nonreflective manner. Convinced that women cannot safely be moral
unless they continually ask themselves questions about the wisdom of
their being moral, Daly encourages women to challenge the "virtuous-
ness" of any virtue society tells them to cultivate. To be sure, women
who keep asking "Why should I be moral?"[30] will be castigated as ob-
noxious children who do not know better than to stop asking "Why?"
But unless women ask themselves why they should be "moral," they will
mistakenly and repeatedly cultivate those "virtues" that make them, always, the obedient handmaidens of patriarchy's conventions.

In addition to reinterpreting the traditional intellectual virtue of prudence, Daly reinterprets the traditional moral virtues of justice, courage, and temperance. Traditional ethicists define justice as "the per-
petual and constant will to render to each one his right."[31] The pronoun
his is not an accidental slip in justice's definition. Historically, women
have been the ones who have had difficulty acquiring their rights. The
group that Daly names the "Boys Club" have been so preoccupied with
their own "petty paternal disputes"[32]—their justices and injustices—that
they have failed to notice the women petitioning outside their doors.

Daly suggests that women move from men's justice to women's
Nemesis. She reminds us that "unlike 'justice,' which is depicted as a
woman blindfolded and holding a sword and scales, Nemesis has her
eyes open and uncovered—especially her Third Eye."[33] Nemesis is less

concerned with punishing rule-breakers than with helping oppressed people overcome the causes of their oppression. Rather than contrasting "female" caring with "male" justice, Daly forwards Nemesis as the appropriate foil for the kind of "justice" that bolsters an oppressive status quo. A caring born of sweet reasonability is not the appropriate antidote for the kind of justice that "is indeed *blind* to racism, sexism, war, and poverty";[34] rather, a Nemesis born of "Rage"[35] is the proper medication.

Another traditional moral virtue that Daly reinterprets is courage. She notes that the word *courage* is derived from *cor,* the Latin word for heart, and it is women's "heart"—their sentiments, feelings, and emotions—that is "at the very core/'heart' of the maze of reversals"[36] from which women must seek their exit. Patriarchal society has told us that woman is the heart and that man is the head in order "to legitimate women's condition of subjection as entombed in the touchable caste."[37] Thus, women should not believe men when they extol the feminine virtues of the heart as somehow better than the masculine virtues of the head, for most men actually regard women's traits as just so much "mush-headed sentimentality requiring control by The Head."[38]

Daly urges women to reunite their hearts to their heads in an act of courage. She claims that:

> It is only by Taking Heart again, by Courage-ing the Sin of reuniting her passion and intellect, that a woman can Realize her powers. Pyrosophical Crones, wrenching the Heart back into our own semantic context, make Courage the core of Women's Movement.[39]

For Daly, "Taking Heart" is the quintessential task of feminists. She cites with approval Elizabeth Cady Stanton's admonition that "Better, far, suffer occasional insults or die outright, than live the life of a *coward,* or never move without a protector."[40] By "Taking Heart" courageous women "Give Heart"[41] to women who have yet to put their heads and hearts together. Because courage is quite contagious, men seek to tame, sap of energy, or otherwise subdue "trouble-making" courageous women. From men's point of view, one courageous woman is bad enough; a society of courageous women is a disaster.

Finally, Daly reinterprets the moral virtue of temperance, a virtue that came to be associated with women partially as a result of the nineteenth-century Women's Temperance Movement. To suggest that this movement was entirely focused on men's alcohol abuse is, in Daly's estimation, to trivialize its significance. The Women's Temperance Movement was more about fighting violence against women and children than about "teetotaling." Indeed, as Daly sees it, today's feminist antipornography campaign is a close analogue to yesterday's Women's Temperance Movement, since, like its predecessor movement, it is much more interested in preventing harm to women than in moralizing about the sins of the flesh.[42]

In an attempt to distinguish her kind of temperance from traditional temperance, Daly does a complete etymology of the word *temperance*. She notes that its source is the Latin word *temperare*, which means "to mix, blend, regulate."[43] As they struggle to become whole persons, women stir up and then combine together all the elements of their lives. This process of stirring—of mixing, blending, and regulating—can get very messy, however. Women who "temper" themselves cannot expect to emerge from patriarchy with their hair in place and makeup unsmeared. They will emerge, if they emerge at all, says Daly, as "Pyromantic" women[44] who burn their bridges behind them with the passionate flame and energy of the Female Self. From the vantage point of patriarchy, then, temperate women are very distemperate, "out of order,"[45] trouble-making women whose stirring motions make far too many waves.

JANICE RAYMOND ON A FEMALE FRIENDSHIP APPROACH TO ETHICS

Much of what philosopher Janice Raymond has to say resonates with Mary Daly's message, but she focuses especially on the role that female friendship plays in women's moral lives. Raymond does not limit female friendship to women who have sexual relations with other women. Women who have sexual relations with men, as well as women who have sexual relations with other women, are able to put other women first; the former as well as the latter women can perceive that the world of "hetero-reality"[46]—Raymond's term for "patriarchy"—does not regard women as intrinsically valuable or as interesting enough to befriend.

So oblivious is hetero-reality to women's value that it has a hard time seeing women who are not somehow linked to men.[47] Most women laugh knowingly when Lily Tomlin tells her joke about the man who comes up to a group of women sitting *together* in a bar and asks them why they are sitting *alone*. Women without men are invisible women. Yet, as women realize all too well, female invisibility is not a laughing matter. It causes many women, as well as most men, to view women as nothing more than men's appendages: ancillary beings whose meaning depends on the identities of the men to whom they are attached. Raymond refers to a review of existentialist Simone de Beauvoir's book *Adieux: A Farewell to Sartre* to make her point. The reviewer comments that with or without de Beauvoir, Sartre would still have been Sartre, the great philosopher, for "His life followed its own trail and its own logic."[48] De Beauvoir, on the other hand, would not have been nearly as great a philosopher without Sartre. Implying that women do not have their own "trail" and "logic," the reviewer suggests that de Beauvoir's philosophy is merely derivative of Sartre's.

As Raymond sees it, however, the world does not have to be seen through men's eyes; it can be seen through women's eyes. She contrasts "hetero-relations," her term for any and all "affective, social, political, and economic relations that are ordained between men and women *by men*,"[49] with "Gyn/affection," her term for all passionate relationships between women—be they sexual or nonsexual. Gyn/affection is "the state of influencing, acting upon, moving, and impressing, and of being influenced, acted upon, moved, and experienced by other women."[50]

Truly Gyn/affective relationships differ, for example, from the kind of female relationships, especially mother-daughter relationships, that Dorothy Dinnerstein and Nancy Chodorow describe in their major works *The Mermaid and the Minotaur* and *The Reproduction of Mothering,* respectively. Following Freud to some degree, both Dinnerstein and Chodorow believe that girls' transition to "normal"—that is, heterosexual—adult sexuality differs dramatically from that of boys. The boy's first love object is a woman, his mother. If all goes "well," his love objects will continue to be women, and the primary source of his boyhood sexual gratification—the penis—will continue to be the primary source of his adult sexual gratification. Like the boy, the girl's first love object is also a woman, her mother. But if all goes "well" in her case, the girl will have to switch from loving a woman to loving a man, and she will also have to change her erotogenic zone from the masculine clitoris to the feminine vagina.[51]

Dinnerstein observes that because mothers and daughters are symbiotically related, and because daughters realize that they will ultimately share their mother's fate of rejection, daughters find it difficult to relinquish to a man "love that rightly and originally belonged to a woman."[52] Chodorow makes the same point even more forcefully. She claims that girls *never* really stop loving their mothers (and/or mother figures)—not even after they get married. Marriage represents only "final commitments of genital object choice"[53] and not "final and absolute commitments to heterosexual *love*, as emotional commitment."[54]

In Raymond's estimation, both Dinnerstein and Chodorow fail to appreciate the women-loving potential of their own remarks about the mother-daughter relationship. So oriented are they toward heterosexuality that neither of them considers seriously the thesis that love, including sexual love, between women is what is really normal—that were it not for patriarchy's demands, girls might not relinquish their mothers (and/or mother figures) for men. Raymond laments that, just as what Adrienne Rich termed the "institution of compulsory heterosexuality"[55] is weakening, Dinnerstein's and Chodorow's proposals for dual parenting, are likely to strengthen it.[56]

On the surface, dual parenting seems like a feminist project. After all, have not women wanted men to help with the children—to spend more time with them? Dinnerstein and Chodorow claim that were men and women to co-parent, children would not make their mothers their first love object but would instead make both their mothers and their fathers their first love objects. As Raymond sees it, however, the problem is not that children identify primarily with their mothers—nor is it that women do most of the parenting. Rather, it is that women parent on men's terms. Were girls blessed with mothers who made women, not men, their first priority, "Gyn/affection would become a prevailing reality."[57] Mothering/parenting would be fun—and not the burden that it has become for women under patriarchy.

Raymond claims that although hetero-reality relies for its justification on the myth that man and woman are two halves that need to be joined together, it actually operates on the assumption that woman is for man, but not vice versa. According to Christian theology, for example, woman is *"ontologically* for man."[58] She was formed for him, and she cannot survive without him. Her destiny and desire are to sate him; her essence and existence are only in relation to him. Man, however, is only *"accidentally* for woman."[59] Because man's destiny and desire is to build empires not with women but with other men, the "secret" that structures hetero-relational culture is man's *homo-relational* identity—he is *of* men and *for* men: "Hetero-reality is the foil for homosexuality."[60]

Raymond emphasizes that hetero-relations and hetero-reality are much more than a matter of *sexual* relations between men and women. In and of themselves, such relations do not cause women's oppression. Rather, the worldview that woman is for man harms women. As

Raymond sees it, hetero-relations, broadly conceived to include economic, political, and social intercourse as well as sexual intercourse, "give men constant access to women and have consistently transformed the worlds of women into hetero-reality."[61] Because men feel a need to exert control over women at all times, they seek to regulate all of their thoughts and actions. Beginning in the nineteenth century, for example, male obstetricians started to take over the birthing process from midwives and female relatives. Raymond claims that the current trend toward "natural" childbirth is the latest development in this takeover, springing much less from a desire to get women bonded with their babies than from a desire to get men included in the birthing process. Even as she gives birth, woman's role is played down.[62]

In this connection, a "Saturday Night Live" skit comes to mind. Two young couples are discussing the one couple's new baby, and finally the one couple offers to show a videotape of the birth. Once the tape is placed in the VCR though, we realize that the *mother* filmed the *father* as she gave birth. We watch from between her legs as the father and the doctor wave. When she goes through some contractions and the camera wobbles, her husband yells at her to keep the picture in focus. The other couple is enthralled. When the other woman (who is pregnant) suddenly goes into labor, the first couple runs to get the camera and shows the pregnant woman how to use it. The scene closes as they all rush to the hospital, the mother filming the father all the way. Now obviously this is a satire—yet satire mocks and criticizes through exaggeration and ironic humor situations that actually occur. The skit paints in all too painful detail Raymond's point about why fathers might want to participate in natural childbirth: Even as the woman struggles to bring new life into the world, the man wants center stage.

So normal does hetero-reality seem to women, that women forget the far greater freedom and benefits of Gyn/affection, which is woman-centered, not man-centered. Gyn/affection occurs "where women turn to their Selves and others like their Selves for empowerment rather than once more seeking help from men."[63] Hetero-reality limits women's growth as feminists, since it causes women to equate success with making it in a man's world. In order to achieve full liberation, women must stop defining their Selves in terms of men's selves. Instead, women must define their Selves and goals in terms of women. As Raymond sees it, feminism is not about women becoming men's equals but about women rediscovering their identities, their powers, their bonds. Any "feminism" that fails to recognize that female friendship is both "a foundation for and a consequence of feminism"[64] cannot succeed.

Raymond believes that the sine qua non for friendship between women is Self-love—the kind of Self-love that is born from thinking. When a woman thinks, she discovers that she is her own best friend and that she can have more friends than just her Self:

> Through thinking, a person discovers that she can be her real Self. In discovering this, she also realizes that the conversation that took place in the duality of thinking activity—that is, the duality of "myself with myself," the "two-in-one," or "the one who asks and the one who answers"—enables conversation with others. When I discover, through thinking, that I can converse with my real Self, I have to realize that such a conversation is possible with others. This is the awakening of female friendship in which the search for others like my Self begins.[65]

In suggesting that female friendship plays an essential role in women's moral lives, Raymond's purpose is not to idealize female friendship, however. Rather, she strives to fight against a misogynist culture that causes women to be indifferent to each other or even to hate each other. Women have been stereotyped as their own worst enemies, as catty creatures incapable of deep relationships with one another.

Admittedly, there are many obstacles to female friendship in a hetero-real world where pleasing *men* is of great importance. Raymond names three in particular: "dissociation from the world," "assimilation to the world," and "victimization in the world."[66] Women can dissociate from the world in one of two ways: a "worldless" way or a "worldly" way.[67] What Raymond objects to is women's *worldless* dissociation from the world. If women abandon the public world for fear of getting their hands dirty, their retreat is imprudent as well as irresponsible. Women can and should play a decision-making role in the public world, for if they do not, men will shape that world to serve men, not women. Women who seek to seclude themselves in a private Epicurean garden of delights misunderstand what Gyn/affection is. Love between women is not merely "a personal matter";[68] it is the source of women's "political power."[69] Gyn/affective women may choose to dissociate themselves from the public world, but when they do so, they do so in a *worldly* manner—that is, in order to gather the strength they need to transform the public world.

Raymond connects *worldless* as opposed to *worldly* dissociation from the world with two syndromes that weaken female friendship: "therapism," or "the tyranny of feelings," and "relationism," or "the tyranny of relations."[70] Therapism forces women to reveal all of their inner feelings to other women, as if there are no secrets too private to share with anyone. As Raymond sees it, however, there is a real difference between forced confessions that pander to people's prurient interests on the one hand and "genuine self-revelation"[71] on the other. When nosy questions take the place of mutual sharing, friendship is cheapened. "Navel-gazing"[72] replaces the kind of "hunger for truth, beginning with the truth of each other"[73] that characterizes close friendships.

Like therapism, relationism is a cheapening of friendship; it is "the reduction of friendship to relationships that get constantly 'examined' and 'dealt with.'"[74] So focused does a woman become on having relationships, that she surrenders her Self unconditionally to anyone who seems even slightly interested in her. In Raymond's estimation, however, others should not be the focus of a woman's life—be these others men *or* women. Rather, the center of a woman's life ought to be her Self. Women who do not have a strong Self—who depend on others for whatever weak Self they are able to hold together—tend to fall apart when their relationships end.

As large an obstacle as dissociation from the world is, it is no larger than what Raymond regards as the second major obstacle to female friendship: assimilation to the world. The "assimilationist woman," says Raymond, is the one who "disidentifies consistently with women."[75] She tries to fit in with "the boys"; to laugh at their sexist jokes; and even to condone their oppression of women. Or she asserts that she is not a feminist, despite the fact that her accomplishments reflect "unconventional capabilities, courage, determination, and persistence."[76] Or she proclaims how sexually liberated she is, even though she says "yes" to sex when she would prefer to say "no."

"Assimilationist women" sometimes claim that "sisterhood" requires women to affirm whatever any woman freely chooses to do in her bedroom simply because she is a woman. As Raymond sees it, however, enforced toleration of anything and everything is simply a form of tyranny. In the name of female friendship, women should not be badgered and bullied into celebrating, for example, either heterosexual or lesbian sadomasochism. Not all sexual practices are necessarily good—even if *women choose* to engage in them. Some of them are bad—especially the ones that mirror the most demeaning and debasing aspects of stereotypical male domination and female subordination. Women need to cultivate what Raymond terms the "virtue of discernment" in order to distinguish between good and bad sexual relationships—and, for that matter, between good and bad female friendships.

The third and final obstacle to female friendship is victimization in the world. Raymond insists that it is a mistake for women to focus only on their experiences of oppression, ignoring their experiences of empowerment: "The range of feminist theory needs to be expanded beyond women's subordinate relation to men to include women's sustaining relations with women."[77] The history of Gyn/affection is about more than women being oppressed and violated by men; it is also about women finding enough courage and strength in their Selves to fight on behalf of women. Women need to develop a philosophy of Gyn/affection, a theory of empowerment even in the face of oppression, suppression, and repression. Women may not be able to control their oppressors—but they can control their Selves.

SARAH LUCIA HOAGLAND ON A FEMALE AGENCY APPROACH TO ETHICS

Sarah Lucia Hoagland, perhaps even more than Raymond and Daly, writes for lesbians. Although she does not insist that what she has to say will be of interest to lesbians only, she admits that heterosexual women fit into her ethical scheme somewhat awkwardly:

. . . they fit in exactly the way lesbians fit in heterosexual society. We fit there, but not as lesbians. Heterosexual women can fit here, though not as heterosexual women—that is, not as members of the category "woman."[78]

Hoagland asks lesbians to begin a moral revolution and to create new moral values. Indeed, as she sees it, women's agency in an oppressive heterosexual society is crucially linked with a lesbian existence. Women must plant in this male-centered society the liberating idea that women can survive without men, that women can survive by themselves. The existence of lesbians proves that this liberating idea of independent women is a reality. Lesbians' survival as lesbians defies heterosexuality's "rules," demonstrating women's ability to overcome the demoralizing effects of what is usually described as patriarchal conditioning.

Hoagland refuses to define the term *lesbian* because to do so requires using heterosexualism as the "norm" and lesbianism as the "aberration." Instead she simply invokes a "lesbian context,"[79] setting that context against heterosexuality. For Hoagland, heterosexuality is about much more than male-female *sexual* intercourse. It is patriarchy, that is, an entire way of life based upon male domination and female subordination:

> The relationship between women and men is considered in anglo-european thought to be the foundation of civilization. I agree. And it normalizes that which is integral to anglo-european civilization to such an extent that we cease to perceive dominance and subordination in any of their benevolent capacities as wrong or harmful: the "loving" relationship between men and women, the "protective" relationship between imperialists and the colonized, the "peace-keeping" relationship between democracy (u.s. capitalism) and threats to democracy. I believe that unless heterosexualism as a way of relating is undermined, there will always remain in social conscience concepts which validate oppression.[80]

Lesbians must challenge—indeed undo—this entire relational framework. Lesbianism is not just a sexual choice; it is a way for women to live as moral agents.

A "female agency" approach to morality differs greatly from a "feminine principle" approach to morality.[81] In an attempt to find a beacon of goodness in the sea of moral corruption that surrounds them, women often turn to the "feminine virtues" of altruism and sacrifice. Although these "feminine virtues" constitute a welcome relief from male pursuit of power and privilege, they are in Hoagland's estimation a trap for women in male-dominated society:

> Under modern phallocratic ethics, virtue is obedience and subservience, and the virtuous are those who remain subordinate (accessible). The function of phallocratic ethics—the master/slave virtues—has been to insulate those on top and facilitate their access to the resources of those under them.[82]

Women succumb to the lures of phallocratic ethics because the "virtues" identified as "feminine" seem important for a more compassionate world. If women do not do the caring, who will? Nonetheless, Hoagland cautions against the current trend to develop feminine approaches to ethics. She sees Noddings's ethics as one that confines female agency to the pursuit of the other's good, and she regards Gilligan's ethics as uncritically celebrating women's capacity for relationships.

Hoagland develops in detail Claudia Card's critique of Gilligan, which applies to any ethics of care. Card urges women to ask themselves why they struggle so hard to maintain their relationships, especially their relationships with men. She suggests that women have been taught that unless they are able to maintain their relationships, they will be miserable indeed. Rape and violent crimes against women, says Card, support a kind of "protection racket" that makes women accessible to men: The message sent is "Hey, honey, let me control and possess your body and I'll stop other men from doing the same thing." As Card notes, "A major task of rape is the subordination and subservience of women to men."[83] Fear of abuse by many men causes women to accept abuse from one "protector." Better an abusive relationship with one man than no relationship at all, for a woman "alone"—that is, a woman without a male guardian—is vulnerable to attack on all sides. Women's fears benefit men by giving them access to and domination over women. As Card comments, "Rackets *create* danger to sell 'protection.'"[84] Women quickly learn that they must sometimes do whatever it takes to get one man—lie, cheat, manipulate. Anything seems better than the alternative of terror and domination by multiple men.

Hoagland pushes this dark picture even further and argues that what currently passes for women's self-sacrifice is often a form of women's self-interest. Women put the needs and desires of men ahead of their own needs and desires because they need men to benefit them—or at least not to harm them. Is, then, the battered wife to be condemned for her "selfishness"—that is, for being so "self-interested" that she caters to her abusive husband's whims to avoid his wrath?[85] So obvious is the answer to this question that it scarcely seems worth asking. Yet, as Hoagland sees it, terms like *self-interest* and *self-sacrifice* (or *selfishness* and *altruism*) can be twisted and turned every which way until a woman begins to think that, yes, it is "selfish"—that is, wrong—for her to do what she has to do.

To challenge this befuddling state of affairs, Hoagland advises lesbians that the kind of selfishness truly hostile to the moral project has little, if anything, to do with their desire to survive the adversities they are likely to encounter in a hetersexual society. Best termed "egocentrism,"[86] the kind of selfishness that Hoagland condemns is the perception that the world and all its agents revolve around one's self—that others are defined only in terms of their relation to one's self. Egocentrists believe that their good is the only good.

Lesbians who suffer from "egocentrism" should not try to overcome their moral myopia by seeking to define themselves exclusively in terms of others, however. Moving from placing one's self to placing others at the center of the universe is hardly an improvement. Lesbians must resist the idea that moral choice is a zero-sum game. Either I get my way or you get yours. In particular, lesbians must resist the feeling that every moment they spend on themselves is a moment they could have spent on others, or vice versa. Such a feeling is destructive. Soon one is able to enjoy neither one's time alone nor one's time with others; no matter what choice one makes, the grass looks greener on the other side.

Hoagland urges lesbians to stop thinking that the time they spend on political work rather than on work around their home, or the time they spend with troubled friends rather than on self-improvement projects, is an act of *self-sacrifice*. On the contrary, it is an act of *self-creation*.

> That I attend certain things and not others, that I focus here and not there, is part of how I create value. Far from sacrificing myself, or part of myself, I am creating; I am weaving lesbian value.[87]

When a woman makes a decision, or chooses something, she is not sacrificing or losing anything. Rather, she is creating and embracing options that were not available before. Her choices expand, rather than limit, her possibilities.

When women come to understand that choice is not punitive—that it is self-creative rather than self-destructive—they begin to realize that heterosexual society has offered women a "choice" that is not really a choice and that one "choice" has been self-sacrifice—particularly that form of self-sacrifice termed "mothering." Defined as "unconditional loving, as a matter of selflessly protecting and nurturing all life,"[88] mothering is not really a choice for women; instead, it is their destiny. Just as cutting is a knife's function, mothering is supposedly a woman's function, a "fact" that Hoagland denies. As she sees it, the statement "Mothering is women's function" is a *value* masquerading as a *fact*. Women can do many more things than mother; their functions are multiple. It is men who have decided that women's function is mothering, for mothering maintains the kind of social structure that best serves men's interests. Indeed, it permits men the time and space they need for their choices—that is, their self-creative activities.

Hoagland states that if she had to name a single function for women, it would be "amazoning."[89] Amazoning is women's creative energies set free from the restrictions of heterosexual society; it is lesbianism. Nevertheless, not only heterosexual women but many lesbian women insist on channeling their creative energies into mothering for a variety of reasons, including the reason of wanting "to work on the next generation."[90]

Although Hoagland concedes that mothering is one of the things a lesbian might choose to do, she still thinks that, given the patriarchal burdens that mothering continues to bear, lesbians (and also heterosexual women) should note that they may be able to accomplish through amazoning what they have yet to be able to accomplish through mothering, namely, "appropriate atmosphere for children, self-esteem for girls, caring, room to grow and flourish."[91]

Among the traps that ensnare mothering women is the ideal of unconditional love, the ultimate stereotype of which is the black mammy. From the point of view of those who benefited from her exploitation, the black mammy's greatest "virtue" was that she passively and faithfully served her white masters. Indeed, she fit the sexist/racist ideal of the slave who loves her master, giving everything and receiving very little, if anything, in return.[92] Saddened by the image of the black mammy, Hoagland rejects the ideal of unconditional love in the name of all the women who give too much and receive too little. She observes that when women equate self-sacrifice with virtue and try to act accordingly, a misguided desire to *control* enters their relationships: "For if we do not perceive ourselves as both separate and related, we will be off-center and forced to control or try to control the arena and those in it in order to retain any sense of agency, of ability to act."[93] To the degree that a woman's identity depends on another person, she may try to control that person's actions and choices. Viewing her whole life as unidirectional, unconditional self-sacrifice, a mother may get caught up in the apparent "success" (in patriarchal terms) of her daughter, for example. She may cease to engage in any projects of her own, relentlessly living her life through her daughter, interpreting every one of her daughter's "failures" as her own failure. Such unconditional "love" only promotes continued oppression and undermines female agency.

Choice limited to self-sacrifice causes women to live their lives vicariously and, ironically, selfishly—that is, egocentrically. Self-sacrifice, unconditional love, and altruism give rise to negative female agency:

> The feminine virtues, virtues which accrue to the less powerful, are developed as strategies for manipulating and gaining control in a relationship of dominance and subordination. When self-sacrifice and altruism—rather than self-understanding—are regarded as prerequisites for ethical behavior, control—rather than integrity—permeates our interactions.[94]

The rationale of the feminine virtues is such that they impede women's effort to be moral: to achieve a positive female agency based on self-understanding that balances the self's desire to be both a separate and a related individual.

Hoagland confesses that, originally, she was not interested in discussing morality. In fact, she refused to discuss ethics, since feminist philosophers are usually assumed to be interested only in ethics. In an act of resistance, Hoagland chose instead to explore feminist approaches to ontology and epistemology; she raised questions about the nature of reality and about the possibilities for knowledge. Then Hoagland was invited to give a weekend workshop on lesbian ethics that involved ideas central to all lesbian lives: power, sabotage, survival, and support. She realized that ethics is "not simply a matter of the boring old male question of whether women should have equal rights."[95] At last convinced that ethics *is* crucial to lesbian self-understanding, Hoagland wanted to explore the field further.

Conceding that lesbians are not perfect human beings, Hoagland notes that lesbians, as well as heterosexual women, must concern themselves with ethics. However, lesbians must resist the lure of a traditional ethics that searches for universal and absolute standards (rules, principles, laws, norms) to guide everyone's conduct. When such standards are named, they give their adherents a measure of false certitude about *the* Good, causing them to stop thinking about what they themselves believe is good. As Hoagland sees it, traditional ethics is a means of social control, the function of which is to inculcate the "antagonistic . . . values of dominance and subordination" and undermine "individual moral ability and agency."[96] In contrast, lesbian ethics is about making choices under oppression. Choices allow lesbians to weave "lesbian meaning,"[97] to develop as moral agents—as selves who are both separate and in relation.

Leaving behind "autonomy," which stems from the Greek words for self (*auto*) and rule (*nomos*), Hoagland creates the concept of "auto-koenony,"[98] which stems from the Greek words for self (*auto*) and community (*koinonia*). To the degree that lesbian interactions do not mirror heterosexual relations of domination and submission, they serve as catalysts for developing a self that is communally related to other selves. Although a lesbian cannot always control the situations in which she finds herself, she is not necessarily doomed to fall victim to these situations. Telling the oppressed that they are total victims does not help them or excuse them; it merely robs them of what little moral agency remains in their hands. Even when the oppressed cannot control situations, they can still *affect* them:

> In focusing on choice and moral agency, I mean to invoke lesbian ability to engage, to act in situations—that we move here now makes a difference. And I mean to suggest that whatever limits we face, our power—ability and agency—lies in choice.[99]

Ethics is not about some people making rules for other people to follow. Instead it is about making choices no matter what the constraints of one's situation.

Hoagland observes that her ethics constitutes a threat to traditional ethics. The very idea of a specifically lesbian ethics denies the relevance of heterosexuality's principles: its purported right to judge everyone on the basis of "universal" criteria. Being a lesbian is not just a sexual orientation; it is a refusal to be defined either sexually or morally through and by men. Rather than striving to discover an approach to ethics that resembles traditional ethics, lesbians must forge their own moral path and start walking down it, even if they are not certain where it leads. To transcend the bounds of heterosexual society and its ethics, however, lesbians must withdraw from heterosexual society. The only way to stop being dominated is to refuse to be subordinated—to leave the scene of the crime, as it were.

CRITICISMS OF LESBIAN ETHICS

As Claudia Card notes, lesbian approaches to ethics are to be distinguished from feminine and maternal approaches to ethics on the one hand and from feminist approaches to ethics on the other. Lesbian ethicists regard feminine and/or maternal approaches to ethics as generally "conservative for women,"[100] that is, as espousing types of caring—especially maternal caring—that contribute to women's oppression. It is not that lesbian ethicists do not value caring. They do. It is just that they insist that lesbians should engage in the kind of caring that is not bogged down in the quicksand of a sense of duty and obligation from which there is no escape. Comments Hoagland:

> The concepts of "duty" and "obligation" do not represent lesbian connection. Obligation does not measure lesbian caring and network. Duty is not the essence of our connection, nor is it the reason we are lesbians. Lesbians do not come together out of duty, nor does obligation hold us together as

lovers, friends, collectives, or community. And neither duty nor obligation will hold us together over time in a way that we become an energy field capable of resisting oppression.

I am suggesting that duty and obligation are not part of Lesbian Ethics. And I am also suggesting that caring, while not the sort of energy that can be forced or guaranteed, nevertheless comprises the heart of lesbian connections.[101]

Caring is not about meeting imposed responsibilities; it is about "look(ing) forward to each other's company."[102]

Similarly, it is not that lesbian ethicists do not value mothers. It is just that they insist that "daughter ethics" is preferable to "mother ethics."[103] Not only does the former ethics signal the obvious—namely, that whereas all women are daughters, only some women are mothers—it also does not presume that all women *should* childbear, childrear, or even babysit.

Like feminine and maternal approaches to ethics, feminist approaches tend to view a relatively wide "range of relationships with men as potentially ethically acceptable, even within a patriarchal society."[104] In contrast, lesbian approaches to ethics manifest a strongly separatist element as a legitimate, if not ideal, moral choice. Comments Hoagland:

> We may withdraw from a particular situation when it threatens to dissolve into a relationship of dominance and subordination. And we may withdraw from a system of dominance and subordination in order to engage in moral revolution.[105]

Although lesbian ethicists believe that heterosexual women, and even men, can, and perhaps should, learn from their approaches to ethics, they do not believe it is their responsibility to share their insights with men or, less certainly, with heterosexual women. Rather, they believe it is their calling to weave lesbian values, leaving it to nonlesbians to create their own meanings and values.

Those who take issue with lesbian approaches to ethics have focused primarily on its separatist tendencies. Their criticisms usually take one of two forms: (1) It is neither feasible nor desirable for lesbians to separate themselves from men, let alone heterosexual women; and (2) it is misguided for lesbian ethicists to develop an ethics for lesbians only, thereby conveying the impression, intentionally or unintentionally, that lesbians are "better" than heterosexual women. Additionally, these same critics have sometimes claimed that (3) lesbian approaches to ethics are not so much guides to moral action, as manuals for self-improvement.

Criticism One

Joan Cocks is among the critics who view separatism, be it lesbian or nonlesbian, as morally irresponsible. As she sees it, there are two ways that women can separate from men's world, neither of which is unproblematic. The first way is the *reformist* way. Some women believe that, provided that women remain among women in their private hours, they will be able to reform men's world—that is, the world of ecological chaos, nuclear disaster, technological excess—without becoming part of that world and its mindset. Insofar as this belief is based on the assumption that women are "purer" than men—that is, less susceptible to the siren calls of power, prestige, and financial gain than men—Joan Cocks criticizes it as naive, as the latest reinstantiation of Catherine Beecher's version of the separate virtue theory.[106]

Realizing that there is no sure way not to be affected by patriarchy unless one separates from it completely, some separatists simply refuse to have anything to do with men's world. Their way is the way of *rejection*. Joan Cocks believes that this separatist path is both unfeasible and undesirable. Total withdrawal from men's world is *unfeasible* unless women are willing to downscale their life-style considerably, to lead a very simple and bucolic life. No matter how much women cooperate, pooling their resources and talents, they will not be able to replicate—at least not for a long time—the positive features of patriarchy. Total withdrawal from men's world is *undesirable* because in severing all their connections to men's world, women come dangerously close to abandoning their social responsibilities. Perhaps envisioning separatists as withdrawing into some sort of Epicurean garden of delights, or haven in a heartless world, Joan Cocks comments that "Insulated from issues of class conflict, racial strife, and international upheaval, feminism's grappling with the personal as political promises to degenerate into an absorption with the personal as personal."[107] The woman who really cares about all women's oppression, and not simply her own, will not leave the public world to its own devices—not if most of her sisters are living their lives and dying their deaths in that world. To do so is to act in a morally nonresponsible manner.

As Joan Cocks interprets separatism, it does seem like a morally irresponsible, as well as pragmatically burdensome, mode of behavior. However, there is reason to believe that her interpretation of separatism does not represent an adequate understanding of its fundamental goals. Joan Cocks objects to what Raymond faulted as women's *worldless* dissociation from the world.[108] Raymond criticized this kind of separatism because it increases rather than decreases women's vulnerability to men. She claimed, for example, that the separatism of worldless dissociation

> is usually accompanied by a "downward mobility" of mind and of money. It often creates an apathy toward political, intellectual, and financial existence as well as an apathy toward one's physical appearance which becomes a symbol of one's disregard for the man-made world. It behaves as if money and status are things that women already have (or could have if they wanted), can easily discard and can easily replace. It calls upon "patriarchy as excuse" to rationalize the inactions of not getting a job, not going to school, not taking economic and professional strides, that would locate a woman in the "real" world.[109]

She also claimed that this kind of separatism drives women toward what she termed "therapism,"[110] the tendency to spend one's every waking moment analyzing one's personal relationships, and/or self-improvement projects as if nothing in the universe were of greater significance.

Having described the separatism of worldless dissociation so negatively, Raymond found it easy to condemn. However, unlike Joan Cocks, Raymond defends that form of separatism, or dissociation from the world, she terms "worldly." Indeed, Raymond believes that it is *necessary* "for women to live 'on the boundary' of hetero-relational society."[111] She urges heterosexual women, as well as lesbians, to become like Virginia Woolf's "insider outsiders."[112] The insider-outsider woman remains within hetero-relational society, despite the fact that she is critical of that society and intent on ultimately disestablishing it. Because she works in man's world, the insider-outsider woman is familiar with men's modus operandi, and, therefore, she is less likely to be taken advantage of by men. She is also in a position to transform man's world—to engage in feminist work there, the kind of work that Raymond believes has already had a "profound impact on the man-made world, changing, for example, the face of patriarchal legislation, health care, and learning, as well as creating more women-centered and institutional structures."[113] Far from being morally irresponsible—that is, self-indulgent—Raymond believes that women's *worldly* dissociation from hetero-reality constitutes a paradigm for moral responsibility.

Although some separatists agree with the kind of distinctions Raymond makes, other separatists wonder whether women really ought to try to be insider-outsiders in man's world. In the end, the better course may be for women to *try* to be outsiders as much as possible, even if they cannot remain entirely outside of man's world.[114] At stake in this disagreement among separatists is what constitutes the necessary preconditions for lesbians (and perhaps also heterosexual women) becoming moral. Hoagland believes that the more physical as well as psychological space lesbians can clear between themselves and heterosexual society, the more opportunities they will have to create lesbian values. She observes that heterosexualism "de-skills a woman, makes her emotionally, socially, and economically dependent, and allows another to dominate her 'for her own good' all in the name of 'love.' "[115] Described as such, heterosexualism is clearly not good for a woman. Thus, it would seem that not only lesbians but also heterosexual women cannot risk remaining inside heterosexualism—that is, inside "the balance between male predation upon and masculine protection of a feminine object of masculine attention."[116] For women to remain inside of the system is for them to deliberately stymie their own moral growth.

All things considered, lesbian separatism is not that different from the choice nuns and monks make to remove themselves from "the world" so that they can weave the value of holiness. Nor is it that different from the choice any group of people makes who seek to spend as much time as possible with each other—and as little time as possible with others—so that they can weave whatever values they find meaningful. Admittedly, the sounds of the relativism-absolutism debate begin to be heard at this point. From the perspective of Sherwin's feminist relativism, for example, lesbians' value weaving is very different from the Ku Klux Klan's value weaving. What makes the former separatist project morally worthy and the latter one morally unworthy is that in removing themselves from heterosexualism, lesbians help erode a system of domination and subordination that has impeded the moral development of the victims of not only sexism but also imperialism, colonialism, and ethnocentrism. The same cannot be said for the Ku Klux Klan's separatist project, the goal of which is to victimize those from whom it holds itself not only *separate* but *superior*. The raison d'être of the Klan is to dominate and subordinate.

Criticism Two

Related to the first criticism of lesbian approaches to ethics is the criticism that these moral pathways are biased against heterosexual women. Some critics claim that implicit, if not explicit, in many lesbian approaches to ethics is the argument that unless a woman tries to distance herself as far as possible from men, she is violating her moral duties to herself by denying herself the opportunity to become her own person rather than a man's appendage. The woman who would be moral—in the Greek sense of a fully integrated person—must, in other words, stop loving men and start loving women, sexually as well as emotionally. In sum, lesbianism is the condition of the possibility of women's being moral agents.

Although some lesbian ethicists may believe that women must refrain from relations with men, especially sexual relations with men, in order to be moral, most lesbian ethicists do not make this strong claim. Rather, they claim that, in order to be moral, women have to refrain from *oppressive* sexual relations, with women as well as men. Raymond makes the point, for example, that just because a woman has sexual relations only with women does not mean that she is a fully morally developed person. She comments that:

> hetero-relations can function quite smoothly in the lives of lesbians who merely "commit" lesbian sex acts or in the lives of women who make of lesbianism a lifestyle. Hetero-relations can function, more specifically, in lesbian role-playing, in lesbian S & M, in the lesbian objectification of other women, or in the lives of lesbians who act in a woman-identified way in Lesbian circles but who, in their work or social lives, for example, act the part of the hetero-relational woman.[117]

Although heterosexual women may find it harder than lesbians to stop relating to other people as either dominates or subordinates, lesbians' ability to overcome this demoralizing style of human relationships should not be "romanticized."[118]

Raymond's realistic assessment of lesbian sexuality reminds us that the goal of lesbian approaches to ethics is not converting heterosexual women to lesbian sexuality. Rather, these moral perspectives want to celebrate the advantages of a gyno-centric life. Although there is considerable debate within the lesbian community about whether heterosexual women as well as lesbian women can lead a fully gyno-centric life, there is generally openness within the lesbian community to heterosexual women. Still, lesbians do not deny either that there are differences between them and heterosexual women or that lesbian approaches to ethics are primarily concerned about what is *good for lesbians*.

For example, Raymond thinks that women who focus their attentions or energies primarily on women are not necessarily what she terms *Lesbians* (capitalized), that is, women who deliberately choose politically aware, woman-to-woman relationships that usually include, though they are certainly not confined to, genital sexual relations. It disturbs her that, in forwarding her ideas about a "lesbian continuum," Adrienne Rich, for example, insists that all "woman-identified" women—regardless of their sexual preference—are situated on it.[119] Raymond regards Rich's desire to broaden the term *lesbian* "to embrace many more forms of primary intensity between and among women, including the sharing of a rich inner life, the bonding against male tyranny, the giving and receiving of practical and political support"[120] as a serious dilution of what it means to be a Lesbian. Raymond does not label as "Lesbian" a heterosexual woman who works tirelessly on behalf of women's reproductive freedom, or even a lesbian woman who chooses another woman as her long-term sexual partner and living companion but who refuses to "publicize" or "politicize" her choice. Rather, she labels them "Gyn/affected" women—women who have affinities for women and/or who struggle on behalf of women. All Lesbians are Gyn/affective women, but not all Gyn/affective women are Lesbians.

Although Raymond's distinctions between Lesbianism and Gyn/affection provide heterosexual women and nonpolitical lesbians with an excuse not to wear the label "Lesbian," not everyone agrees that it is morally appropriate to provide women who are not Lesbians with this escape mechanism. Card points out that even Gyn/affected women can suffer from "Lesbophobia"—that is, the fear of women being more than friends, of loving each other erotically though not necessarily sexually. Thus, it is vital that heterosexual women and nonpolitical lesbians situate themselves on Rich's lesbian continuum not only to express their sisterly support for Lesbians but also to overcome their Lesbophobia. Lesbianism may, after all, be the condition of the possibility for women's full moral development in the sense that a woman cannot respect, esteem, admire, and love others for who they are unless she can publicly respect, esteem, admire, and love herself for who she is: a woman. When women come to realize how ordinary their physical and psychological attractions to each other are, they will be able to wear the label "Lesbian" comfortably.[121]

Criticism Three

The last criticism, not that it is always intended as a criticism, is that lesbian ethics is not really an ethics. As Marilyn Frye sees it, the need for ethics tends to arise among people who have a vested interest "in being good and/or in others' being good."[122] For example, a white, Christian, middle-class, American bases his conception of himself as a "judge, teacher/preacher, director, administrator, manager, and in this mode, as a decision maker, planner, policymaker, organizer"[123] on his conviction that he is in the right—that he knows what is good for himself and others. As long as women continue to accept this "male" conception of moral agency, they have one of two choices: (1) to become men so that they can exert *men's* moral authority over others or (2) to become female moral authorities who then make it their business to exert *women's* moral authority over others.

That Frye should regard both of these options as unacceptable is not surprising. The first option forces women to negate themselves, and the second sends women down the same moral blind alley that men have gone. If ethics is about some people not only proclaiming to other people what is "good" for them but imposing that "good" on them, then it is doubtful, in Frye's mind at least, whether what lesbians are approaching is *ethics* as it has traditionally been conceived. Frye comments that the only people who need what has been known as ethics are those "situated just so in culture, economy, and history."[124] Those who have a vested interest in the status quo—in the powerful remaining powerful—are precisely the people who require certitude about their righteousness—about their warrant to "direct" and "administer" everything.[125] But because lesbians do not want this kind of power—because they appreciate what immoralities it generates—they require neither proof of their "goodness" nor the "right" to impose it on anyone but themselves. Thus, it is doubtful that lesbians need ethics.

Careful reflection on Frye's words enables us to appreciate just how different lesbian approaches to ethics are from traditional approaches to ethics. Given that lesbian ethicists tend to emphasize the concept of freedom more than the concept of the good, their work bears some resemblance to so-called "existentialist ethics." Like the existentialists Jean-Paul Sartre and Simone de Beauvoir, many lesbian ethicists claim that ethics is not about moral agents following divinely and/or humanly imposed rules and regulations but about moral agents creating their own values. In particular, Hoagland emphasizes that the very act of choosing gives meaning to lesbian existence. Realizing that lesbians are not always free to make precisely the choices they want to make, Hoagland is concerned with specifying lesbians' freedom to make choices "from where we stand—as finite beings who will die (who will end this life) and who live within the boundaries of a finite world as well as under significant restrictions, including oppression."[126] When lesbians assess their daily life, situation, abilities, and limitations—and then *choose* to do or not do something—this is freedom; this is the creation of values; this is ethics.

Created values stand in contrast to discovered or revealed values. There is no universal Good to pronounce judgment on the "goods" that lesbians choose. Does this mean, then, that any choice a lesbian makes, no matter how trivial, is of moral consequence? Or does it mean instead that lesbians are subject to the same criticism that has been directed against existentialists in the past: namely, that "if choosing freely for oneself is the highest value, the free choice to wear red socks is as valuable as the free choice to murder ones' father or sacrifice yourself for one's friend"?[127]

To those queries Hoagland has no definitive answer, except to remind us that so many limitations and boundaries have been imposed on lesbian choice that perhaps for now choice *is*, in and of itself, more important than the things chosen. Still, Hoagland does not mean to suggest, nor is there anything in her lesbian approach to ethics that suggests, there are no limits on lesbian choice. At one point in her analysis of what constitutes moral agency and interaction, Hoagland notes that de Beauvoir believes that "to be ethical . . . we must not only embrace our own freedom and create value through our choices, we must also choose the freedom of others."[128] Later, in the course of the same analysis, Hoagland continually affirms that in choosing for herself, a lesbian chooses for other lesbians, who in turn choose for her. Lesbians do not weave value in isolation from each other; they weave value together. Ethics is not an individualistic quest; moral value does not emerge from somewhere deep within one's self or from far outside of one's self. On the contrary, moral value—that is, meaning—emerges from what Hoagland terms "lesbian context," or "an energy field capable of resisting oppression."[129] A lesbian approach to ethics is about lesbians becoming beings "who are not accustomed to participating in relationships of domination and subordination." Insofar as these last named relationships are a very bad thing, what heterosexual women and men can learn from a lesbian approach to ethics is what Hoagland and other lesbian ethicists—Maria Lugones in particular—term "playfulness,"[130] that is, "our ability to travel in and out of each other's world."[131] In fact, Hoagland believes that playfulness is the essence of a lesbian approach to ethics—a welcome relief, I suppose, to the deadly and deadening seriousness of many traditional approaches to ethics. In Hoagland's estimation, emphasis on playfulness—on "adventure, curiosity, desire"[132]— "seems to take the power out of [traditional] ethics, of being able to make each other behave; ethics ceases to be a tool of control."[133] What ethics becomes instead is an open question, the answer to which may emerge only when lesbians—and other playful souls—have had time to weave enough tapestries of meaning. One thing is certain, however; lesbian approaches to ethics do demand that we rethink the nature and function of morality itself.

NOTES

1. Claudia Card, "Lesbian Ethics," in *Encyclopedia of Ethics*, Lawrence Becker with Charlotte Becker, eds., II (New York: Garland, 1992), 693.
2. Ibid.
3. Ibid.
4. Mary Daly, *Gyn/ecology: The Metaethics of Radical Feminism* (Boston: Beacon Press, 1978), xiii.
5. Ibid., 3–4.
6. Ibid., 13.
7. Ibid., 15.
8. Ibid.
9. Ibid., 20.
10. Ibid.
11. Ibid.
12. Mary Daly, *Pure Lust: Elemental Feminist Philosophy* (Boston: Beacon Press, 1984), 198.
13. Ibid., 200.
14. Ibid.
15. Ibid.
16. Ibid., 204.
17. Ibid.
18. Ibid., 206.
19. Ibid., 215.
20. Ibid., 216.
21. Ibid.
22. Ibid., 261.
23. Ibid.
24. Ibid., 262.

25. Valerie Solanas, *SCUM Manifesto*, with an introduction by Vivian Gornick (New York: Olympia Press, 1967, 1968, 1970), 7.
26. Ibid.
27. Daly, *Pure Lust,* 263.
28. Ibid.
29. Ibid.
30. Ibid., 264.
31. Ibid., 274.
32. Ibid., 275.
33. Ibid.
34. Ibid., 278 (emphasis mine).
35. Ibid., 279.
36. Ibid., 280.
37. Ibid.
38. Ibid., 281.
39. Ibid.
40. Ibid.
41. Ibid.
42. Ibid., 287.
43. Ibid., 287.
44. Ibid., 115.
45. Ibid., 288.
46. Janice G. Raymond, *A Passion for Friends: Toward a Philosophy of Female Affection* (Boston: Beacon Press, 1986), 3.
47. Ibid.
48. As quoted in ibid., 4.
49. Ibid., my emphasis.
50. Ibid., 7–8.
51. Sigmund Freud, "Femininity," in Sigmund Freud, *The Complete Introductory Lectures on Psychoanalysis,* James Strachey, trans. and ed. (New York: W. W. Norton, 1966), 580.
52. Dorothy Dinnerstein, *The Mermaid and the Minotaur: Sexual Arrangements and Human Malaise* (New York: Harper Colophon Books, 1977), 65.
53. Nancy Chodorow, *The Reproduction of Mothering* (Berkeley: University of California Press, 1978), 140.
54. Ibid.
55. Adrienne Rich, "Compulsory Heterosexuality and Lesbian Existence," *Signs: Journal of Women in Culture and Society* 5 (1980):648.
56. Raymond, *A Passion for Friends,* 52.
57. Ibid., 53.
58. Ibid., 10.
59. Ibid.
60. Ibid.
61. Ibid., 11.
62. Ibid., 11–12.

63. Ibid., 13.
64. Ibid.
65. Ibid., 222.
66. Ibid., 153, 164, 181.
67. Ibid., 154.
68. Ibid., 155.
69. Ibid.
70. Ibid., 155, 161.
71. Ibid., 156.
72. Ibid., 159.
73. Ibid.
74. Ibid., 161.
75. Ibid., 164.
76. Ibid., 165.
77. Ibid., 22.
78. Sarah Lucia Hoagland, *Lesbian Ethics* (Palo Alto, Calif.: Institute of Lesbian Studies, 1989), 8.
79. Ibid.
80. Ibid., 7–8.
81. Ibid., 82.
82. Ibid.
83. Claudia Card, "Rape as a Terrorist Institution," in R. G. Frey and Christopher W. Morris, eds., *Violence, Terrorism, and Justice* (Cambridge, Mass.: Cambridge University Press, 1991), 299.
84. Ibid., 304.
85. Hoagland, *Lesbian Ethics*, 87.
86. Ibid., 89.
87. Ibid., 91–92.
88. Ibid., 93.
89. Ibid., 94.
90. Ibid., 97.
91. Ibid., 94.
92. Ibid., 98, see Bell Hooks's quotation.
93. Ibid., 99.
94. Ibid., 100.
95. Ibid., 9.
96. Ibid., 12.
97. Ibid.
98. Ibid.
99. Ibid., 13.
100. Card, "Lesbian Ethics," 694.
101. Hoagland, *Lesbian Ethics*, 284.
102. Ibid., 280.
103. Card, "Lesbian Ethics," 694.
104. Ibid.

105. Hoagland, *Lesbian Ethics,* 54–55.
106. Joan Cocks, "Worldless Emotions: Some Critical Reflections on Radical Feminism," *Politics and Society* 13, no. 1 (1984):37.
107. Ibid.
108. Raymond, *A Passion for Friends,* 154.
109. Ibid.
110. Ibid., 155.
111. Ibid., 154.
112. Ibid., 232.
113. Ibid., 234.
114. Claudia Card, "Female Friendships: Separations and Continua," *Hypatia* 3, no. 2 (Summer 1988):128.
115. Hoagland, *Lesbian Ethics,* 67.
116. Ibid.
117. Raymond, *A Passion for Friends,* 14.
118. Ibid.
119. Ibid., 16.
120. Rich, "Compulsory Heterosexuality and Lesbian Existence," 648.
121. Card, "Female Friendships: Separations and Continua," 128.
122. Marilyn Frye, "A Response to *Lesbian Ethics:* Why Ethics?" in Claudia Card, ed., *Feminist Ethics* (Lawrence, Kans.: University Press of Kansas, 1991), 53.
123. Ibid., 54.
124. Ibid.
125. Ibid.
126. Hoagland, *Lesbian Ethics,* 203–204.
127. Mary Warnock, *Existentialist Ethics* (London: MacMillan, 1967), 54.
128. Hoagland, *Lesbian Ethics,* 205.
129. Ibid., 241.
130. Maria Lugones, "Playfulness, 'World'-travelling, and Loving Perception," *Hypatia* 2, no. 2 (Summer 1987):13.
131. Hoagland, *Lesbian Ethics,* 246.
132. Ibid.
133. Ibid.

10

Conclusion

To a greater or lesser extent, feminine, maternal, feminist, and lesbian approaches to ethics are reshaping the contours of traditional approaches to ethics. As we have seen, this process of transformation is not entirely a contemporary development. In the eighteenth and nineteenth centuries, thinkers such as Mary Wollstonecraft, John Stuart Mill, Harriet Taylor, Catherine Beecher, Charlotte Perkins Gilman, and Elizabeth Cady Stanton raised questions about "women's" and "men's" morality, debating whether morality is or is not gendered.

The results of their speculations were quite mixed. Wollstonecraft, Mill, and Taylor vociferously objected to any form of the separate virtue theory, according to which women have different moral values and character traits than men. What they tended *not* to notice, however, was that the virtues they most often classified as worthy of all human beings usually had a strong "masculine" flavor. Wollstonecraft, for example, was particularly insistent on the relationship between rationality and morality. She went as far as to suggest that women had to suppress their feelings—their female "emotionality"—in order to act in recognizable moral ways. The more a woman thinks and acts like a man, the better chance she has to develop as a moral agent.

In contrast to Wollstonecraft, Mill, and Taylor, thinkers such as Beecher and Gilman not only underscored the ways in which women's moral identities and behaviors differed from men's, they celebrated women's virtues as being at least as good as men's virtues. In fact, Beecher and Gilman manifested some separatist tendencies based on the suspicion that men's moral values were not quite as good as women's. As long as society accords women's moral world the same respect and admiration it accords men's moral world, they believed there was no need to combine women's and men's moralities. On the contrary, to the degree that society is relying on women to be more moral than men, it is better that women remain separate from men, as they did in *Herland*.

Finally, Stanton stressed that although women's traditional virtue of benevolent self-sacrifice is necessary for society to survive, let alone thrive, she emphasized that women are not obligated to always practice this virtue any more than men are. Under certain circumstances, a woman's duty to develop herself takes precedence over her duty to be "good" to others—to contribute to their happiness and to foster their perfection. One's own self is no less important than anyone else's.

Clearly, all these early thinkers and others like them set the stage for today's "feminine" and "maternal" thinkers to discuss whether "women's ethics" is indeed one of *care* and "men's ethics" one of *justice* and to debate whether women's traditional role as childbearers and child-rearers—that is, as mothers—has caused women, but not men, to think "maternally." Rather than denigrating the "feminine" characteristics of nurturing, caring, compassion, benevolence, kindness, and the like as soft and sentimental virtues for weak and vulnerable people, proponents of feminine approaches to ethics have shown how demanding—physically, psychologically, and spiritually—it is to be a caring person. Care demands no less in the way of integrity, commitment, and heroism than justice. Similarly, rather than dismissing the mother child relationship as a mindless, thoughtless, "natural" symbiosis, proponents of maternal approaches to ethics have argued that this largely non-voluntary relationship between unequals is a more realistic paradigm for human relationships than the kind of legalistic, formalistic contracts that consenting adults enter into deliberately, consciously, and presumably equally. Because most of our morally significant human relationships are more like mother-child relationships than business partnerships, traditional ethicists have misled us by judging relations mainly in terms of how they serve our best interests.

Whatever the appeal of twentieth-century feminine and maternal approaches to ethics may be, they have not gone unchallenged; however, nonfeminist critics have argued that "feminine" approaches to ethics are not *new*—that is, that many traditional approaches to ethics encompass a "care" as well as a "justice" perspective without making what amounts to unsubstantiated gender claims. "Justice," say these critics, is no more the prerogative of men, than "care" is the prerogative of women. For example, George Sher claims that Carol Gilligan's contrast between women's approach to morality—an approach that is supposedly concrete, nonprincipled, personal, care-driven, and responsibility

oriented—and men's approach to morality—an approach that is supposedly abstract, principled, impersonal, duty-driven, and rights oriented—is a distinction that traditional ethicists such as Kant and
Schopenhauer have already made. Comments Sher: "The opposition of
concrete and abstract, personal and impersonal, duty and care are not
empirical discoveries but generic determinants of the moral problematic."[1] The opposition of care and justice, say such critics, is nothing
new under the moral sun.

Unlike their nonfeminist counterparts, feminist critics do think that
feminine approaches to ethics are *new*—that Gilligan and Noddings
are, indeed, speaking in a different voice. Moreover, they do not dismiss the hypothesis that men's and women's moral perspectives differ
at least at the level of norms and symbols if not also at the level of empirical fact. Even if some men actually value their communal relationships more than their personal rights, and even if some women actually
value justice more than caring, Western culture does seem to associate
traits like strength of will, ambition, courage, independence, assertiveness, hardiness, rationality, and emotional control with men, and traits
like gentleness, modesty, humility, supportiveness, empathy, compassion, tenderness, nurturance, intuitiveness, sensitivity and unselfishness
with women.[2] No matter how "androgynous" our personal tastes in virtues may be, most of us are still able to classify virtues as ordinarily, usually, typically, or normally "masculine" or "feminine."

What disturbs feminist critics of feminine approaches to ethics, then,
is something quite different from what concerns nonfeminist critics of
these moral pathways. As we noted in our analysis of Gilligan and
Noddings, for example, feminist critics of them often worry that the
ethics of care/caring is an ethics for oppressed or otherwise vulnerable
people. Oppressed people often cater to the needs and desires of their
oppressors in order to survive. Servants who please their masters usually fare much better than servants who do not. To the extent that
women have, in Sandra Bartky's opinion, fed men's egos and tended
men's wounds without any hope of being reciprocated, women have imperiled themselves "epistemically" and "ethically."[3] Proper self-respect
demands that one be a receiver as well as a giver. Moral maturity requires that we ask the question "What is care?" with the same intensity
we have historically asked the question "What is justice?" Caring is subject to the same excesses and defects as justice.

Nonfeminist and feminist critics have also challenged "maternal" approaches to ethics. Proponents of maternal ethics offer a care-based, re-

lational ethics that uses the mother-child relationship to explore the
necessary, if not also sufficient, conditions for *good* human relationships. Sara Ruddick, for example, analyzes the kind of thought that enables a woman to preserve her children, to help them grow, and to
make them socially acceptable. As she sees it, applying maternal thinking to all human relationships—be they in the private or public world—
makes them more fully human.

Traditional ethicists doubt, however, that any one relationship either
can, or should, serve as the paradigm for all human relationships. As
they see it, any human relationship—be it one of husband-wife, parent-
child, sibling-sibling, friend-friend, or ruler-subject—is simply too specific to provide a general model for how people should treat each and
every person with equal respect and consideration. Certainly, relationships between unequals should not serve as the model for relationships
between equals or vice versa. Feminist critics express similar reservations, adding the point that the mother-child relationship is a particularly problematic choice for a moral paradigm, freighted as it is with
enough patriarchal baggage to weigh down even the strongest of
women. Although feminist critics concede that the mother-child relationship is a better model for human and humanizing relationships than
the traditional rational contractor model, they believe that even better
models are available. After all, the mother-child relationship is not the
only kind of human relationship that is based more on need than on desire, more on love than on obligation, and more on trust than on freedom. For example, friendship relationships, especially ones that are
based on shared goals and aspirations, as well as on having a good time
and/or providing emotional and economic support, offer all that the
mother-child relationship offers and more. Held together by tears,
laughter, and sweat rather than waivers, subpoenas, and depositions,
friendship relations seem to hold out more possibilities for moral development than contractual relations. They are also less imbalanced than
mother-child relationships in that the parties to them are near equals;
they can give to each other approximately as much as they take from
each other.

Like feminine and maternal approaches to ethics, feminist approaches to ethics are also subject to criticism. Because feminist approaches to ethics focus on *women's* moral concerns, critics complain
that they are "female biased." Ethics, insist the critics, cannot proceed
from a specific standpoint—in this case, from the standpoint of women
—and still be regarded as an ethics. Indeed, traditional ethics has

proceeded on the assumption that its values and rules apply to all rational persons equally. Yet, any number of the "Great Philosophers'" moral theories seem to be based on men's moral experience as opposed to women's. For example, Aristotle's ethics reflects the values of Athenian citizens: that is, property-owning Greek males. It does not reflect the values of Greek females or of slaves/foreigners—be they male or female. Nevertheless, traditional ethicists have tried to make the case that, properly interpreted, Aristotle's ethics applies equally well to both women and men, to both non-Greeks and Greeks, and that it would be misguided to *deliberately*—as opposed to *nonreflectively*—construct an ethics that focuses on a specific group of people.

Related to the above controversy are similar controversies about women's history and literature courses, for example. A person developing a feminist approach to ethics could argue, for example, that she is simply doing what Aristotle, Mill, and Kant should have done in the first place—namely, paying as much attention to women's moral experience as to men's. In the same way that historians have ignored the stresses, strains, and struggles of the private world of "children, church, and kitchen" to focus on the economic revolutions, political upheavals, and military conquests of the public world, traditional ethicists have focused on men's moral interests, issues, and values, failing to notice just how significant and interesting women's moral interests, issues, and values were. Therefore, when a proponent of feminist ethics insists on highlighting "women's morality," she may be doing little more than some corrective surgery—adding moral experiences to a male-biased ethical tradition sorely in need of them.

However, she may be doing more than this. She may be suggesting that it is not enough for traditional ethics to incorporate women's interests and issues and to recognize women as moral agents who must be taken seriously. On the contrary, she may be urging the "Tradition" to rethink all of the ontological and epistemological assumptions on which it is based and even to consider the possibility that far from being sources of human liberation, its principles, rules, regulations, norms, and criteria actually serve to support patterns of domination and subordination that "de-moralize" everyone. What makes an ethics feminist, as opposed to feminine or maternal, then, is, as Alison Jaggar has observed, its utter opposition to structures of oppression; its willingness "(1) to articulate moral critiques of actions and practices that perpetuate women's subordination; (2) to prescribe morally justifiable ways of resisting such actions and practices; (3) to envision morally desirable alternatives that will promote women's emancipation; and (4) to take the moral experience of all women seriously, though not, of course, uncritically."[4] In addition to theorizing about the causes of oppression, a feminist approach to ethics offers specific ways to eliminate it.

To be sure, as Laura Purdy has argued, there are other approaches to ethics that have practical goals. She gives the example of utilitarianism, one of whose most urgent charges is to diminish suffering "by choosing actions and social policies entailing the least possible suffering."[5] But there is an enormous difference between seeking to diminish everyone's suffering *in general,* all the while neglecting to ask *who* it is that suffers, and seeking to diminish women's suffering *in particular.* Once again, feminists favor the concrete approach of binding the wounds of a specific oppressed group over the abstract idea of fighting suffering qua suffering. A feminist approach to ethics, unlike other practical approaches to ethics, mobilizes women to take charge of their moral destinies: to overcome the causes of their unfreedom.

That feminist approaches to ethics should be so bold as to focus on women is part of what makes them unique and controversial. In a similar vein, lesbian approaches to ethics dare to focus on lesbians, in what may represent the greatest assault on the Tradition. First, by speaking to lesbians primarily or exclusively, these approaches carry "particularity" to what even some feminists may believe is a fault. There is concern, for example, that lesbian ethics privileges lesbians' moral concerns over those of heterosexual women. Yet, we must ask ourselves whether there is really that much difference between an ethics that focuses on lesbians in particular and one that focuses on women in general. In both instances, the purpose of the narrow focus is to identify and overcome structures of domination and subordination.

Second, lesbian approaches to ethics threaten the Tradition because thinkers like Mary Daly offer a transvaluation of values that would frighten even Friedrich Nietzsche. We will recall that Nietzsche's disenchantment with Western civilization—its good-naturedness, mediocrity, egalitarianism, softness—led him to redefine and counter prevailing notions of good and bad. Virtue, said Nietzsche, does not consist in what the Jews, Christians, democrats, and socialists believe it consists: namely, kindness, humility, and sympathy. Rather, it consists in what noble aristocrats, or übermenschen, regard as good: namely, assertiveness, aloofness, and pridefulness. What Western civilization has come to accept as "good" is in actuality very bad. Value must be transvalued. What is praised as "virtue" must be exposed as *vice,* and what is condemned as "vice" must be revealed as *virtue.*

Daly is Nietzchean not because she posits two types of morality—a superior female morality and an inferior male morality—but because she insists that when it comes to women, she whom the patriarch calls "evil" is in fact good, whereas she whom the patriarch calls "good" is in fact bad. If a woman is to escape the traps men have laid for her—if she is to assert her power, to be all that she can be—then she must realize that it is not good for her to sacrifice, deny, and deprive herself for the sake of the men and children in her life. What *is* actually good for women, observes Daly, is precisely what patriarchy identifies as evil for women: namely, becoming whole persons.

Third, and finally, complementing and completing Daly's earthquake, Sarah Lucia Hoagland releases the too-long suppressed female freedom to question and choose. Women must replace the questions "Am I good?" and "Is this good?" with the question "Does this contribute to my self-creation, freedom, and liberation?" Rejecting heterosexual society's values, lesbians use free choice to weave their own values.

Given the differences among feminine, maternal, feminist, and lesbian approaches to ethics, what worries me is the Tradition's willingness, even eagerness, to accommodate feminine and maternal approaches to ethics. Optimistically interpreted, the Tradition's increasing acceptance of these "newcomers" may stem from a recognition that it needs to explore care as well as justice, the mother-child paradigm as well as the contractarian paradigm, and to consider women's as well as men's ways of knowing and acting. Pessimistically interpreted, however, the Tradition's "welcome party" may be motivated by the realization that feminine and maternal ethics are unlikely to end its moral monopoly. If men as well as women are caring, then the Tradition can claim caring as its own, and if men are not as caring as women, then the Tradition can encourage women to develop an ethics of care that will keep women within patriarchy's clutch.

In contrast, feminist and lesbian approaches to ethics deeply disturb the Tradition. Committed to exposing the politics of domination and subordination, feminist and lesbian approaches reveal the corruption of status quo ethics. They make critics nervous *precisely because* they proceed from the point of view of historically situated women rather than from the point of view of an Ideal Observer who transcends time and space. The Tradition's champions argue that every system of ethics demands respect for persons. Kantian ethics, especially, demands that we be unbiased, that we treat everyone with the same care and concern, *regardless* of our relationship to them. Yet if this is so, why have women and minorities been exploited for centuries? Is the principle willing but the people weak?

The feminist and/or lesbian ethicist makes traditional ethics accountable for centuries of lack of respect for persons: Justice has been blind all right; *he* has not seen equality crumbling in front of his face. Daly may be right. Not solicitous care but raging Nemesis, with her Third Eye open to spot oppression, may be the proper replacement for a justice blind to anything but upholding the status quo.[6] Feminist and lesbian approaches to ethics show the importance of women's *perspective* and *experience* in seeing what the Tradition has missed. The Ideal Observer cannot see anything in particular because *he* is too busy seeing everything in general. To successfully develop an ethics that compensates for the Tradition's tunnel vision, women—and others like women —must first come to a feminist consciousness or some equivalent thereof. As Sheila Mullett says, such awareness begins with the kind of moral sensitivity to the particularities of a situation that occasions a moment of ontological shock powerful enough to commit one to action.[7]

The ontological jolt that opened my eyes to the need for a feminist approach to ethics came unexpectedly, through discussion of Akira Kurosawa's film *Rashomon*. In this story a husband and wife traveling through the forest are attacked: The husband is killed, the wife raped. Through a series of flashbacks, the director shows us four people's different perspectives on the event. What struck me in all four versions of the story was how the woman, not the assailant, ended up being blamed or reviled for the tragedy. The bandit recounts the classic male fantasy of rape: She fought at first, but once he started she loved it. He fights her husband in hope of "winning" her as a prize. Yet when she runs away, he forgets her, because he feels no attraction to a cowardly woman. He declares to the police that she was not worth chasing. The wife claims that after the rape the bandit left her crying on the forest floor. When she looked to her husband for compassion, she found only hatred and contempt in his eyes. She begged him to kill her, to do anything but look at her with those eyes. He remained stonily silent, and she fainted. Clearly, he blamed her for the rape. The dead husband, speaking through a medium, testifies that his wife agreed to run away with the bandit after he took advantage of her. Indeed, she asked the bandit to kill her husband, as she could not go with him while her spouse lived. The rapist, disgusted by such womanish "treachery," tells her husband that he will kill or spare her, as the injured husband sees fit. The criminal is all too ready to punish the victim. The final version of the story comes from a witness, a firewood gatherer who stumbled on the scene while walking through the woods. On his account, the bandit first tried to gain the woman's love and promise of marriage but ultimately rejected her after her husband called her a "shameless whore" and refused to fight for her. After all, if rape is seen as a power struggle between men, and the husband refuses to risk death for the woman, he takes all the adventure out of it!

For me, the different stories only showed that no matter what a woman does before, during, or after a rape, in patriarchal society she will often be blamed for her own victimization. I saw *Rashomon* as a movie about the horror of rape and the powerlessness of women. While talking with a male colleague, however, he mentioned to me that he used *Rashomon* in his philosophy class to demonstrate the fluid nature of truth. Just as in a court of law different witnesses tell different stories, the director masterfully shows us how different truths are seen with different eyes. The facts of the case forever elude us. Objectivity is continually melting into subjectivity. What my male friend apparently did not see, however, was the event that the observers actually *saw:* They witnessed or participated in a *rape*. Enamored with the beauty of the myriad nature of abstract truth, he was oblivious to the horror of the concrete event of the young woman's rape. Indeed, he told me that it did not matter what the film was about. It could be about anything provided that it let his class discuss the differences between reality and interpretation. In a moment of shock I realized that whereas I, as a woman, thought the film was about rape, he, as a man, thought the film was about truth. From then on I believed in the necessity of developing feminist approaches to ethics.

Of course, if we accept feminist and lesbian ethicists' tacit suggestion that we must have certain experiences to gain moral vision, we return to a gendered claim. Only women—or groups oppressed like women— can understand the flaws of the Tradition. Only those who have been the victims of domination and subordination can have the moral vision to create an ethics that transcends such abuse. I realize that the Tradition is threatened by a moral claim with an experiential prerequisite. Yet, should it be? Even Aristotle said that ethical decisions rest in perception—in perceiving, in *seeing through one's experiences* to the moral truth beneath appearances.

Looking at the history of the exploitation and degradation of women and others like women, I do not think it is astonishing to say that philosophy's revered Ideal Observer—and also some of the greatest philosophers—failed in their abstract moral vision because they failed in their daily moral vision. Not seeing the oppression that surrounded them, they shaped an abstract ethics that may have served to protect the interests of those in power. Feminist and lesbian approaches to ethics try to re-vision the moral world to make up for the gaps in traditional ethics. They try to fight oppression by making the powerful accountable for ignoring the oppressed. Now they challenge us to do the same.

NOTES

1. George Sher, "Other Voices, Other Rooms? Women's Psychology and Moral Theory," in Eva Kittay and Diana Meyers, eds., *Women and Moral Theory* (Totowa, N.J.: Rowman & Littlefield, 1987), 187–188.
2. This list of psychological traits is found in Mary Vetterling-Braggin, ed., *"Femininity," "Masculinity," and "Androgyny"* (Totowa, N.J.: Littlefield, Adams, and Co., 1982), 5–6.
3. See Sandra Lee Bartky, *Femininity and Domination: Studies in the Phenomenology of Oppression* (New York: Routledge, 1990), 111.
4. Alison Jaggar, "Feminist Ethics: Projects, Problems, Prospects," in Claudia Card, ed., *Feminist Ethics* (Lawrence, Kans.: University of Kansas Press, 1991), 366.
5. Laura Purdy, in *Their Best Interest: The Case Against Equal Rights for Children* (Ithaca: Cornell University Press, 1992), 239.
6. Mary Daly, *Pure Lust: Elemental Feminist Philosophy* (Boston: Beacon Press, 1984), 275.
7. Sheila Mullett, "Shifting Perspectives: A New Approach to Ethics," in Lorraine Code, Sheila Mullett, and Christine Overall, eds., *Feminist Perspectives: Philosophical Essays on Method and Morals* (Toronto: University of Toronto Press, 1988), 114.

Index

Dual careers, 9
Dual parenting, 9, 150, 197
Dumb View, 70
Duties
  absolute, 22
  conflicts, 22
  defined, 19–23
  deontology, 19–23
  morally nonworthy, 19
  morally unworthy, 19
  parental, 22–23
  prime, 170
  self-sacrifice, 41, 130
Dworkin, Andrea, 170

E

Economic man, 52–55. *See also*
    Autonomous man paradigm
Egocentrism, 203
Emile (Rousseau), 31
Emotion, 70–77
Emotional woman vs. rational man,
    31
Engels, Frederick, 7
Episodic autonomy, 62
Epistemology
  abstract vs. concrete, 63–65
  Blum, 72–77
  criticisms of traditional views, 63–77
  impartiality vs. partiality, 68–70
  Jaggar, 70–72
  reason vs. emotion, 70–77
  universality vs. particularity, 65–68
Equality, in relationships, 36–37
Equal parenting, 146
Eros, 109
Ethical caring, 112
Ethical diminishment, 124, 120, 158
Ethical ideal, 130
Ethics, defined, 13
Eudaemonia, 26
Euthanasia, 115–116
Evacuation of motherhood, 155
Evil, 112–114, 120–122
Existentialist ethics, 214–215

F

FACT (Feminist Anti-Censorship
    Taskforce), 172
False consciousness, 59
Female agency approach to ethics,
    201–207
Female bias, 188, 223
Female friendship approach to ethics,
    195–201, 223
Female self, 189
Female virtue, 29–30
Feminine, defined, 4, 221
Feminine consciousness, 4–6
Feminine ethics, 4–6, 10–11
  ethics of care, 80–103
  relational ethics, 108–132
Feminine Mystique, The (Friedan),
    191
Femininity and Domination (Bartky),
    100
Feminism
  Baier, 56–57, 97–98, 175–179
  Beecher, 37–39, 45, 164–165, 220
  Gilligan, 158, 221
  Gilman, 41–44, 220
  Jaggar, 161–165, 181, 224
  liberal, 7
  Marxist, 7
  Mill, 7, 15–16, 34–37, 220
  Mullett, 103, 165–169, 227
  Noddings, 158
  postmodern, 10
  psychoanalytic, 8–9
  radical, 7–9
  relativist, 173
  Sherwin, 4, 159, 167–175
  Stanton, 39–41, 194
  Taylor, 33–37, 220
  Wollstonecraft, 7, 33–34, 44–45,
    220
Feminist, defined, 4
Feminist Anti-Censorship Taskforce
    (FACT), 172
Feminist consciousness, 4, 6–10, 165–
    169

K

Kant, Immanuel
  categorical imperative, 19–23, 27,
    222
  deontology, 19–23
  emotions, 73–77
  ethical caring, 112
  respect for persons, 64
  universality view, 65–66
Kerber, Linda, 98
Knowledge, 80
Kohlberg, Lawrence, 82–83, 96, 163
Koinonia, 206
Kristeva, Julia, 10

L

Ladies' Home Journal, 172
Lauritzen, Paul, 150–152
Lesbian, defined, 213
Lesbian ethics
  criticisms of, 207–216, 225, 227
  Daly, 189–195
  female agency, 201–207
  female friendship, 195–201
  Hoagland, 201–207
  Raymond, 195–201, 210–213
  and self-creation, 189–192
  and traditional virtue, 192–195
Lesbophobia, 213
Lessing, Doris, 113
Liberal feminism, 7
Logos, 109
Love, 14
Lugones, Maria, 216

M

Maccoby, Eleanor E., 89
MacIntyre, Alasdair, 36, 137–138
MacKinnon, Catharine, 170
Male bias, 163
Male thinking, 10
Male virtue, 29–30
Mapping the Moral Domain
    (Gilligan), 87, 108, 111
Marxist feminist, 7

Masculine traits, 44, 163
Maternal-child health, 51
Maternal ethics
  criticisms, 148–155, 222–223
  Held, 143–148
  MacIntyre, 137–138
  maternal instinct, 148
  maternal thinking and, 136–143,
    223
  mothering persons, 144–148
  private morality, 143–144
  Rich, 138–139
  Ruddick, 136–143, 223
  Whitbeck, 148
Maternal instinct, 148
Maternal peacefulness, 142
Maternal practice, 136–143
Maternal thinking, 136–143, 221
Maternal Thinking (Ruddick), 148–
    149
McCloskey, H. J., 18
Medical ethics, 179–180
Men, and care, 80–81
Mermaid and the Minotaur, The
    (Dinnerstein), 196
Metaethics, 189–190
Metavirtue, 141
Meyers, Diane, 58–63
Mill, John Stuart, 7, 15–16, 34–37, 220
Millet, Kate, 58, 60
Miscarriages, 118
Mitchell, Juliet, 9–10
Moody-Adams, Michelle M., 94
Moral absolutism, 171–172
Moral development, 82–83, 87–88,
    96, 163
Moral impartiality, 68
Moral inferiority, 81–82
Morality
  Aristotle, 26–28, 163
  Beecher, 37–39, 45, 164–165, 220
  complementary approaches, 89
  female agency approach, 201–207
  Gilman, 41–45
  and human weakness, 73–74

Phallogocentric thought, 10
Plastic passions, 191–192
Plato, 183
Playfulness, 216
Pleasure, 16–17, 23–24
Pojman, Louis P., 13–15
Polar opposites, 50–51
Political agendas, 182–183
Politicizing morality, 169–175
Politics and ethics, 183
Politics of resistance, 143
Pornography, 170, 172
Positive rights, 54
Postmodern feminist, 10
Potted passions, 191–192
Poverty, and relational ethics, 118–119
Power, 160, 176
Practical wisdom, 27
Practice, 136–143
Preference utilitarians, 16–17
Pregnancy, and mothering, 145–148, 161
Prescription, 13
Prescriptivists, 166
Preserving maternal practice, 139
Prime duty, of women, 170
Principles, 65
Private property, and oppression, 7, 170–171
Private realm, 143–145
Programmatic autonomy, 61
Protection racket, 203
Protestant tradition of morality, 73
Prudence, 193
Pseudopassions, 191
Psychoanalysis and Feminism (Mitchell), 9
Psychoanalytic feminist, 8–9
Psychological development, 5–6
Psychological traits, 44, 94–95
gendered, 29
Psychosexual development, 5, 84
Puka, Bill, 94–96, 101–102
Purdy, Laura, 225
Pyromantic women, 195

R
Radical feminist, 7–9
Rape, 24, 125, 203, 227–228
Rashomon, 227–228
Rational man, 31
Raymond, Janice G., 195–201, 210–213
Reason vs. emotion, 70–77
Receptivity, 127–128
Reciprocity, 127–128
Reformist approach to separatism, 209
Rejection, 209
Relation, 109
Relational ethics, 108–132
Relationism, 200
Relationship
abusive, 129, 131, 158, 162, 203
agape, 127, 130–131
caring, 88–89
caring/relying, 55
colonial, 124
dependency, 127
destructive, 129
domination-subordination, 55
equality in, 36–37
growth potential, 130
parenting, 88–89
trusting, 175–179
unequal, 124–127, 223
Relationship-based morality, 52
Relativism, moral, 171–175, 211
Reproduction of Mothering, The (Chodorow), 196
Reproductive technology, 167–169
Republic (Plato), 183
Rich, Adrienne, 56, 138–139, 196, 213
Rights, 15–16, 54, 83–84
Rights-based morality, 51–52
Romanticism, 150–152
Rousseau, Jean-Jacques, 31–33, 45, 161
Ruddick, Sara, 136–143, 223
Rules, 14, 19, 22, 64
Rule utilitarians, 18–19